MY REVISION NOTES

AQA

A-level

COMPUTER SCIENCE

THIRD EDITION

Mark Clarkson

Boost

HODDER
EDUCATION
AN HACHETTE UK COMPANY

Although every effort has been made to ensure that website addresses are correct at time of going to press, Hodder Education cannot be held responsible for the content of any website mentioned in this book. It is sometimes possible to find a relocated web page by typing in the address of the home page for a website in the URL window of your browser.

Hachette UK's policy is to use papers that are natural, renewable and recyclable products and made from wood grown in well-managed forests and other controlled sources. The logging and manufacturing processes are expected to conform to the environmental regulations of the country of origin.

Orders: please contact Hachette UK Distribution, Hely Hutchinson Centre, Milton Road, Didcot, Oxfordshire, OX11 7HH. Telephone: +44 (0)1235 827827.
Email education@hachette.co.uk. Lines are open from 9 a.m. to 5 p.m., Monday to Friday.
You can also order through our website: www.hoddereducation.co.uk

ISBN: 978 1 3983 2548 7
© Mark Clarkson 2021
First edition published in 2016. This edition published in 2021 by
Hodder Education,
An Hachette UK Company
Carmelite House
50 Victoria Embankment
London EC4Y 0DZ

www.hoddereducation.co.uk

Impression number   10 9 8 7 6 5 4 3 2

Year   2025 2024 2023

Cover photo © Maksym Yemelyanov - stock.adobe.com

Illustrations by Aptara, Inc.

Typeset in India by Aptara, Inc.

Printed and bound by CPI Group (UK) Ltd, Croydon, CR0 4YY

A catalogue record for this title is available from the British Library.

Get the most from this book

Everyone has to decide his or her own revision strategy, but it is essential to review your work, learn it and test your understanding. These Revision Notes will help you to do that in a planned way, topic by topic. Use this book as the cornerstone of your revision and don't hesitate to write in it — personalise your notes and check your progress by ticking off each section as you revise.

Tick to track your progress

Use the revision planner on pages 4–7 to plan your revision, topic by topic. Tick each box when you have:

✚ revised and understood a topic
✚ tested yourself
✚ practised the exam questions and gone online to check your answers and complete the quick quizzes

You can also keep track of your revision by ticking off each topic heading in the book. You may find it helpful to add your own notes as you work through each topic.

Features to help you succeed

Exam tips

Expert tips are given throughout the book to help you polish your exam technique in order to maximise your chances in the exam.

Now test yourself

These short, knowledge-based questions provide the first step in testing your learning. Answers are available online at **www.hoddereducation.co.uk/ myrevisionnotesdownloads**

Definitions and key words

Clear, concise definitions of essential key terms are provided where they first appear.

Key words from the specification are highlighted in bold throughout the book.

Making links

This feature identifies specific connections between topics and tells you how revising these will aid your exam answers.

Exam skills

These summaries highlight how to specific skills identified or applicable in that chapter can be applied to your exam answers.

Revision activities

These activities will help you to understand each topic in an interactive way.

Exam practice

Practice exam questions are provided for each topic. Use them to consolidate your revision and practise your exam skills.

Summaries

The summaries provide a quick-check bullet list for each topic.

Online

Go online to check your answers to the exam questions and try out the extra quick quizzes at **www.hoddereducation.co.uk/ myrevisionnotesdownloads**

My Revision Planner

REVISED   TESTED   EXAM READY

Check your understanding and progress at **www.hoddereducation.co.uk/myrevisionnotesdownloads**

Introduction

As a student of computer science, it is important that you understand three things in relation to the A-level examinations.

✤ Assessment objectives
✤ Command words
✤ Exams and NEA

Assessment objectives

✤ AO1 You should be able to demonstrate **knowledge and understanding** of the principles and concepts of computer science, including abstraction, logic, algorithms and data representation.
✤ AO2 You must be able to **apply** your knowledge and understanding of the principles and concepts of computer science, including to analyse problems in computation terms.
✤ AO3 You must be able to **design, program and evaluate** computer systems that solve problems, making reasoned judgements about these and presenting conclusions.

Command words

Familiarity with the relevant command words is important. It helps you to avoid wasting time in the exam room (for example, trying to evaluate when there is no requirement for it). The most frequently used command words used for the A-level papers are listed here.

✤ **Calculate...** requires you to work out the value of something. A correct final answer, to the required degree of accuracy and with the correct units, will score full marks. Working is usually required, and correct working can score marks. (AO2)
✤ **Compare...** requires you to identify similarities and differences between ideas, technologies, or approaches. (AO1)
✤ **Create...** requires you to write program code that solves a problem. Even if you struggle to get the syntax correct, marks are awarded for evidence of the approach taken as well as for working code. (AO3)
✤ **Define...** requires you to specify the meaning of a technical term in order to show that you understand what it means. (AO1)
✤ **Describe...** requires you to set out the characteristics of a device or a computing concept. These can be very short questions worth 1 mark, or long-answer questions worth up to 12 marks. (AO1)
✤ **Discuss...** requires you to present the key points. These questions are typically of medium length, worth 4-6 marks. You should aim to present as many points as you can and, where appropriate, provide balance between advantages and disadvantages. (AO1)
✤ **Draw...** requires you to produce a diagram. These are usually technical diagrams such an E-R diagram for a database, or a logic circuit diagram. (AO2)
✤ **Explain...** requires you to provide purposes or reasons. These questions are used to assess your knowledge of a topic and can sometimes be used within a specific context. If a question is asked in relation to a particular scenario then you should always make sure you link to the scenario in your answer. (AO1, AO2)
✤ **Express...** requires you to convert an input into a particular format. Examples might include encrypting a message or calculating a value. (AO2)
✤ **Modify...** requires you to take an existing section of program code and add to or edit it. This is commonly asked as part of Section D in Component 1, involving changes to the skeleton program. (AO3)
✤ **State...** requires you to express some knowledge in clear terms. These questions are usually short answer questions and are usually worth 1 mark. (AO1)

Check your understanding and progress at **www.hoddereducation.co.uk/myrevisionnotesdownloads**

+ **Suggest...** requires you to present a suitable case or solution. (AO1, AO2)
+ **Test...** requires that you run the code that you have written in order to check that it functions as it should. This is usually combined with a write/create/modify question in component 1 and screenshots of the testing process should be included. (AO3)
+ **Write...** requires you to create a program or a Boolean expression to solve a specific problem. These questions can be quite lengthy and partially complete answers are usually worth a significant proportion of the marks. (AO2, AO3)

Exams and NEA

The AQA A-level in Computer Science is assessed using three components. There are two exams, both taken at the end of the course, and one piece of non-examination assessment (NEA) which is based on a programming project.

Component 1	Component 2	Component 3
On-screen exam	Written exam	Programming project (NEA)
2.5 hours	2.5 hours	Internally assessed
40% weighting	40% weighting	20% weighting

Component 1

Component 1 is an on-screen exam, largely focused on programming and computation. In advance of the exam, you and your teachers will be provided with a skeleton program and a small pack of background information.

The exam will be taken using a programming language you have studied throughout the course, and will be pre-selected by your teacher. The available languages are:
+ C#
+ Python
+ Java
+ VB.net
+ Pascal/Delphi

The skeleton program is a working program that is functional but could be improved. Typical examples include text-based role-playing games or simulations.

For A-level students the pre-release information is available from September of that academic year (typically Year 13).

The pre-release information should be given to you by your teacher, but they may choose not to give the information out straight away, depending on how and when they plan to deliver the content.

The A-level exam is split into four sections:
1 **Section A:** Questions about programming and computation; for example, finite state machines, standard algorithms, trace tables, Turing machines and computation logic.
2 **Section B:** A programming problem (unrelated to the skeleton program); for example, writing a program to convert between binary and denary numbers.
3 **Section C:** Questions about the skeleton program; for example, identifying specific variables or programming constructs, hierarchy charts, class diagrams and explaining the purpose of specific elements.
4 **Section D:** Improving the skeleton code; for example, adding an extra menu option, improving exception handling, adding new functionality.

Component 1 tests programming ability as well as theoretical knowledge covered in Chapters 1–4, and the skills covered in Chapter 13.

Programming syntax

Some questions in Component 1 will include algorithms written using AQA pseudo-code. It is important to be able to read and understand this pseudo-code and, in some cases, to write program code in your chosen programming language based on the pseudo-code algorithms provided.

This book is not intended to teach you how to program using one specific language and uses pseudo-code similar to that used by AQA. Any code that is not labelled as being from a particular language is instead written in AQA pseudo-code.

Component 2

Component 2 is a traditional-style written paper, largely focused on the more theoretical components of this course.

The topics covered in this paper test subject content from Chapters 5–12, and typically include:
+ data representation
+ computer systems
+ computer hardware
+ consequences of computing
+ networking
+ databases and Big Data
+ functional programming.

As this is a written paper, no practical programming activities are assessed, though some practical elements such as calculations, data conversions and trace tables (especially for assembly language and instruction sets) are likely to appear.

This paper will generally include short answer questions (1–2 marks) that will assess your knowledge, questions that will assess your ability to apply your knowledge (3–4 marks), and a small number of longer-answer questions that require detailed discussion (6–12 marks).

For these longer-answer discussion questions, credit is awarded for identifying, discussing and evaluating potential issues.
+ Marks are awarded for identifying relevant knowledge; for example, suggesting appropriate input devices for collecting data or identifying the methods by which wireless data transmissions can be intercepted.
+ To reach the top mark bands it is important to follow a line of reasoning, using your knowledge to write in connected sentences in a way that makes sense and relates to the context of the question. Explaining how each point links to the scenario and adding as much technical detail and vocabulary as you can makes it more likely that you will score well on this type of question.
+ Always make sure you back up any arguments or suggestions you make with facts, logical arguments and technical details, as unsubstantiated statements don't demonstrate your understanding.

Component 3

Component 3 is a non-examination assessment (NEA) component, based on completing a programming project.

The programming project is extremely open-ended, and it is up to you to identify a real-world problem and then work through each phase of the systems development lifecycle in order to solve it.

It is beyond the scope of this book to go into detail in terms of completing the programming project, but typical examples include online booking and scheduling systems, computer games with a simple AI component, animal population simulations, and so on. There is no definitive list of expected or excluded projects and your teacher will be able to provide with much more specific guidance.

Check your understanding and progress at **www.hoddereducation.co.uk/myrevisionnotesdownloads**

Programming

Data types

It is important to declare variables using the correct data type. This will make sure that memory is not wasted, and that the program is able to process the data correctly.

Different data types are processed in different ways; for example, adding two strings produces a different result to adding two integers.

```
"123" + "456" = "123456"

123 + 456 = 579
```

The main data types are:

Data type	Suitable for	Examples
integer	whole numbers	7, 9, 163
real/float	fractional numbers	7.3, 9.6, 0.5
Boolean	True/False	True, False
character	a single letter or other character	'b', 'W', '@'
string	text	"word", "EC4Y 0DZ"
date/time	a date, time, or combination	14:18, 17/10/2004
pointer	a memory address	#bf4e3a67
record	a collection of fields	RECORD username, password
array	a table of data	[1,3,5,7,11,13,17]

Different data types use different amounts of memory. If a numeric variable will always hold a whole number, it will use less memory stored as an integer than it will if stored as a real or float.

> **Note**
>
> All programming languages deal with data types slightly differently.
>
> It is important to note that Python does not support the character data type, using only a string to store text of any length. Python also does not support the array data type. The closest alternative is a list data type.

Most of the data types are quite straightforward.
+ Records are more complex as they allow the programmer to group together attributes of different types; for example, a user record may have attributes for Username, Password and Last_Login.
+ An array is a table-like structure. Each field in an array must be of the same data type (e.g. an array of integers, or an array of strings).

> **Making links**
>
> Arrays are an important data structure that are used to store sets of data together. The use of arrays can increase the efficiency of programs when processing lots of data. Arrays are covered in detail in the chapter on data structures.

> **Exam tip**
>
> There are many additional data types, some quite specific (for example, for whole numbers Java has a choice of byte, short, int or long). The mark schemes allow for any appropriate answer though only those listed above are strictly required.

9

Built-in and user-defined data types

Built-in data types are those already defined by a programming language. The exact list varies from language to language, but most of those in the table above are built-in to most programming languages.

It is possible for a user to define their own data types, combining more than one value per variable. The use of user-defined data types means that program code can be simplified, with attributes being grouped together. This can be carried out in various ways in different languages. A good example might be a user data type that is made up of a username and a password.

Now test yourself   TESTED ⬤

1   What data type is most suitable for storing a whole number?
2   What is the difference between a character and a string?
3   What sort of data would be stored in a pointer?
4   Suggest two fields that could be included in a user-defined record for recording high scores on a game.

Answers available online

Programming concepts

REVISED ⬤

For each of the programming concepts you should be familiar with both the pseudo-code used by AQA and the syntax used in your own programming language.

Declaration

Variable declaration is the process of creating a variable.

In languages which are strongly typed (for example, C#, Pascal/Delphi, Java and VB.net) the data type of the variable is stated, followed by the variable's identifier. In these languages it is possible to declare a variable without initially assigning a value to it.
➕ `int Age;`   (C# and Java)
➕ `var Age: integer;`   (Delphi and Pascal)
➕ `Dim Age As Integer`   (VB.net)

In languages which are weakly typed (for example, Python) a value must be assigned to a new variable, and no data type is declared as the data type can be changed during the course of the program.
➕ `Age = 18` (Python)

Constants are declared in a similar way, but with a key word that indicates the variable cannot be changed. Because the value of a constant cannot be changed later, they must be declared with an initial value:
➕ `const int MAX = 3;` (C#)
➕ `Const MAX = 3;` (Pascal/Delphi)
➕ `final int MIN = 3;` (Java)
➕ `Const MAX As Integer = 3` (VB.net)

Python does not support the use of constants and therefore it is not possible to prevent the accidental assignment of a new value to a constant.

Making links

It is important to consider where a variable is declared. A variable declared inside an `IF` statement, loop or subroutine can only be used within that section of the code and will be destroyed once that section has ended. This issue is dealt with more in the section on local and global variables.

Pseudo-code A format for program code that is not specific to one programming language. Used extensively in Component 1. Pseudo-code is useful for describing an algorithm that could be coded in one of several different languages.

Syntax The strict rules and structures used within a specific programming language. You will only be assessed in the syntax of one programming language for Component 1.

Declaration The creation of a variable in memory.

Check your understanding and progress at **www.hoddereducation.co.uk/myrevisionnotesdownloads**

Assignment

Changing the value of a variable is called assignment.

✦ Assignment in AQA pseudo-code often uses a left arrow (for example, Score ← 12).

✦ Assignment in most programming languages uses an equals sign (for example, Score = 12)

> **Now test yourself**   TESTED ○
>
> 5 What is meant by the term *declaration*?
>
> 6 Describe one difference between the declaration of a variable and the declaration of a constant.
>
> 7 What symbol is used to indicate assignment in AQA pseudo-code?
>
> 8 What symbol is used to indicate assignment in most programming languages?
>
> **Answers available online**

Sequencing

Program code is executed in the order in which it appears. For example, given the code:

```
x ← 5

OUTPUT x

x ← x + 1
```

The value 5 will be output before the value of x is increased.

Selection

All but the simplest computer programs need to include decisions. A simple decision of whether to execute a particular block of code is controlled by a selection statement, often implemented using an IF statement.

```
IF score > 90 THEN

    OUTPUT "Top marks!"

ELSE IF score > 60 THEN

    OUTPUT "Good job."

ELSE

    OUTPUT "Try again."

END IF
```

There are no limits to how many ELSE IF statements can be used, but with a large number it is possible to use a SWITCH statement instead. A SWITCH statement is slightly faster to execute if used with single values (rather than checking for a range)

```
SWITCH (grade)

CASE "A*" THEN

    OUTPUT "Top marks!"

    BREAK

CASE "A" THEN

    OUTPUT "Very good job."

    BREAK

...

END SWITCH
```

Selection A program structure that makes a decision about which block of code to execute, typically implemented using an IF statement.

SWITCH An alternative selection structure to an IF statement that is slightly quicker to execute if used with exact values rather than a range.

Exam tips

Remember that IF and ELSE IF commands need a conditional statement with a Boolean (True/False) answer. The ELSE command doesn't as it will catch all other possibilities.

You are not required to use a SWITCH statement and can score full marks using IF-ELSE IF-ELSE. The skeleton code or pseudo-code may include a SWITCH statement so you should make sure you are familiar with the concept.

Nested selection

Nested IF statements occur when an IF statement is placed inside an IF statement.

```
IF animal = "dog" THEN

    IF target = "sheep" THEN

        OUTPUT "Dog chases sheep"

    ELSE

        OUTPUT "Dog wags tail"

    END IF

END IF
```

> **Revision activity**
>
> + Write a program in your chosen programming language that uses an IF statement to allow the user to choose one of four options.
> + Re-write the program to use a SWITCH statement.

Now test yourself

TESTED

9 What programming concept is implemented using an IF statement?

10 Which part of an IF statement does not need a condition?

11 What alternative to an IF statement is sometimes used if there are several possible options?

12 What is meant by a nested IF statement?

Answers available online

Iteration

When a block of code needs to be repeated, this is referred to as iteration.

Definite iteration

Definite iteration, or count-controlled iteration, refers to the use a FOR loop, where the number of times to repeat is known. Even if the number of times to repeat isn't always the same, if it is known at the start of the loop then a FOR loop should be used.

You should be familiar with the syntax of a FOR loop in your own programming language as well as the pseudo-code you might see in an exam:

```
FOR i ← 1 TO 5

    OUTPUT "This is step " + i

ENDFOR
```

Indefinite iteration

Indefinite iteration or condition-controlled iteration refers to a loop where the number of iterations is not known. A typical example might be a validation loop, asking a user to enter a valid input and repeating while their answer is invalid.

Indefinite loops can be further split into those that assess the condition at the start of the loop (a WHILE loop) and those that assess the condition at the end of the loop (a DO-WHILE loop).

In AQA pseudo-code:

A WHILE loop will have the condition at the top of the loop, allowing the program to bypass the code inside completely. For example:

```
value ← 5

WHILE value < 100 DO

    value ← value * 2

ENDWHILE
```

> **Exam tips**
>
> Be very careful with the start and end conditions when creating FOR loops. While a pseudo-code algorithm may explicitly start and end at given values, the implementation for a FOR loop may be less clear (for example, in Python `for i in range(1,5)` would stop at `i = 4` and in Java `for (int i = 1; i < 5; i++)` would also stop at `i = 4`).
>
> Although the specification refers to definite and indefinite iteration, question papers typically use the terms count-controlled and condition-controlled iteration.

> **Iteration** The repetition of a process or block of code.
>
> **Definite iteration, or count-controlled iteration** Iterating a fixed number of times (also known as a count-controlled loop, implemented as a FOR loop).
>
> **Indefinite iteration, or condition-controlled iteration** Iterating until a condition is met (also known as a condition-controlled loop, implemented in AQA pseudo-code as a WHILE loop or DO-WHILE loop).

Check your understanding and progress at **www.hoddereducation.co.uk/myrevisionnotesdownloads**

A DO-WHILE loop will have the condition at the bottom of the loop, forcing the program to pass through the code at least once. For example:

```
DO
    OUTPUT "Enter shoe size:"
    ShoeSize ← INPUT
WHILE ShoeSize > 12
```

Note

Python does not support the use of a DO-WHILE loop, but students are still expected to be familiar with the concept. One solution to this problem is to copy and paste the first iteration of the code before a WHILE loop. Another is to create a REPEAT ... UNTIL structure.

Nested iteration

Nested iteration means having a loop within a loop. This is used in a number of applications, including when working with 2D arrays, and in a number of standard algorithms including the bubble sort.

```
FOR i ← 1 TO 3
    FOR j ← 1 TO 5
        OUTPUT "Outer loop = " + i + " | Inner loop = " + j
    ENDFOR
ENDFOR
```

Remember

Remember that if you know how many times to loop you should use a FOR loop. If you don't know how many times then use a WHILE or DO-WHILE loop.

Remember that the inner loop is completed multiple times for each step around the outer loop. Selection and iteration statements can be nested inside each other, potentially many layers deep.

Now test yourself   TESTED

13 What type of loop is also called a count-controlled loop?

14 When should you use a condition-controlled loop?

15 Describe the difference between a WHILE loop and a DO-WHILE loop.

16 Suggest **two** possible uses for nested iteration.

Answers available online

Revision activity

✦ Write a program that uses iteration to print out the 12 times table.

✦ Write a program that uses nested iteration to print out all of the times tables from 1 to 12.

Debug The process of identifying and removing errors from program code.

Self-documenting code Program code that uses naming conventions and programming conventions that help other programmers to understand the code without needing to read additional documentation.

Meaningful identifier names

It is important to choose identifiers for variables (and subroutines) that tell other programmers something about the purpose of that variable (or subroutine).

✦ Var1, Var2 and Var3 are very poor choices as they make it very hard to read the code and to debug if there are any errors.

✦ UserName, UserAge and DateUserLastLoggedIn are much more meaningful and are key to writing self-documenting code.

It is not usually possible to use spaces in identifier names. Common strategies to aid readability include the use of CamelCase, Kebab-Case or Snake_Case.

Exam tip

In Component 1, Section B and Section D, it is very important to use any identifier names exactly as they are provided in the question. If the identifier name is not given explicitly then remember that making it easier for the examiner to understand the code makes it more likely you will pick up the marks.

Now test yourself

17 Describe **two** advantages of using meaningful identifier names.

18 Explain the term *self-documenting code.*

Answers available online
                                    TESTED ◯

Note

The use of meaningful identifier names to produce self-documenting code can have a significant impact on the marks available in the NEA.

Subroutines

Information on subroutines can be found in the section Purpose of subroutines.

Arithmetic operations

There are several key operators you should make sure you are familiar with.

Simple arithmetic operators include those for addition (+), subtraction (-), multiplication (*) and division (/).

It is important to understand the different types of division operation that can be carried out:

+ Real or float division will result in a real or float answer; for example,
  `5 / 2 = 2.5`
+ Integer division will strip any fractional part of the answer, effectively rounding down; for example, `5 DIV 2 = 2`
+ The modulo operator will find the modulus – the remainder of an integer division, as a whole number; for example, `5 MOD 2 = 1`

DIV and MOD are useful for converting between different number systems, including conversion between units of time, imperial measurements, and between numbers using different bases (for example, denary and hexadecimal).

Exponentiation refers to powers; for example, $2\char`^3 = 2*2*2 = 8$

Rounding can be carried to a given number of decimal places or significant figures, generally using a function; for example, `round(3.14,1) = 3.1`, `round(3.16,1) = 3.2`

Additional functions can be used that always round up or always round down; for example, `roundup(3.142,1) = 3.2`

Rounding down has the same effect as truncation.

> **Exam tip**
>
> Some questions in Component 1 will assess your understanding of programming principles in general and may involve having to read and show understanding of pseudo-code. Other questions will require you to write your own program code in your chosen programming language, so it is important to make sure you are familiar with the specific operators and functions that are used in that programming language.

> **Exam tip**
>
> DIV and MOD are common terms for integer division and modulo. Make sure you are comfortable with how they function.

> **Operators** Symbols used to indicate a function.
>
> **Modulus** The remainder of the division of one number by another.
>
> **Exponentiation** The raising of one number to the power of another.
>
> **Rounding** Reducing the number of digits used to represent a value while maintaining its approximate value.
>
> **Truncation** Removing any value after a certain number of decimal places.

> **Now test yourself**   TESTED
>
> 19 What is the difference between float division and integer division?
>
> 20 What is the value of 7.86 when rounded to one decimal place?
>
> 21 What is the value of 7.86 when truncated to one decimal place?
>
> **Answers available online**

> **Revision activity**
>
> Write a program that uses DIV and MOD to convert a given number of hours into a number of days.

Relational operations

Relational operators are used in comparisons, typically in selection statements and condition-controlled loops. A relational operation, or comparison operation, will always return either True or False.

The relational operators are as follows:

= or ==	Equal to
!= or <> or ≠	Not equal to
>	Greater than
>=	Greater than or equal to
<	Less than
<=	Less than or equal to

Check your understanding and progress at **www.hoddereducation.co.uk/myrevisionnotesdownloads**

Now test yourself TESTED

State whether each of these is True or False when x ← 60.

22 x != 60

23 x < 60

24 x >= 60

25 x = 60

Answers available online

Making links

C# and Java are not able to make use of the standard relational operators when comparing strings. String handling operations are discussed on page 16.

Boolean operations

REVISED

Boolean operations can be used to invert the logic of a conditional statement, or to combine two or more conditions together.

NOT	Will invert the logic (that is, a condition that returns True will become False).
AND	Both conditions must be True.
OR	Either one condition must be True, or both.
XOR	One condition must be True and the other False.

Making links

The exam for Component 2 assesses understanding of Boolean logic in much more detail, including questions on Boolean algebra. The same basic principles apply whether combining logical statements in a practical programming setting or solving Boolean equations. For a more in-depth examination of Boolean logic see Chapter 6.

Now test yourself TESTED

Where a = 50 and b = 100, would each overall condition be True or False?

26 NOT (a = b)

27 a < 100 AND b > 100

28 a > b OR b = 2*a

29 a < b XOR b = 100

Answers available online

Revision activity

Write a program to calculate the output of simple logic circuits for NOT, AND, OR and XOR.

Variables and constants

REVISED

Concept of a variable

Computer programs are essentially sequences of instructions for how to process data. This data must be stored in memory in order to be accessed and the computer program will save and retrieve data as needed.

Variables are made up of four components:
+ A memory address – the location of the variable in memory.
+ An identifier – a name used to identify the variable in the program code.
+ A data type – a definition of what type of data can be stored in that variable.
+ A value – the actual value of the variable at that moment in time.

Memory The location where instructions and data are stored in a computer.

Identifier A technical term for the name of a variable.

Data type A definition of what type of data can be stored in that variable.

15

Variables are used to store values that are used in a computer program. The value of a variable can be changed while the program is running (such as a score, a running total, a user's name).

A named constant is a variable whose value cannot be changed while the program is running. Examples might include constants used in calculations (such as Pi) or user-defined values that should be used throughout the program (such as a maximum number of turns or a maximum size).

It is a common convention to use all caps in the identifier for a constant; for example, MAX_SIZE or MIN_VALUE and to declare constants at the start of a program.

Named constants are useful because:
+ they make it easier to update the program if the value of the constant needs to be changed
+ it reduces the need to use absolute values (that is, it is better to use a constant in the condition for a loop than a hard-coded number)
+ it stops the value being changed accidentally
+ it makes code more readable.

Exam tip

Component 1, Section C will often start with asking you to 'state the identifier for...' some variable or subroutine in the skeleton code.
For those questions you must only write down the identifier, and not the whole line of code.

Named constant A variable whose value cannot be changed while the program is running.

Exam tip

Remembering two or three standard advantages for each aspect of programming (such as named constants) will help you answer those questions quickly and accurately in the exam.

Now test yourself

TESTED

30 What **four** components make up a variable?

31 What is the meaning of the term *identifier* for a variable?

32 What is the main difference between a variable and named constant?

33 What are the advantages of using a named constant?

Answers available online

String handling operations

REVISED

Working with strings is an important part of programming, and it is very important to be familiar with the specific syntax used in different languages.

Comparing strings is handled using different syntax in different languages.
+ In AQA pseudo-code and VB.net, a single equals (=) is used to test for equality
+ In Pascal/Delphi and Python, a double equals (==) is used to test for equality.
+ In C# and Java a function must be used; for example, if (StringOne.equals(StringTwo)) (C# and Java).

There are several other string handling operations with which you should be familiar. The exact syntax will vary significantly depending on your chosen programming language and it is important to make sure you are confident in carrying out all of these operations in that language. Some examples are included below, in a variety of different languages, in order to demonstrate each operation.

Concatenate Join two (or more) strings together; for example, ABC + DEF = ABCDEF.

The key operations are as follows.

Key operator	Example
Finding length of a string	len(string) or string.length()
Finding a character at a given position	string.charAt(3) or string[3]
Retrieving a substring	string[0:6] or string.Substring(0,6)
Concatenating two or more strings	stringOne + stringTwo or concat(stringOne,stringTwo)
Finding the numeric code for a character	ord('D') or (int)'D'
Finding the character from a given numeric code	char(68) or chr(68)
Converting strings into different formats, and vice-versa	converting a string into an integer, float or date/time format

Check your understanding and progress at **www.hoddereducation.co.uk/myrevisionnotesdownloads**

Exam tips

Substring methods in different languages use different parameters.

+ Python and Java require the start and end positions.
+ C#, Delphi and VB.net require the start position and the length.

Make sure you read any pseudo-code questions that involve substrings carefully, and make sure you are comfortable programming with substrings using the language chosen for your exam.

Some languages treat a string as an array of characters and can use an index array to refer to a specific character; for example, `string[3]`. Some languages require the use of functions such as `charAt(int)`.

Make sure you are familiar with all of the operations above in your own language in advance of the Component 1 exam.

Now test yourself

TESTED ◯

34 Explain what is meant by *concatenation*.

35 Which string handling operation should be used to extract a person's first name from the string `FullName`?

36 State and describe **two** other string handling operations.

Answers available online

Revision activity

+ Write a program that will ask for a string and display each character's numeric code.
+ Write a program that will ask for a series of numeric codes and convert them into a single string which is displayed.

Random number generation

REVISED ◯

A large number of programs rely on random number generation.

Most languages have the ability to generate a random float between 0 and 1; for example, in Delphi:

```
float: Random;
```

Generating a random number in a specific range can then be achieved using multiplication; for example, to find a random float between 0 and 3 using VB.net:

```
Rnd() * 3
```

Most languages have a function for finding a random integer; for example, in Python:

```
random.randint(1,3)
```

Exam tip

In most years there is some random number generation included in the skeleton code. If you forget the correct syntax during the exam then make sure you know where to find a working example from the skeleton code to help you.

Revision activity

+ Write a program that will ask for a minimum and maximum number and will generate a float between those two values.
+ Write a program like that one above that will generate an integer between those two values.

17

Exception handling

Exception handling is used to deal with situations where a program may crash. The program should try to execute a block of code and then catch the error and deal with it appropriately.

Although the exact syntax may vary between languages, the basic construct typically reads:

```
try
{
        strInput = input("Enter a number")
        numInput = int(strInput)
}
catch (Exception)
{
        print("Error, did not recognise a number")
        numInput = -1
}
```

Exam tip

Make sure you can explain the purpose of any exception handling found in the skeleton code as this may be a question asked in Section C.

Making links

Using exception handling in your NEA programming project is a good way to demonstrate good programming techniques.

Revision activity

Write a program that asks users to enter a 2-digit number as a string (such as '12'), convert it to an integer, and then double it. Use exception handling to catch errors such as a non-digit entry (such as 'twelve').

Now test yourself

TESTED

37 What does the initialism RNG typically refer to?

38 What runtime error might occur in a program that asks a user to enter numeric values?

39 What programming structure should be used to deal with these types of errors?

Answers available online

Purpose of subroutines

A fundamental aspect of improving the efficiency of program code is the use of subroutines.

A subroutine allows a programmer to take a section of program code that performs a specific task and move it out of line of the rest of the program. This means that the programmer can call the subroutine in order to run that block of code at any point.

Subroutines are called using the subroutine's identifier, followed by any arguments that must be passed in parentheses; for example, `DisplayGreeting(name)`.

Subroutines that do not require any parameters must still be called using parentheses; for example, `DisplayDate()`.

The advantages of subroutines are:
+ the subroutine can be called multiple times without needing to duplicate the code
+ changes to the subroutine only need to be made once
+ it is easier to read the code
+ it is easier to debug the code if there is a problem
+ subroutines can be re-used in other programs
+ the job of writing a program can be split, with each programmer tackling their own subroutines.

Exam tip

Make sure you are able to explain the difference between a function and a procedure, and that you can identify which subroutines are which in the skeleton code. This is a common topic in section C.

Subroutine A named block of code designed to carry out one specific task.
Call The process of running a subroutine by stating its identifier, followed by any required arguments in parentheses.
Pass The transfer of a value, or the value of a variable, to a subroutine.

Making links

Using meaningful, self-documenting identifiers for subroutines is important to make your code more readable. It is essential to do this as part of your NEA.

Subroutines are broken down into two types: functions and procedures.

A function is a subroutine that returns a value once it has finished executing. A typical use of a function is to carry out a calculation and return the result.

A procedure is a subroutine that does not return a value. A typical use of a procedure is to display some data and/or prompts to the user.

Subroutines can be grouped together in a file to form a module or library. These subroutines can then be re-used in other programs.

It is common to import libraries that have already been written to help solve problems; for example, in Java `import java.util.*` or, in Python, `import random`.

> **Function** A subroutine that returns a value.
> **Procedure** A subroutine that does not return a value.
> **Module** A file that contains one or more subroutines that can be imported and used in another program.
> **Library** A collection of modules that provide related functionality.

Now test yourself TESTED

40 State **three** advantages for using subroutines.
41 Explain why it is important for subroutines to have meaningful identifiers.
42 What is the name for a subroutine that doesn't return a value?
43 What is the name for a subroutine that does return a value?

Answers available online

Parameters

REVISED

The parameters of a subroutine are the variables that must be passed to a subroutine when it is called. This is declared when the subroutine is written.

For example, in the code `Procedure DisplayTemperature(int Temp, bool Celsius)`, the subroutine called DisplayTemperature needs to be passed an integer value and a Boolean value.

When a subroutine is called, the values must be passed as arguments; for example, `DisplayTemperature(20,True)`.

> **Parameters** The variables that a subroutine needs in order for the subroutine to run.
> **Arguments** The actual values that are passed to the subroutine at runtime.

Returning a value

REVISED

Functions must always return a value at the end of their execution. This is carried out with a return statement.

For example:

```
Function Double(int StartVal)

        return 2*StartVal

End function
```

The value that is returned is passed back to the part of the program that called the function.

It is possible for a subroutine to have several different return statements – for example, within a selection structure – but the subroutine will stop once a value has been returned.

> **Return** To pass a value or the contents of a variable back to the place in the program where the function was called.

Now test yourself

44 Describe what is meant by the term *parameter*.
45 Explain the purpose of a return statement.

Answers available online
TESTED

Local variables

REVISED

When a subroutine is called, any variables passed as parameters and any variables declared within that subroutine are referred to as local variables. These variables can only be accessed within that subroutine and will be destroyed once the subroutine has finished executing. This is referred to as the scope of the variable.

> **Local variables** Variables that are declared within a subroutine and can only be accessed by the subroutine during the execution of that subroutine.
> **Scope** The visibility of variables (either local or global).

19

The advantages of local variables are:

+ uses less memory as local variables are destroyed once the subroutine has finished executing
+ less likely to accidentally change the value of a variable somewhere else in the program
+ easier to debug
+ variable identifiers can be re-used in separate subroutines
+ subroutines can be more easily re-used (subroutines are modular).

Knowing that local variables are destroyed once that section of code has finished executing, it is important to note that variables declared within a selection statement or iteration structure will also be destroyed at the end of that section of code. It is therefore very important to choose carefully where in the program a variable will be declared.

> **Modular** Independent of other subroutines.

Global variables

REVISED

Global variables are variables that are declared in the main program and can be read or altered in any subroutine.

Accessing global variables from within subroutines reduces the need for passing parameters and using return statements but should generally be avoided where possible.

Global variables are, however, useful for named constants.

> **Global variables** Variables that can be accessed from any subroutine.

> **Making links**
>
> Try to limit your use of global variables when working on your NEA programming project. Using a modular structure for your subroutines will increase the range of marks you are able to access.

> **Now test yourself** TESTED
>
> 46 Explain what is meant by the *scope* of a variable.
> 47 Explain **three** advantages of using local variables.
> 48 Explain **three** disadvantages of using global variables.
> 49 Describe a situation where it would be appropriate to use a global variable
>
> **Answers available online**

Stack frames

REVISED

When a subroutine is called a stack frame is created. This stack frame contains:

+ the return address – where to return to in the program once the subroutine has finished executing
+ parameters – the variables to which data was passed when the subroutine was called
+ local variables – any variables declared within that subroutine.

Newly called subroutines are added to the top of the call stack and the top stack frame is removed once that subroutine has been completed.

> **Stack frame** The collection of data associated with a subroutine call.
> **Call stack** A data structure that stores the stack frames for each active subroutine while the program is running.

> **Making links**
>
> Stacks are a complex data structure with a variety of uses in programming. Stacks and other complex data structures are explored further in Chapter 2.

> **Exam tip**
>
> Make sure you can recall the three things stored in a stack frame as this is a common question in Section A.

> **Now test yourself** TESTED
>
> 50 What **three** things are stored in a stack frame?
> 51 When is a new stack frame created?
> 52 Where are stack frames stored?
>
> **Answers available online**

> **Note**
>
> If a program becomes stuck in a loop that continually calls one or more subroutines then eventually the call stack will become too full, triggering a stack overflow error.

Check your understanding and progress at **www.hoddereducation.co.uk/myrevisionnotesdownloads**

Recursive techniques

Some algorithms are best solved by solving smaller and smaller instances of the same problem. To achieve this, a function must call itself repeatedly – this is known as recursion. One example of recursion is used in calculating a factorial.

A factorial is calculated by multiplying a number by all of the integers less than itself. The '!' is used as the mathematical symbol for 'factorial'. For example:

$5! = 5 \times 4 \times 3 \times 2 \times 1$

This can be simplified as $5 \times 4!$

$4! = 4 \times 3!$

$3! = 3 \times 2!$

$2! = 2 \times 1!$

$1! = 1$

A recursive subroutine will continue to call itself (known as the general case) until it reaches a decision that returns a value without calling itself (known as the base case or terminating case).

The pseudo-code algorithm for a factorial calculator might read:

```
Function Factorial (int n)

        IF n <= 1 THEN

                RETURN 1

        ELSE

                RETURN n * Factorial (n-1)

        END IF

End Function
```

If n = 1 or less then the function cannot attempt to break the task down any further, and should stop calling itself recursively, returning the result of 1 (1! = 1). This is the base case.

In all other cases the function will call itself. This is the general case.

It is possible to have more than one general case and more than one base case.

> **Recursion** The process of a function repeatedly calling itself.

> **General case** A case in which a recursive function is called and must call itself.
> **Base case** The case in which a recursive function terminates and does not call itself.

> **Exam tips**
>
> Following a recursive algorithm can be very tricky and it is important to get lots of practice using trace tables to step through recursive algorithms.
>
> Section B questions can require the use of recursion to achieve full marks, though a non-recursive solution will always be possible.

> **Making links**
>
> While Sections B and D may assess your ability to write program code using recursive techniques, Sections A and C may require you to demonstrate your ability to hand trace a recursive algorithm. Trace tables are covered in more detail in Chapter 4.

Now test yourself

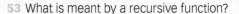

53 What is meant by a recursive function?

54 Explain what is meant by the base case in a recursive algorithm.

55 Explain what is meant by the general case of an algorithm.

56 Using the pseudo-code for a factorial calculator, above, state the maximum number of stack frames on the stack when calculating `Factorial(4)`.

Answers available online

Revision activity

+ Use the pseudo-code provided to program and test a working factorial calculator.
+ Use a debugger to step through the factorial calculator and inspect the stack frames.
+ Create a program that uses recursion to display the Fibonacci sequence (in which the previous two numbers are added to get the next one; for example, 1,1,2,3,5,8,13…).

1 Fundamentals of programming

21

Programming paradigms

Programming paradigms

REVISED

A programming paradigm is a way to classify a programming style or approach, based on its features and its approach. For Component 1 you are expected to have studied:

+ procedural-oriented programming
+ object-oriented programming.

Each paradigm is discussed in more detail below, and it is expected that you will have had practice programming using both paradigms throughout your preparation for the exam.

> **Exam tip**
>
> Study the skeleton program carefully to help predict what kinds of questions you might be asked. If the skeleton program uses object-oriented techniques then it is more likely that any questions on this topic will appear in Section C and will refer to the skeleton code and pre-release scenario. If the skeleton code doesn't use object-oriented techniques then it is more likely that questions on procedural-oriented programming will appear in Section C, and Section A will include some more generic questions on object-oriented programming.

> **Paradigm** A particular style or approach to designing a solution to a problem.
> **Procedural-oriented programming** An approach to solving a problem using subroutines to tackle smaller sub-problems.
> **Object-oriented programming** An approach to solving a problem using a model based on real-world objects that are designed to interact in a realistic way.

> **Now test yourself** TESTED
>
> 57 What is the meaning of the term *programming paradigm*?
> 58 What are the two programming paradigms that you should know?
> 59 Which paradigm uses a model based on real-world objects?
>
> **Answers available online**

Procedural-oriented programming

REVISED

Procedural-oriented programming is designed to allow programmers to use a structured, top-down approach to solve a given problem.

The program designer uses decomposition to break the problem down into increasingly small sub-problems, each of which can then be solved using a subroutine (either a function or a procedure).

The main program will then be constructed by calling subroutines which will, in turn, call other subroutines in order to solve the original problem.

Data can be passed to subroutines and values can be returned from them, allowing the different parts of the program to interact with each other.

This type of computer program is generally simpler to understand and the subroutines can be re-used at different points in the program without needing to copy it. This type of program is very modular and can easily be updated by changing one subroutine.

Hierarchy charts

Procedural-oriented programs can be represented using hierarchy charts. Simple hierarchy charts show the relationship between subroutines, such as the chart shown in Figure 1.1, with lines used to connect subroutines wherever one subroutine calls another.

> **Making links**
>
> For more on subroutines see the section *Purpose of subroutines* above on page 18.

> **Top-down approach** A method of planning solutions that starts with the big picture and breaks it down into smaller sub-problems.
> **Decomposition** A method of solving a larger problem by breaking it up into smaller and smaller problems until each problem can't be broken down any further.
> **Hierarchy charts** A diagram that shows which subroutines call which other subroutines. More complex versions will also show what data is passed and returned.

1 Fundamentals of programming

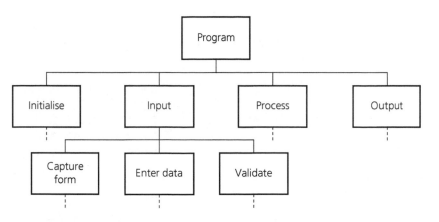

Figure 1.1 A simple hierarchy chart

> **Exam tip**
>
> Questions involving hierarchy charts almost exclusively appear in Section C, referring to the skeleton program, and usually involve a 'fill the gaps' style of question. Make your own hierarchy charts when studying the skeleton code to help you understand how the subroutines fit together and see past papers for example of this style of question.

Now test yourself   TESTED ◯

60 How is decomposition used when designing solutions using procedural-oriented programming?

61 In a hierarchy chart, what is the meaning of a line connecting two subroutines?

Answers available online

Revision activity

+ Open a complex program you have been working on in your lessons and create a hierarchy chart to show the relationships between each subroutine.
+ Consider the steps involved in a two-player game such as Rock-Paper-Scissors or Noughts & Crosses. Create a hierarchy chart to show how the game could be broken down into subroutines and how those subroutines would be related.

Object-oriented programming   REVISED ◯

Classes

Object-oriented programming (often referred to as OOP) uses a different approach to programming.

The programmer thinks about real-world objects and creates a class to describe the attributes and methods for that type of object. For instance, in Figure 1.2, the class called Customer has:
+ the attributes: Name, Address, and Date of birth
+ the methods: Edit customer and Delete customer.

> **Class** The definition of the attributes and methods of a group of similar objects.
> **Attributes** The properties that an object of that type has, implemented using variables.
> **Methods** Processes or actions that an object of that type can do, implemented using subroutines.

Customer		Account
Name		
Address	←—— Attributes ——→	Account number
Date of birth		Balance
Edit customer		Check balance
Delete customer	←—— Methods ——→	Add interest

Figure 1.2 Classes containing attributes and methods

Attributes are implemented using variables to hold the relevant data.

Methods are implemented using subroutines to carry out each action.

Objects

When the program is run, objects are instantiated (created) based on the class definitions. Once instantiated, the object is stored in a variable.

> **Note**
>
> The object is stored in memory and the variable stores the memory address of that object so that it can be accessed.

When an object is created, a special method called the constructor is called, and this will initialise the object, typically setting the attributes and sometimes calling other methods.

Each instance of an object will have its own values for each attribute, but all instances of that object will be able to carry out the same methods. For instance, in Figure 1.3:

+ the object Account1 is an instance of the class Account, with Account number 12345 and a balance of £7.63
+ Account2 is a different instance of the class Account, with a different account number and balance.

All objects of this type have the same attributes, however the value of the attributes can vary from object to object.

Account1	Account2	Account3
Account number: 12345	Account number: 73526	Account number: 92649
Balance +7.63	Balance -3,107.12	Balance +11,836.01
Check balance	Check balance	Check balance
Add interest	Add interest	Add interest

Figure 1.3 Three unique instances of an Account object

> **Now test yourself** TESTED ◯
>
> 62 What **two** features are defined in a class?
> 63 Describe the relationship between an object and its class.
> 64 What method is called when an object is instantiated?
> 65 When two objects of the same class are instantiated, describe the features of each object which will definitely be the same and which might be different.
>
> **Answers available online**

Encapsulation

Deciding how to structure and organise classes can be difficult, but the main rule is to group together objects with common characteristics (attributes) and behaviours (methods). Keeping these features together in one class is called encapsulation.

Encapsulation is useful because it means that program code is more modular. This means that the code is easier to debug, can be re-used more easily and teams of programmers can work on individual classes without needing to know how other classes are programmed – they only need to know what methods can be accessed.

Encapsulation is also helpful as it allows for information hiding, in which the data stored in the attributes can be kept within that object and access to that data can be controlled.

Object A specific instance of a class.
Instantiation The process of creating an object based on its class definition.
Constructor A special method (with the same name as the class) that is called when the object is instantiated.

Encapsulation The concept of grouping similar attributes, data, and methods together in one object.
Information hiding Controlling access to data stored within an object.

Check your understanding and progress at **www.hoddereducation.co.uk/myrevisionnotesdownloads**

Access specifiers

Each attribute (variable) and method (subroutine) within a class has an access specifier (also commonly known as an access modifier) which controls whether other objects are able to directly interact with it.

Access specifier	Symbol	Attributes	Methods
public	+	can be viewed or updated by any object of any class	can be called by any object of any class
private	-	cannot be viewed or updated by any other object, regardless of class	cannot be called by any other object, regardless of class
protected	#	can only be viewed or updated by this object or another object of that class, or a subclass	can only be called by this object or another object of that class, or a subclass

The convention is to declare attributes as private so that other objects cannot directly interact or affect the values that are stored. This make it less likely that a class written by another programmer could adversely affect the overall program.

To allow access to those data, a class should include getters and setters – public methods that allow other objects to ask an object to return the value of a specific attribute, or that ask an object to update a value.

One example might be a game character that has a score and a number of lives which are both set to private, and uses public methods to allow other objects to interact with those values:

```
Character = Class

    Private:

            Score: Int

            Lives: Int

    Public:

            Function GetScore()

            Function GetLives()

            Procedure AddPoints()

            Procedure LoseALife()

            Procedure GainExtraLife()

End Class
```

Access specifier (or access modifier) A keyword that sets the accessibility of an attribute or method.
Public An access specifier that allows that attribute or method to be accessed by any other object.
Private An access specifier that protects that attribute or method from being accessed by any other object.
Protected An access specifier that protects that attribute or method from being accessed by other objects unless they are instances of that class or a subclass.
Getter A function used to return the value of an attribute to another object.
Setter A procedure used to allow another object to set or update the value of an attribute.

Revision activity

+ Using pseudo-code, describe the class attributes and methods required for a virtual pet.
+ Design and build an object-oriented program that uses a Calculator class with methods such as Press0, Press1, PressPlus and PressEquals.

Now test yourself · TESTED ○

66 Identify **three** things that are grouped together using encapsulation.

67 Suggest **two** advantages of using encapsulation.

68 State the name, symbol and meaning for the three main access specifiers.

69 Which access specifier should be used, by default, for attributes?

70 Explain how it is possible for private attributes or methods to be accessed by other objects.

Answers available online

Inheritance

Inheritance describes an 'is a' relationship between classes. For example, a horse is a type of animal.

To implement this, subclasses (or child classes) inherit attributes and methods from a base class (or parent class).

Inheritance The idea that one class can use the attributes and methods defined in another class.
Subclass (or child class) A class that inherits the attributes and methods from another class.
Base class (or parent class) A class whose attributes and methods are inherited by another class.

25

This means that the same code can be re-used without needing to be copied, and if the code needs to be changed then it only needs to be changed in the base class, reducing the risk of errors and making it easier to debug.

In class diagrams, inheritance is showing using a hollow arrow, which always points towards the base class.

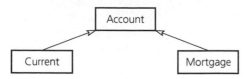

Figure 1.4 An inheritance diagram

Figure 1.4 shows a class structure in which two types of account (Current and Mortgage) are subclasses will inherit the attributes and methods from the Account base class.

> **Exam tip**
>
> In AQA Pseudo-code, subclasses are declared by adding the base class name in parentheses; for example:
>
>   Dog = Class (Animal)
>
> It is rare for the exam to ask students to describe a class using pseudo-code. However, when this is the case, then language-specific syntax is accepted; for example:
>
>   Dog = Class extends Animal

Subclasses will have additional properties and methods specific to that type of object (for example, a current account might have a withdrawal limit or the ability to allow an overdraft, whereas a mortgage account might have a fixed end-date and the ability to allow a payment holiday).

Both subclasses will inherit the attributes and methods from the base class (that is, they both have an account number and a balance and both have methods for checking the balance and adding interest).

> **Now test yourself** TESTED ◯
>
> 71 Suggest equivalent terms for *child class* and *parent class*.
>
> 72 What symbol is used to show an inheritance relationship on a class diagram, and which direction does it point?
>
> 73 Suggest **two** advantages of using inheritance.
>
> **Answers available online**

Aggregation

Aggregation describes a 'has a' relationship between classes; for example, a building has a room.

In the implementation of aggregation, one container object contains a reference to an associated object as an attribute (variable).

There are two types of aggregation:

+ association aggregation
+ inheritance aggregation.

Association aggregation

In association aggregation the two types of object are associated with each other, but not dependent on each other.

If the container object is removed or destroyed, the associated objects are undamaged. In a real-world example, employers and managers in a business all have a job role. A business that is changing the way it works may decide a certain role is no longer needed. However removing the job role does not remove the employees and managers – they are still part of the business.

> **Exam tip**
>
> The terms subclass and child class are interchangeable and both mean the same thing. The terms base class and parent class are also interchangeable. It is helpful to either use the terms subclass and base class OR child class and parent class for consistency, but both sets of terminology are acceptable.

Aggregation The idea that one class can be related to another using a 'has a' relationship.
Container class (or **container object**) A class or object that contains, or is made up of, other objects.
Associated class (or **associated object**) A class or object that is used to make up another object.
Association aggregation A type of aggregation where the container object can be destroyed without destroying its associated objects.
Composition aggregation A type of aggregation where, if the container object is destroyed, its associated objects are also destroyed.

Check your understanding and progress at **www.hoddereducation.co.uk/myrevisionnotesdownloads**

In class diagrams, association aggregation is shown using a hollow diamond, which always points towards the container class.

Figure 1.5 Class diagram showing association aggregation

Composition aggregation

Composition aggregation describes a more dependant relationship in which the container object is directly made up (composed) of the associated objects.

If the container object is removed or destroyed then so are the associated objects. In our example the container object Workforce is made up of managers and employers. Removing Workforce from the model altogether results in the removal of the employees and managers.

In class diagrams, composition aggregation is shown using a filled diamond, which always points towards the container class.

Figure 1.6 Class diagram showing composition aggregation

Now test yourself   **TESTED** ◯

74 What is the difference between *inheritance* and *aggregation*?
75 Describe the difference between association aggregation and composition aggregation.
76 State which symbols are used to show each type of aggregation on a class diagram.
77 In a computer model featuring a Room class, a Window class and a Door class, which class is the container class?

Answers available online

Polymorphism

Polymorphism means 'many forms'. It covers the potential scenario of having two or more methods with the same name.
+ A method to ring(PhoneNumber) would involve dialling that specific number.
+ A method to ring(Name) would involve looking up the phone number for the person you want to ring and then ringing that number.

Both methods have the same name, but different parameters. By looking at the data type of the value that is passed, the object can identify which method to use.

Having methods with the same names but different parameters means that the same basic goal can be achieved using different steps, or methods, and is a common feature in object-oriented programming.

Overriding

Overriding is the situation where a base class has a method and a subclass has a method of the same name, but with different steps. The subclass method overrides (takes priority over) the method from the base class.

For example, an Account class can have a method CloseAccount that transfers the remaining balance to the customer.

> **Polymorphism** Literally 'many forms' – the ability for two methods with the same name to carry out their actions using different code.
> **Overriding** A method in a subclass re-defining a method inherited from a base class.

> **Exam tip**
> Look carefully through the skeleton code for any examples of polymorphism. If there are any then this is a likely question to appear in Section C.

A Mortgage class is a subclass and inherits the `CloseAccount` method, but in this case the `CloseAccount` method needs to be re-written so that the account can only be closed if the mortgage has been paid off.

Revision activity

+ Create flashcards for each piece of key vocabulary in this chapter.
+ Examine the skeleton program for your Component 1 exam, or a previous skeleton program, and identify as many examples of instantiation, inheritance, aggregation, polymorphism and overriding as possible.

Why object-oriented programming is used

There are several advantages for choosing object-oriented programming over procedural-oriented programming.

+ OOP more closely represents the real world, which is made up of objects of various types.
+ Program code is easier to debug as each class is modular.
+ Classes can be re-used in other programs.
+ Code can be re-used through inheritance and aggregation.

Object-oriented design principles

There are three main design principles you are expected to be familiar with:

+ encapsulate what varies
+ favour composition over inheritance
+ program to interfaces, not implementation.

Encapsulate what varies

This means that in the design stage a programmer should try to identify the features of a model that are likely to change in the future and encapsulate those features.

One example is a method designed to display the number of wheels that a vehicle has, using a selection statement:

```
IF Vehicle.Type = "bicycle" THEN

    OUTPUT "Vehicle has 2 wheels"

ELSE IF Vehicle.Type = "car" THEN

    OUTPUT "Vehicle has 4 wheels"

ELSE IF Vehicle.Type = "boat" THEN

    OUTPUT "Vehicle has 0 wheels"

ENDIF
```

A better design would use encapsulation to store the number of wheels as part of a vehicle class:

```
OUTPUT "Vehicle has " + Vehicle.NumberOfWheels + " wheels"
```

This means that if the program is changed to add a tricycle vehicle type, there is no need to change the existing code.

The use of inheritance can also make it much easier to encapsulate features or behaviours that vary, using the technique of overriding within subclasses.

Making links

Object-oriented design principles go alongside software development principles, covered in Chapter 13. Clear definition and analysis of a problem will directly inform the object-oriented code design.

Favour composition over inheritance

Composition aggregation and association aggregation provide a more flexible relationship between classes than inheritance.

This is advantageous because each class can be tested independently of other classes, which is not true for subclasses.

Changing a base class can cause unexpected side-effects in subclasses, so using composition rather than inheritance means it is safer to update program code in the future.

A particular problem with inheritance is that a subclass can't inherit from two different classes at once. This means that if a new behaviour is common to two different classes then it may not be easier to re-use code without copying it into both classes.

Program to interfaces, not implementation

Interfaces are a special concept which can be used to group similar behaviours together and make them available to unrelated classes that have access to that interface.

> **Interface** A collection of subroutines that can be implemented by unrelated classes.

For example, a `Dog` class might have access to an interface called `Annoy`, which will call the methods `Bark` and `ChewSlippers`. A `Person` class might also have access to the interface called `Annoy`, and in this class it will call the methods `TalkLoudly` and `PickNose`.

By grouping both sets of behaviours into one interface, a programmer can make either type of object 'annoy' without concerning themselves with the actual implementation of how each unrelated class will carry out that process.

This technique uses a mixture of encapsulation (grouping similar behaviours together) and abstraction (hiding the complexity of what is happening).

Now test yourself   TESTED ◯

81 Describe **three** advantages of using object-oriented programming.

82 Explain why composition is preferable to inheritance.

83 Which design principle involves the grouping together of similar behaviours with unrelated classes?

84 Which design principle involves the grouping together attributes or methods that are likely to be changed in the future?

Answers available online

Writing object-oriented programs

It is important to be familiar with the syntax of your chosen programming language.

For each of the following, these techniques may be present in the skeleton program and you may be required to make use of them, but you are unlikely to be asked direct questions about them.

Abstract methods are declared but contain no program code. These are sometimes used in base classes to create the requirement to override a method. An example may be a `Speak` method in an `Animal` class that must be overridden for each of the `Dog`, `Cat` and `Parrot` subclasses.

Virtual methods are methods that may be overridden. In some languages (Java and Python) all methods are virtual by default. In other languages (C#, Delphi/Pascal and Visual Basic) methods must be declared as virtual in the base class if they are to be overridden.

Static methods are methods that can be called within a class without the need to create an object of that class. This means less memory usage as the program doesn't need to create the object in order to be able to run those methods and should be used when any object should be able to make use of those methods.

> **Abstract method** A method that has no program code and is intended to be overridden.
> **Virtual method** A method that may be overridden (this is the default in many languages).
> **Static method** A method within a class that can be called without the need to create an object of that class.

Class diagrams

The design of classes can be described using a class diagram, using arrows and diamonds to describe the relationships

Simple class diagrams just show the names of classes and the relationships between them.

More detailed class diagrams show the attributes and methods within each class as well.

These diagrams show the name of the class in the top section, attributes in the middle section and methods in the bottom section, along with access specifiers.

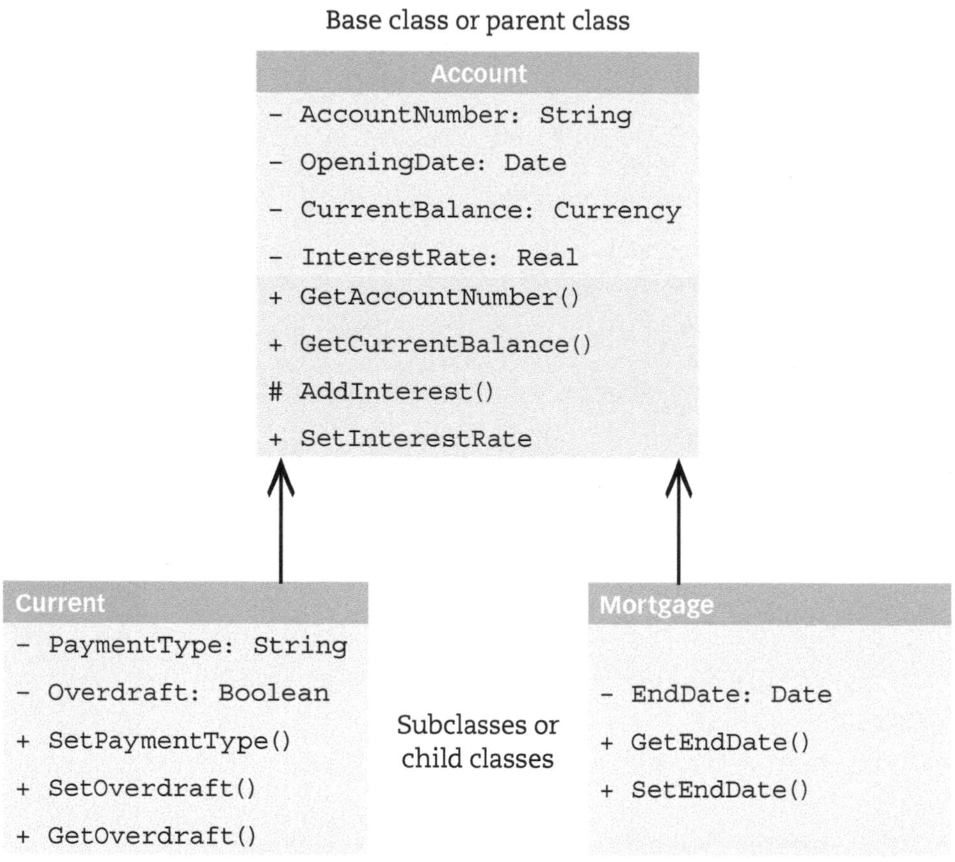

Base class or parent class

Account

```
- AccountNumber: String
- OpeningDate: Date
- CurrentBalance: Currency
- InterestRate: Real
+ GetAccountNumber()
+ GetCurrentBalance()
# AddInterest()
+ SetInterestRate
```

Current

```
- PaymentType: String
- Overdraft: Boolean
+ SetPaymentType()
+ SetOverdraft()
+ GetOverdraft()
```

Subclasses or child classes

Mortgage

```
- EndDate: Date
+ GetEndDate()
+ SetEndDate()
```

Figure 1.7 A class diagram showing the design for different types of account

Note the way that attributes are described using Identifier: Data Type.

Now test yourself   TESTED ◯

85 What type of method can be called even if an object of that class has not been instantiated?

86 What key word means that a method can be overridden?

87 What type of method must be overridden?

88 Identify six things should be included in a detailed class diagram.

Answers available online

Summary

Programming

+ Each variable has an address in memory, an identifier, a data type and a value. It is important to choose a meaningful identifier
+ Named constants are variables whose values cannot be changed while the program is running
+ Selection is used to decide which block of code to execute and is implemented using an IF or SWITCH statement
+ Iteration is used to repeat a block of code and either uses a count-controlled (FOR) loop if the number of repetitions is known or a condition-controlled (WHILE or DO-WHILE) loop if the number of repetitions is not known
+ Arithmetic operators include basic arithmetic, plus rounding, truncation and the use of DIV and MOD
+ Relational operators can be combined with Boolean operators to create more complex conditions
+ String handling operations include the basic skills of finding the length, addressing specific positions and concatenation (joining) of strings, as well as extracting substrings, converting to and from the numeric character codes and converting data types
+ It is important to be able to use random number generation and exception handling in your programming
+ Exception handling is an important tool when a block of code has a chance of failure (for example, opening a file that may not exist, or processing user inputs that may be in the wrong format)
+ Subroutines allow for code to be re-used. Parameters describe the data that must be passed to a subroutine when it is called
+ Functions are subroutines that return a value. Procedures are subroutines that do not return a value
+ Local variables are preferable to global variables in most cases as they use less memory, make subroutines more modular and make programs easier to read and debug.
+ Stack frames contain the return address, parameters, and local variables of a subroutine call while it is running
+ A recursive function is a function that calls itself. It must include at least one base case, a point at which the function will stop calling itself

Programming paradigms

+ There are two main programming paradigms to study – procedural-oriented programming and object-oriented programming
+ In procedural-oriented programming the main problem is broken down into smaller sub-problems, each of which is solved using a subroutine
+ Hierarchy charts are used to show which subroutines call other subroutines

+ In object-oriented programming the programmer designs a program around the attributes and behaviours of real-world objects
+ A class contains the attributes (variables) and methods (subroutines) associated with that type of object and functions as a blueprint for how objects of that class will behave
+ Objects are instances of a specific class and instantiated by calling their constructor
+ The process of grouping objects with common attributes and behaviours together is called encapsulation
+ Access to an object's attributes and methods is controlled using access specifiers
+ It is common for all attributes to be declared as private, and for setter and getter methods to be declared as public in order to allow other objects to interact in a controlled manner
+ Inheritance describes an 'is a' relationship. A subclass will inherit the attributes and methods of a base class
+ Aggregation describes a 'has a' relationship. A container class will be linked to one or more associated classes
+ In association aggregation, if the container class is destroyed then the associated classes will be untouched
+ In composition aggregation, if the container class is destroyed then the associated classes will be destroyed as well.
+ Polymorphism is the term for using having two or more methods with the same identifier in the same class, but using different parameters to allow the program to decide which method to run
+ Overriding is the term for a subclass having a method with the same identifier as a method in the base class; the method in the subclass will always take precedence
+ There are three design principles to remember: 'Encapsulate what varies', 'Favour composition over inheritance' and 'Program to interfaces, not implementation'
+ You should not be asked about abstract, virtual and static methods but these may appear in the skeleton code
+ Class diagrams should always show the name of the class, the attributes for that class (including data types and access modifiers) and the methods for that class (including access modifiers)
+ Inheritance is shown using a hollow arrow that points towards the base class
+ Association aggregation is shown using a hollow diamond that points towards the container class
+ Composition aggregation is shown using a filled diamond that points towards the container class

Exam practice

1   Dave has been asked to write a program as part of a project looking at rainfall. At the end of a week the user of the program will enter the total rainfall (measured in mm) for each one of the last seven days as a number with one decimal place. The program should calculate and then output:
    + The amount of rain that fell on the day with the least rainfall.
    + The amount of rain that fell on the day with the most rainfall.
    + The total amount of rainfall for that week.
    + The mean average amount of rainfall for that week.

    a) An iterative structure should be used in the program described above. Explain whether a count-controlled or condition-controlled iteration structure would be most suitable, and why.   [2]
    b) Write a program using your chosen programming language that will solve the problem described above.   [10]
    c) Show the output of the program when the following values are input.   [1]

        2.2   7.6   1.4   3.1   2.7   1.5   3.2

2   In the following table, the first column contains pseudo-code for an algorithm that will check to see if a piece of text is a palindrome (a word or phrase that reads the same forwards or backwards).

    The second column contains pseudo-code for a recursive algorithm that will carry out the check.

    The subroutine `Length()` will return the number of characters in a given string.

    The subroutine `Substring(start,end)` will return the string starting from position start and ending at position end. For example `"Message".Substring(2,5)` will return `"ssag"`.

```
FUNCTION Palindrome()

   OUTPUT "Enter a word or phrase"

   Phrase ← INPUT

   Result ← PCheck(Phrase)

   IF Result = TRUE THEN

      OUTPUT "This is a palindrome"

   ELSE

      OUTPUT "This is not a palindrome"

   ENDIF

ENDFUNCTION
```

```
FUNCTION PCheck(Phrase)

   NumChars = Length(Phrase)

   IF NumChars < 2 THEN

     RETURN TRUE

   ELSEIF Phrase[0] = Phrase[NumChars-1] THEN

      RETURN PCheck(Phrase.Substring(1,NumChars-2))

   ELSE

      RETURN FALSE

ENDFUNCTION
```

   a) Explain what is meant by a recursive algorithm.   [1]
   b) Explain what is meant by a base case, and describe one base case from the subroutine `PCheck`.   [2]
   c) Write a program in your chosen language that will ask the user to enter a word or phrase and check if it is a palindrome without using recursion.   [7]
   d) Show the output of the program when the word "RACECAR" is entered.   [1]
   e) Show the output of the program when the word "BEAR" is entered.   [1]

3 This class diagram is a partial representation of the relationships between some of the classes in a program for a garage.

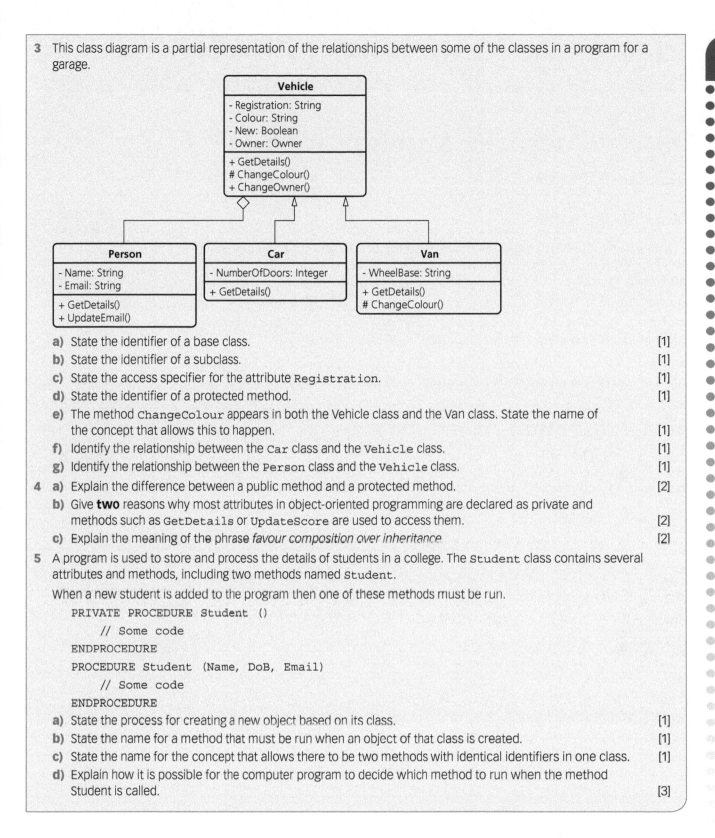

a) State the identifier of a base class. [1]

b) State the identifier of a subclass. [1]

c) State the access specifier for the attribute `Registration`. [1]

d) State the identifier of a protected method. [1]

e) The method `ChangeColour` appears in both the Vehicle class and the Van class. State the name of the concept that allows this to happen. [1]

f) Identify the relationship between the `Car` class and the `Vehicle` class. [1]

g) Identify the relationship between the `Person` class and the `Vehicle` class. [1]

4 a) Explain the difference between a public method and a protected method. [2]

b) Give **two** reasons why most attributes in object-oriented programming are declared as private and methods such as `GetDetails` or `UpdateScore` are used to access them. [2]

c) Explain the meaning of the phrase *favour composition over inheritance* [2]

5 A program is used to store and process the details of students in a college. The `Student` class contains several attributes and methods, including two methods named `Student`.

When a new student is added to the program then one of these methods must be run.

```
PRIVATE PROCEDURE Student ()
    // Some code
ENDPROCEDURE
PROCEDURE Student (Name, DoB, Email)
    // Some code
ENDPROCEDURE
```

a) State the process for creating a new object based on its class. [1]

b) State the name for a method that must be run when an object of that class is created. [1]

c) State the name for the concept that allows there to be two methods with identical identifiers in one class. [1]

d) Explain how it is possible for the computer program to decide which method to run when the method Student is called. [3]

2 Fundamentals of data structures

Data structures and abstract data types

Data structures

REVISED

Data structures are designed to hold several items of data at a time. This makes it easier to manage, find, update and process data than to work with individual variables.

For instance, finding the biggest value from ten separate variables would require a separate selection statement to interrogate each one, and additional code would be needed each time the number of variables increased.

Using a data structure called an array means that it is possible to step through each item using a loop, reducing the amount of code and making the code much more flexible .

> **Data structure** The concept of storing multiple values together with a single identifier.
>
> **Array** A data structure for holding values in a table.

Single- and multi-dimensional arrays (or equivalent)

REVISED

An array is a fixed-size collection of values, all of the same data type.

Single-dimensional arrays

A single-dimensional array can be written down as a single row of a table.

Each individual item in the array is referred to using the identifier (or variable name) of the array, followed by the index in brackets (usually square brackets). Each index position can hold data.

> **Index** A value indicating the position of a value with in an array or list.
>
> **List** A data structure similar to an array, commonly used in Python in place of an array.

Index	[0]	[1]	[2]	[3]	[4]
Data	1	3	5	7	11

> **Note**
>
> Arrays are always declared as a fixed size and cannot be changed later in the program. In an array, all data must be of the same data type.
>
> **Lists** are very similar to arrays, however it is possible to alter the size of a list while the program is running and it is possible to store data of differing types in the same list.
>
> In some languages (notably including Python) it is much more common to use a list, whereas in others it is much more common to use an array.
>
> You are not expected or required to show your understanding of the difference between the two, and you should use whichever version is most suitable for your chosen programming language.

> **Exam tip**
>
> In most languages (including C#, Delphi/Pascal, Java & VB.Net) the array index starts at 0, but be very careful when reading exam questions as some languages and some scenarios will have the array index starting at 1.

Arrays are an effective solution for storing several values because a FOR loop can be used to iterate (or loop) over an array.

In this example Numbers is the name of an array and Length(Numbers) returns the size of the array (the number of items is contains).

```
FOR i ← 0 TO Length(Numbers)
    OUTPUT Numbers[i]
ENDFOR
```

Check your understanding and progress at **www.hoddereducation.co.uk/myrevisionnotesdownloads**

This code will step through the items in the array n times, where n is the size of the array. This code would work for all arrays regardless of their size. This is far more efficient than stepping through several variables one at a time, as this would require a separate line of code for each variable and the program would need to be edited every time the number of items changed.

Multi-dimensional arrays

A two-dimensional array can be written down as a table.

A two-dimensional array can be thought of as an array of one-dimensional arrays.

By identifying which row is being addressed using one array index, a particular value can be addressed within that row using a second array index.

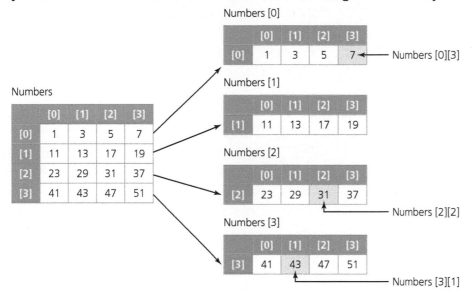

Figure 2.1 A two-dimensional array called Numbers

In the example above the contents of Numbers[0][3] can be found by isolating row 0 and then finding the item in position 3.

A two-dimensional array is useful because it can store more complex data; for example, the scores for different students or values for different days.

It is possible to find the size of a two-dimensional array using the Length function (exact syntax varies by programming language).

For an array with indexes defined as [row][column], to find the number of rows, find the number of one-dimensional arrays the table can be split into:

```
NumberOfRows ← Length(ArrayName)
```

To find the number of columns, find the length of a row in the table:

```
NumberOfColumns ← Length(ArrayName[0])
```

To interrogate a two-dimensional array it is necessary to use nested loops.

```
FOR i ← 0 to Length(Numbers)        // Step through each row

    FOR j ← 0 to Length(Numbers[i]) // Step through each
value in that row

        OUTPUT Numbers[i][j]

    ENDFOR

ENDFOR
```

Using the principle above, it is possible to think of a three-dimensional array as an array of two-dimensional arrays.

Making links

One-dimensional arrays can be an effective way of representing a vector. Vectors are used in many games and physical models, and are discussed in more detail towards the end of this chapter.

Exam tip

Arrays can also be defined using the first index to find the column and the second index to find the item in that column. Always read the question carefully as any ambiguities should be made clear.

Making links

One common use for a two-dimensional array is storing a **matrix**. Matrices are often used in complex maths, and can also be used to represent a graph data structure. This is explored further later in this chapter.

Matrix A rectangular, two-dimensional collection of values.

Nested A selection statement or loop inside another selection statement or loop.

Exam tip

Make sure you are able to hand trace a program such as the one above to fully understand which counter variable is addressing the row or column index of the table.

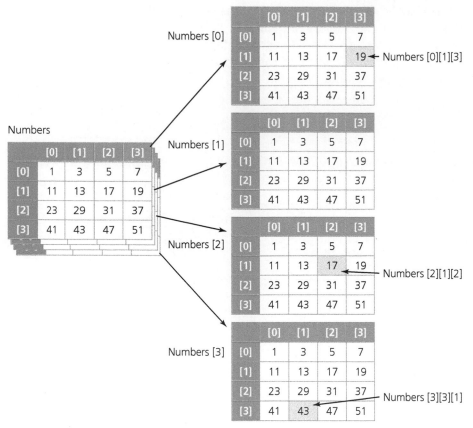

Numbers

Numbers [0]

Numbers [0][1][3]

Numbers [1]

Numbers [2]

Numbers [2][1][2]

Numbers [3]

Numbers [3][3][1]

Figure 2.2 A three-dimensional array represented as an array of two-dimensional arrays

Similarly, an array of n-dimensions is possible, where n is any positive integer.

Now test yourself

1 Explain the purpose of an index in an array
2 Describe **two** advantages for using an array of integers instead of several integer variables.
3 True or false? All arrays start counting from 0.
4 What data structure is typically used instead of an array in Python?
5 True or false? It is not possible to have an array of more than four dimensions.
6 How many FOR loops need to be nested in order to interrogate a two-dimensional array?

Answers available online

Revision activity

+ Create a two-dimensional array called `MovieRatings`. Populate the array with film review ratings, with each row representing one review website and each column representing one film.
+ Create a menu and write program code that will allow the user to:
    + find the min, max and mean average review score for each film
    + find the min, max and mean average review score from each website
    + find a specific review rating given the name of the film and the review website.
+ Create a 2-dimensional array to store the game state for a game of noughts and crosses.

Check your understanding and progress at **www.hoddereducation.co.uk/myrevisionnotesdownloads**

Fields, records and files

A record holds groups of related items together, using fields. An example might be a user record, containing fields to store the first name, last name and username for people logging onto a website.

First name	Last name	Username
Dave	Smith	Davo263
Nicola	Tandy	NicTandy
Stephen	Duffy	DuffS17

Each item in a record can be a different data type, making a record more complex than an array, but also more flexible.

There are many ways to implement a record, and this is handled differently in different programming languages. Understanding and recognising records of data and which fields are being used is the key concept.

One common concept when considering records is the importance of writing records to a file.

Files are a way of permanently storing data which would otherwise be lost once the program or subroutine has finished executing.

Text files use a character set (such as ASCII or Unicode) to store the data as text and typically use a delimiter such as a comma (,) or colon (:) to separate the individual items of data. These files are usually saved with a .txt or .csv (comma separated value) file extension.

A saved file from a game of Noughts and Crosses might be saved like this as a .csv file, where a comma is used to separate each item of data.

	X	
	O	X
	X	O

```
-,X,-,-,O,X,-,X,O
```

An alternative is to save the game as a binary file. A binary file only stores binary information, and needs a key to translate binary into particular items of data. For instance, for the Noughts and Crosses game, using two bits per cell, the following key could be used:

00	Empty
01	X
10	O
11	Not used

Then the saved game file would be stored as:

000100

001001

000110

The advantages of using a text file to store this data are that the data can be:
+ read by other programs
+ easily understood.

Record A collection of related data.

Field A category of data within a record or group of records.

File A persistent collection of data, saved for access and accessible once the program or subroutine has finished running.

Text file A file that uses text encoding (such as ASCII or Unicode) to store data.

Binary file A file that uses binary values to represent each item of data.

Exam tip

Make sure you can identify the advantages and disadvantages of using binary files versus text files. It is extremely unlikely that you will be asked to write code to work directly with binary files, though you may choose to explore this as part of your NEA programming project.

2 Fundamentals of data structures

37

The advantages of using a binary file to store this data are:
+ smaller file size
+ data cannot be read by other programs (more secure).

> **Note**
>
> For A-level it is only necessary to consider sequential file access. That is, reading files from start to end, in order.

> **Exam tip**
>
> The syntax for writing to and reading from files varies significantly in different programming languages. It is important to be familiar with file handling routines in your chosen programming language and to look carefully for any file handling that takes place in the skeleton program.

> **Now test yourself** TESTED
>
> 7 What are the two types of file?
> 8 Describe **one** advantage and **one** disadvantage for using a binary file.
> 9 What is used to separate individual values in a .csv file?
> 10 Which of the following is correct: a field is made up of records, or a record is made up of fields?
>
> **Answers available online**

> **Revision activity**
>
> + Create a two-dimensional array to represent the state of a game of noughts and crosses. Write program code that will:
>   + save the game state as a text file
>   + load a game state from a text file
>   + save the game state as a binary file
>   + load a game state as a binary file.
> + Compare the file size of the text and binary files. Try opening both types of file in a simple text editor (such as *Notepad*) and compare the contents.

Abstract data types/data structures

REVISED

While most programming languages have built in data structures such as arrays (or similar), more complex data structures are not always directly supported.

Abstract data types can be implemented using a collection of existing tools, typically involving the use of an array and one or more other variables. Each one is discussed in more detail below.

They are referred to as abstract data types because the complexity of the data structure is hidden and a programmer can make use of them without needing to be directly concerned with how they are implemented.
+ Some data structures (including arrays) are static. That means that, once declared, their size is fixed and cannot be increased or decreased.
+ Static data structures are assigned a fixed amount of memory when declared, making access to the values quick, however memory can be wasted if some spaces are left empty.
+ Some data structures (including lists) are dynamic. That means that their size is not fixed and they can grow and shrink as necessary.

Dynamic data structures are assigned memory as needed which uses memory more efficiently, but accessing the data can be slower as the memory assigned to the data structure may become fragmented.

> **Abstract data type** A complex data structure in which the complexity of how the data is stored or accessed is typically hidden from the programmer.
>
> **Static** The size of, and the memory assigned to that data structure is fixed and cannot be changed.
>
> **Dynamic** The size of, and the memory assigned to that data structure can change.

Check your understanding and progress at **www.hoddereducation.co.uk/myrevisionnotesdownloads**

Queues

A queue data structure works in a very similar way to a queue in the real world.

Items are retrieved from the front of the queue and new items are added at the rear of the queue.

The term for this type of data structure is First In, First Out (FIFO).

Common uses for queues include:
+ buffering (storing data as it arrives until it can be processed)
+ simulating a card game (cards are drawn from the front and replaced at the back).

> **Making links**
>
> Queues are a fundamental part of the breadth first search (BFS) which is explored in Chapter 3.

Queue A data structure in which items are stored in the order in which they should be accessed.

First In, First Out (FIFO) Those items placed into the queue first will be the first ones to be accessed.

Pointer A value that stores an address. In the context of queues this is usually the index of the front or rear item.

A queue can be implemented using a single-dimensional array and two integer variables, referred to as the Front Pointer (FP) and the Rear Pointer (RP).

FP		RP			
[0]	[1]	[2]	[3]	[4]	[5]
Dave	Angelina	Faaris			

FP	0
RP	2

There are several actions that can be carried out on a queue:

Enqueue	add new data to the rear of the queue
Dequeue	remove one item from the front of the queue
Peek (or Top)	look at, but don't remove, one item from the front of the queue
IsEmpty	check to see if the queue is empty
IsFull	check to see if the queue is full

The IsFull and IsEmpty actions are necessary because a program will crash if there is an attempt to enqueue data when the queue is already full or to dequeue data from an empty queue.

There are three types of queue:
+ Linear queue
+ Circular queue
+ Priority queue

Linear queue A queue in which data is stored in a line.

Circular queue A queue which wraps around in a circle. If implemented using an array, the last index is followed by the first index.

Priority queue A queue which stores a priority for each value so that the items with the highest priority can be accessed first.

Implementing a linear queue

REVISED

In a linear queue a front pointer is not needed.

			RP		
[0]	[1]	[2]	[3]	[4]	[5]
Dave	Angelina	Faaris	Kev		

RP	3

Items are retrieved from the front of the queue by moving each item forward in the array:

		RP			
[0]	[1]	[2]	[3]	[4]	[5]
Angelina	Faaris	Kev			

RP	2

This can be inefficient, especially for large queues, as moving each item in the array takes time.

39

Implementing a circular queue

In a circular queue a front pointer is needed.

The front pointer is moved whenever an item is dequeued:

	FP		RP		
[0]	[1]	[2]	[3]	[4]	[5]
Dave	Angelina	Faaris	Kev		

FP	1
RP	3

> **Note**
>
> In a circular queue there is no need to delete the value from the array, only to move the pointers. The data that has been dequeued will eventually be overwritten when the rear pointer comes back around.

When a pointer reaches the end of the array, it wraps around back to the start. For example, given the following state of a circular queue:

		FP			RP
[0]	[1]	[2]	[3]	[4]	[5]
		Dave	Angelina	Faaris	Kev

FP	2
RP	5

When a new item is enqueued, the rear pointer will wrap around to 0.

RP		FP			
[0]	[1]	[2]	[3]	[4]	[5]
Aadya		Dave	Angelina	Faaris	Kev

FP	2
RP	0

> **Note**
>
> Exact implementations vary slightly, for example some implementations have the rear pointer pointing to the first empty space rather than the last full space.

A circular queue is much more efficient that a linear queue when the queue is large as it avoids the need to move each item each time a value is dequeued.

A circular queue is also a more complex data structure and a linear queue may be more appropriate for a smaller queue.

Implementing a priority queue

A priority queue enqueues items to the rear of the queue, but also records a priority level.

When an item is enqueued the new item's priority will be compared to each item in the list, starting at the back, in order to find the correct position to insert the item. This means that the items with the highest priority will always be dequeued first.

In the example below, a priority queue is used to store the inputs to a processing system on an aircraft. The bottom row represents the priority level, where a higher number means a higher priority.

FP		RP			
[0]	[1]	[2]	[3]	[4]	[5]
Engine Warning	Steering Input	Calculate Position			
5	4	3			

Check your understanding and progress at **www.hoddereducation.co.uk/myrevisionnotesdownloads**

A new item, Rudder Input, is added to the queue, with priority 4.

Starting at the rear of the queue, the priority is compared to Calculate Position. Because the priority is higher, this item is moved back one space.

The priority is then compared to Steering Input. Because the priority is the same (or higher), the new item is inserted into the list behind it.

FP			RP		
[0]	[1]	[2]	[3]	[4]	[5]
Engine Warning	Steering Input	Rudder Input	Calculate Position		
5	4	4	3		

Exam tip

Questions relating to queues may focus on hand-tracing algorithms, discussing the circumstances in which different types of queues are needed (Section A), suggesting what changes may be needed to adapt one type of queue into another (Section C) or making changes to an existing implementation (Section D).

Revision activity

✦ Create a `Queue` class in your chosen programming language. Include the following methods.
  ✦ `IsFull`
  ✦ `IsEmpty`
  ✦ `Enqueue`
  ✦ `Dequeue`
  ✦ `Peek`
✦ Implement a linear queue, a circular queue and a priority queue.

Stacks

A stack is a Last In, First Out (LIFO) data structure.

Much as with a stack of plates, new items are placed at the top of the stack and items are also removed from the top of the stack.

Common uses for stacks include:
✦ reversing a list of values
✦ performing undo operations
✦ as a call stack for keeping track of subroutine calls.

A stack can be implemented using a single-dimensional array and a single integer variable to point at the top of the stack.

Stack A data structure in which items are added to the top and removed from the top, much like a stack of plates.

Last In, First Out (LIFO) Those items placed into the stack most recently will be the first ones to be accessed.

			Top	2
[5]				
[4]				
[3]				
[2]	Change font	Top		
[1]	Make bold			
[0]	Type			

There are several actions that can be carried out on a queue:

Push	add new data to the top of the stack
Pop	remove one item from the top of the stack
Peek (or Top)	look at, but don't remove, one item from the top of the stack
IsEmpty	check to see if the stack is empty
IsFull	check to see if the stack is full

Making links

Stacks are a fundamental part of the depth first search (DFS) which is explored in Chapter 3.

The IsFull and IsEmpty actions are necessary because a program will crash if there is an attempt to push data when the stack is already full or to pop data from an empty stack.

When a value is pushed onto the stack it is placed at the top position and the value of the top pointer is incremented.

[5]	
[4]	
[3]	Delete selection
[2]	Change font
[1]	Make bold
[0]	Type

Top

Top	3

When a value is popped from the stack the value at the top position is returned and the top pointer is decremented.

[5]	
[4]	
[3]	Delete selection
[2]	Change font
[1]	Make bold
[0]	Type

Top

Top	2

Now test yourself   TESTED

17 State the acronym used to classify a stack data structure, and state the words this stands for.

18 Describe **two** potential uses for a stack.

19 What error could occur when trying to Push an item? State how this situation could be dealt with.

20 Describe the difference between *Pop* and *Peek*.

Answers available online

Note

In a stack there is no need to delete the value from the array, only to move the pointer. The data that has been popped will eventually be overwritten when new data is pushed and the top pointer moves back up.

Revision activity

+ Create a `stack` class in your chosen programming language. Include the following methods:
  + `IsFull`
  + `IsEmpty`
  + `Push`
  + `Pop`
  + `Peek`
+ Take a program that you have written that makes use of subroutines and write down the state of the call stack each time a new subroutine is called or a value returned.
+ Repeat the first bullet for a recursive program that you have written.

Graphs

A graph is a data structure designed to represent more complex relationships.

Typical uses for graphs include:
+ route finding
+ representing relationships in human networks (such as in social networks)
+ computer networks
+ project management
+ game theory (mathematical modelling of strategic decisions).

Each graph is made up of nodes (or vertices) and edges (or arcs).

There are several types of graph.

Types of graph

Unweighted and undirected graphs
A simple graph (unweighted and undirected) shows how two or more items are connected.

Figure 2.3 An unweighted, undirected graph

Weighted graphs
A weighted graph is used where the connection between the two nodes has a cost or value (such as a distance).

Figure 2.4 A weighted graph

> **Weighted graph** A graph in which each edge has a value or cost associated with it.
>
> **Directed graph** A graph some edges can only be traversed in one direction, shown with an arrow head.
>
> **Disconnected graph** A graph in which two or more nodes are not connected to the rest of the graph.

Directed graphs
In a directed graph, one or more edges has an arrow which shows that this edge can only be traversed in one direct.

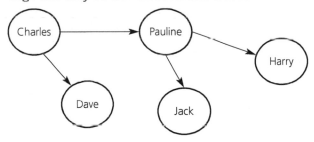

Figure 2.5 A directed graph

In a directed graph, not all edges need to be one-directional.

Disconnected graphs
A disconnected graph is one in which two or more vertices are not connected to the rest of the graph.

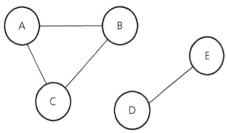

Figure 2.6 A disconnected graph

> **Graph** A data structure designed to represent the relationships between items.
>
> **Node** Used to represent an item of data, drawn as a circle. Also known as a vertex.
>
> **Edge** A line used to represent the relationship between two nodes. Also known as an arc.

Exam tip

Make sure you can identify the different types of graph. Be careful with the term 'edge'. This doesn't mean the outskirts of the graph, but the connections between each node.

Now test yourself

21 Explain the following terms.
  a Weighted graph
  b Directed graph
  c Disconnected graph
22 State **two** other terms for a line or a connector in a graph.
23 What symbol is only used in a directed graph?
24 Suggest **two** possible uses for a graph data structure.

Answers available online

TESTED

Adjacency lists and adjacency matrices

While graphs can be an effective visual way to represent a system for humans, to store them in a computer system uses one of two methods: an adjacency list or adjacency matrix

An adjacency list uses a list for each node to store details of adjacent nodes.

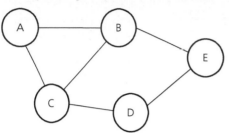

Vertex	Adjacent vertices
A	B,C
B	A,C,E
C	A,B,D
D	C,E
E	B,D

> **Adjacency list** A method of representing a graph by listing, for each node, just the nodes that are connected to it directly.

Figure 2.7 An adjacency list for an unweighted graph

For a weighted graph, this list also includes the cost of travelling along each edge.

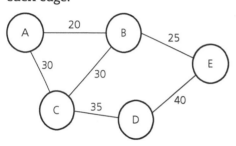

Vertex	Adjacent vertices
A	B,20,C,30
B	A,20,C,30,E,25
C	A,30,B,30,D,35
D	C,35,E,40
E	B,25,D,40

Figure 2.8 An adjacency list for a weighted graph

This is efficient for sparse graphs, where the presence of edges does not need to be tested often, because sparse graphs have very few edges and so not much storage space is needed. However reading and processing each item in an adjacency list can be inefficient if the list is large.

An adjacency matrix uses a grid to store details of adjacent nodes.

For an unweighted graph the adjacency matrix uses a binary number to show the presence or lack of an edge.

> **Sparse graph** A graph with few edges.
>
> **Adjacency matrix** A method of representing a graph using a grid with values in each cell to show which nodes are connected to each other.
>
> **Dense graph** A graph with many edges.

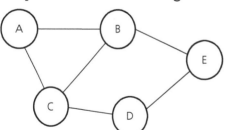

	A	B	C	D	E
A	0	1	1	0	0
B	1	0	1	0	1
C	1	1	0	1	0
D	0	0	1	0	1
E	0	1	0	1	0

Figure 2.9 An adjacency matrix for an unweighted, undirected graph

This is efficient for dense graphs, where the presence of edges needs to be tested often, because the adjacency matrix is simple to step through. However a lot of space can be wasted if the graph has few edges.

Undirected graphs will produce an adjacency matrix with a diagonal line of symmetry.

Directed graphs will produce an adjacency matrix without symmetry, as not all edges can be traversed in either direction.

2 Fundamentals of data structures

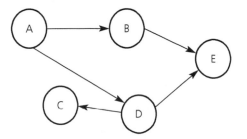

	A	B	C	D	E
A	0	1	0	1	0
B	0	0	0	0	1
C	0	0	0	0	0
D	0	0	1	0	1
E	0	0	0	0	0

Figure 2.10 An adjacency matrix for a directed graph

Weighted graphs will produce an adjacency matrix that stores the cost of each edge.

Where nodes are not adjacent the cost of traversing is infinite.

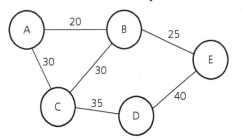

	A	B	C	D	E
A	∞	20	30	∞	∞
B	20	∞	30	∞	25
C	30	30	∞	35	∞
D	∞	∞	35	∞	40
E	∞	25	∞	40	∞

Figure 2.11 An adjacency matrix for a weighted graph

The number of edges is the main consideration when deciding whether an adjacency list or an adjacency matrix is the most appropriate data structure for recording the details of a graph.

	Advantages	Disadvantages
Adjacency list	Good for sparse graphs (few edges) or situations where edges don't need to be tested often as it takes up less storage space.	Poor for dense graphs as it takes longer to process each value.
Adjacency matrix	Good for dense graphs (many edges) or situations where edges do need to be tested often as it is easier to process each value.	Poor for sparse graphs as it wastes storage space.

Now test yourself   TESTED ◯

25 Which representation for a graph, when written down, looks most like a grid?

26 Which representation for a graph is most suitable for a sparse graph?

27 When else would that representation be most suitable?

28 When would an adjacency matrix not be symmetrical?

29 True or false? An adjacency list cannot be used for a weighted graph.

Answers available online

> **Exam tips**
>
> Make sure you are confident recalling the pros and cons of adjacency lists and adjacency matrices, as this is a common question.
>
> The difference between a graph and a tree is that a tree has no cycles. This question comes up quite often.

> **Revision activity**
>
> + Create a weighted graph showing the time taken to travel between five towns near your home.
> + Create an adjacency matrix and an adjacency list to represent the graph.

Trees

A tree is a special example of a graph which has no cycles (or loops).

Trees are always connected (no disconnected nodes) and undirected (edges can be traversed in both directions).

A rooted tree has one node as the root, or starting point, and all of the edges tend to lead away from the root. Rooted trees are commonly used to represent a hierarchical structure, such as the chapters in this book. They are very commonly used as binary search trees, as described below.

> **Tree** A graph which has no cycles (it is not possible to loop back around to a previously traversed part of the tree).
>
> **Rooted tree** A tree with a rooted node, from which all edges leading away from that root.

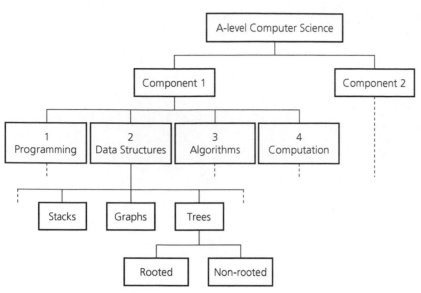

Figure 2.12 A rooted tree to represent chapters and topics in this book

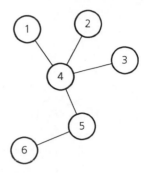

Figure 2.13 A non-rooted tree

A non-rooted tree doesn't have a clear start point and appears at a glance to be more like a graph, though with no cycles.

A binary tree is a rooted tree in which each node has a maximum of two children.

Binary trees consist of:

Root	the node that is the starting point for the tree
Branch	a node that comes after the root and has one or more children
Leaf	a node that does not have any children

Binary search trees are especially useful for storing data in an ordered way and can be quickly and easily traversed to provide an ordered list.

When adding data to a binary search tree, each new node is added according to its order.

In the example in Figure 2.14, where pets are stored alphabetically, to insert the value Dog we would:

+ Compare to the root: Dog comes after Cat so follow the right edge
+ Compare to the next node: Dog comes before Fish in the alphabet so we follow the left node
+ If there is no child node in that direction, then we add one:

The order in which the nodes are written will be different depending on the order in which nodes are added. However the binary search tree will always be able to provide a correctly ordered list.

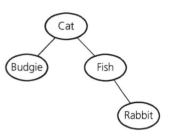

Figure 2.14 A binary search tree for storing pets in alphabetical order

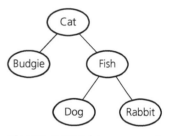

Figure 2.15 A binary search tree with the addition of a node for Dog

> **Binary tree** A tree in which each node has a maximum of two children.
>
> **Root** A node that has no parent nodes.
>
> **Branch** A node that has a parent node and at least one child node.
>
> **Leaf** A node that has no child nodes.
>
> **Binary search tree** A binary tree used to store data in order so that it can be quickly and easily searched.

Note

Binary trees are also useful for representing equations and can be traversed in such a way as to produce equations in infix notation, Polish notation and reverse Polish notation (RPN).

Now test yourself   TESTED ◯

30 What is the difference between a graph and a tree?

31 What is the main feature of a binary tree?

32 Describe **two** advantages of using a binary search tree to store data.

Answers available online

Making links

Infix and reverse Polish notation are explored in Chapter 3.

Hash tables

A hash table is a data structure in which values are found by looking up their associated key by following a hashing algorithm.

When the data is added to the hash table the hashing algorithm is applied to the value in order to generate its key.

A simple hashing algorithm for an ID number might be to add the digits together, divide by 6 and record the remainder. (This is known as modulo 6 division).

For example:

ID number 25463	ID number 34255
Sum of digits = 2 + 5 + 4 + 6 + 3 = 20	Sum of digits = 3 + 4 + 2 + 5 + 5 = 19
Remainder = 20 % 6 = 2	Remainder = 19 % 6 = 1

The key can then be used as the index for the value in the hash table.

In a large hash table this allows for a value to be found quickly.

If the program were to search for the ID number 25463 then it could be run through the hashing algorithm and the index number calculated rather than having to perform a search. This reduces the search time.

A problem can occur where two values generate the same key. This is referred to as a collision.

In the event of a collision, a simple solution is to store the value in the next available index.

Once a hash table is more than half full there will be many collisions, and so it is wise to rehash the table.

This involves designing a new hashing algorithm that will provide more possible values (for example, using modulo 20 rather than modulo 6) and re-calculating the hashes for each existing value.

Ideally a hashing algorithm should be designed to avoid this problem, however rehashing might be needed if data storage requirements grow over the life of a programming project.

0	
1	34255
2	25463
3	
4	
5	

Hash table A data structure for holding data that is indexed according to its key.

Hashing algorithm An algorithm for calculating a key for each value.

Collision The situation where two different items of data produce the same key.

Rehashing The process of recalculating the keys for all existing data using a new hashing algorithm.

Making links

Hashing algorithms are also used for checksums (to check the validity of a file or other piece of data) and for encryption (hashed passwords are typically stored in databases rather than plaintext passwords). Checksums and other error checking processes, and encryption, are described in Chapter 5.

Now test yourself

TESTED ◯

33 Describe the relationship between a value and its key in a hash table.

34 What is meant by a collision in a hash table?

35 Describe **two** steps that must be taken when rehashing.

36 Describe **three** potential uses for a hashing algorithm.

37 A hashing algorithm for an ID number is written as 'sum of each digit MOD 6'. Calculate the hashes for each of the following values.

a 7216

b 5891

c 0275

Answers available online

Dictionaries

A dictionary is a collection of key–value pairs, in which the value is found by looking up the key.

Keys must be unique, but values can be duplicated.

One use for a dictionary is information retrieval, for example in frequency analysis (storing the value of how many instances of a word, letter or other key appears) or as a high score table:

{"Dave" : 23, "Kev" : 37, "Angelina" : 42}

Another use for a dictionary is lossless compression where a dictionary of values is stored and the original file is represented with just the keys, in order.

For instance using the following dictionary:

Key	Value
1	ask
2	not
3	what
4	your
5	country
6	can
7	do
8	for
9	you
10	,
11	.

We can compress the sentence:

"Ask not what your country can do for you, ask what you can do for your country."

This sentence can be stored as:

1	2	3	4	5	6	7	8	9	10	1	3	6	7	8	4	5	12

> **Dictionary** A data structure based on key–value pairs.
>
> **Frequency analysis** The process of examining how often something occurs. A useful tool for trying to break some encryption methods.
>
> **Lossless compression** Reducing the size of a file without the loss of any data.

Now test yourself

TESTED ◯

38 Describe the essential concept of a dictionary using exactly three words.

39 Identify which field is which in a dictionary designed to store data for frequency analysis.

40 Identify which field is which in a dictionary designed to store what type of food each dog staying at a kennels should be fed with.

Answers available online

Vectors

Vector representation

REVISED ◯

In mathematics, scalars are simple numbers that only have a size. Vectors on the other hand are numbers that have both a magnitude and a direction.

Vectors are often used to represent a position. For example, a 2D vector can be used to can be represent a position on a 2D plane.

Vectors can be shown in the list representation – when it is represented as a list of numbers, such as [3,5]. In this two-dimensional vector the

> **Scalar** A single number used to represent or adjust the scale of a vector.
>
> **Vector** A data structure used to represent a position (for example, a 2D vector represents a position on a 2D plane).

Check your understanding and progress at **www.hoddereducation.co.uk/myrevisionnotesdownloads**

first number represents the horizontal position, and the second number represents the vertical position.

The same vector can be represented visually as a position on a two-dimensional grid, or as an arrow.

A two-dimensional vector is known as a 2-vector. The symbol for all possible real numbers is R. A two-dimensional vector made up of real numbers exists in a two-dimensional space called R2.

A function maps one set of numbers to another. In formal mathematics, a function f can map a set of numbers, S, to a co-domain R, where S represents a set of simple numbers and R represents the set of all real numbers:

$$f : S \rightarrow R$$

Using a function representation the position vector [3,5] could be written as:

✚ $0 \mapsto 3$
✚ $1 \mapsto 5$

In this case S is the set of numbers {0,1}. The symbol $\mapsto$ means 'map to'.

And as a dictionary representation this vector could be written as {0 : 3, 1 : 5} and could be thought of as 'move along 3, then move up 5'.

A three dimensional vector would follow the same pattern; for example, [7, 2, 5] could be written as {0 : 7, 1 : 2, 2 : 5} and thought of as 'move along 7, up 2 and back 5'.

A three-dimensional vector made up of real numbers is known as a 3-vector over R, and exists in a three-dimensional space called R3. A four-dimensional vector made up of real numbers is known as a 4-vector over R and exists in a four-dimensional space called R4.

Figure 2.16 A graphical representation of the vector [3,5]

> **Note**
>
> A list representation is equivalent to a 1D array representation.

> **Exam tip**
>
> Although there are numerous ways to represent a vector, a list of values is the most frequently used model in exam papers.

Vector manipulation

REVISED ◯

Because vectors are not normal numbers, the have special rules when adding and multiplying. Vector addition involves adding the equivalent values together. For example,

    [3, 5] + [7, 1] =

    [3+7, 5+1] =

    [10, 6]

The result of vector addition is translation; for example, taking the vector [3, 5] and moving (or translating) by [7, 1].

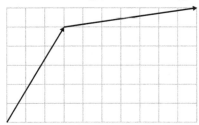

Figure 2.17 Vector addition

Scalar-vector multiplication means multiplying each value in a vector by a single number (or scalar).

    2x [3, 5] =

    [2x3, 2x5] =

    [6, 10]

The result of scalar-vector multiplication is scaling; for example, taking the vector [3, 5] and scaling it by 2.

> **Vector addition** Adding two vectors together in order to perform a translation.
> **Translation** Moving a vector by adding another vector to it.
> **Scalar-vector multiplication** Multiplying each element of a vector by a number in order to increase the scale of a vector.
> **Scaling** Changing the scale of a vector by multiplying the vector by a scalar.

49

The convex combination of two vectors means that two vectors must be multiplied by two scalar numbers which add up to exactly 1 and are both positive (greater than or equal to 0).

```
0.2 x [3, 5] + 0.8 x [7, 1] =

[0.6, 1.0] + [5.6, 0.8] =

[6.2, 1.8]
```

The result of the convex combination of 2 vectors will always be a vector that is on the straight line between the two original vectors.

Convex combination is often written as $\alpha u + \beta v$, where u and v are vectors and $\alpha + \beta = 1$ and $\alpha \geq 0$ and $\beta \geq 0$.

The dot product, or scalar product, of two vectors is written as $u \bullet v$, for example

```
[3,5] • [7,1]
```

The result is found by multiplying the values within each position of the vector together and adding the results.

```
[3,5] • [7,1] =

3x7 + 5x1 =

21 + 5 =

26
```

The result of a dot product is always a scalar, not a vector.

The dot product of two vectors can be used to calculate the angle between the two vectors.

It is not necessary to know how to calculate the exact angle, but the table below gives a general indication.

Dot product	Angle between the vectors
0	Exactly 90°
Bigger than 0	Between 0 and 90°
Less than 0	Between 90° and 180°

> **Note**
>
> The dot product of two vectors is used in many computer games to calculate the angles between characters in order to check whether sentries can see an intruder or to help non-player characters make decisions relating to route finding.

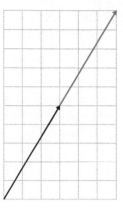

Figure 2.18 Scalar-vector multiplication

> **Convex combination** The process of multiplying two (or more) vectors by scalar values that are both positive and add up to exactly 1.
> **Dot product** A calculation used to help find the angle between two vectors.

> **Note**
>
> The result of the convex combination of 3 (or more) vectors will always be a vector that is within the shape described by the original vectors.

> **Now test yourself**   TESTED ◯
>
> 41 What is the difference between a vector and a scalar?
>
> 42 Describe **four** different ways a vector can be represented.
>
> 43 Add the vectors [-3,2] and [6,-4].
>
> 44 State the effect of multiplying a vector by a scalar value.
>
> 45 If a convex combination of two vectors is calculated using the formula $\alpha u + \beta v$, what two rules dictate the possible values of α and β?
>
> 46 Describe the significance of the value of any convex combination of two vectors.
>
> 47 Describe the purpose of calculating the dot product of two vectors.
>
> **Answers available online**

Check your understanding and progress at **www.hoddereducation.co.uk/myrevisionnotesdownloads**

Summary

+ Data structures provide a way to store collections of data together rather than in individual variables
+ Arrays are designed to store tables of data and can be single-dimensional or multi-dimensional
+ Two-dimensional arrays can be accessed using two nested FOR loops
+ Text files store data using ordinary text (for example, ASCII or Unicode)
+ Binary files store binary codes for each value
+ Binary files are usually smaller in size but cannot be read by other programs
+ Abstract data types are more complex data structures
+ Queues are a FIFO (First In, First Out) data structure
    + Items are enqueued at the back of the queue and dequeued from the front of the queue
    + Common uses include buffers, card games and breadth first searches
    + In linear queues the items are shuffled forward when the front item is dequeued
    + In circular queues the rear pointer and front pointer are moved back when items are enqueued or dequeued and wrap around to the beginning of the queue again
    + In priority queues each item is given a priority and items with higher priorities are dequeued first
+ Stacks are a LIFO (Last In, First Out) data structure
    + Items are pushed onto the top of the stack and popped from the top of the stack
    + Common uses include the undo feature, call stacks in programming and the depth first search
+ The graph data structure uses vertices/nodes and edges/arcs to represent relationships between items
+ Graphs can be weighted or unweighted, directed or undirected, connected or disconnected
+ Sparse graphs, or graphs where the existence of edges doesn't need to be checked often, should be represented using an adjacency list
+ Dense graphs, or graphs where the existence of edges does need to be checked often, should be represented using an adjacency matrix

+ Trees are graphs that don't include any cycles (loops)
+ A rooted tree has one vertex which is the root and all edges flow away from that root
+ In a binary tree each vertex can have a maximum of two children
+ A hash table is a data structure that creates a map between keys and values
+ Hash tables are used to organise data by using a hashing algorithm to generate a key
+ A collision occurs when two values generate the same hash
+ Collisions can be handled by rehashing – designing a new hashing algorithm and recalculating the hash for each item
+ Dictionaries are a collection of key–value pairs
+ Dictionaries can be used for information retrieval or for lossless encryption
+ Vectors are quantities that have a size and a direction
+ Vectors can be represented as a list of numbers, a position or arrow on a chart or as a dictionary
+ Adding vectors results in translation
+ Multiplying vectors by a (scalar) number results in scaling
+ The convex combination of two vectors means multiplying each by a number between 0 and 1, where both numbers add up to exactly one
+ The resulting vector from a convex combination will always be a point on the straight line between the two original vectors
+ The dot product of two vectors is found my multiplying each first term, second term, etc. and adding the results together
+ The dot product can be used to calculate the angle between two vectors
+ Vectors can be in multiple dimensions: a three-dimensional vector is known as a 3-vector over R, which exists in a three-dimensional space called R3

Exam practice

1 A programmer is writing a program to simulate a card game using a circular queue data structure to represent a deck of 52 cards. Cards are dealt from the top of the deck and replaced at the bottom of the deck.

   a) State why a queue is the most appropriate data structure to represent the deck of cards. [1]

   b) Explain why a circular queue is the most appropriate implementation of a queue in this situation. [2]

   c) Describe **one** problem that could occur when a card is drawn from the deck and suggest how this problem could be dealt with. [2]

   d) A player is allowed to check the top card in the deck without taking that card. State the name of the function in a queue which allows this to happen. [1]

2 This graph represents flight routes between five cities.

a) Tick **one** box that best describes this graph. [1]

Directed ☐
Unweighted ☐
Tree ☐
Disconnected ☐

b) Copy and complete the adjacency list for this graph. [2]

A	
B	
C	
D	
E	

c) Copy and complete the adjacency matrix for this graph. [2]

	A	B	C	D	E
A	0	1			
B					
C					
D					
E					

d) Describe **two** situations where an adjacency matrix would be more appropriate than an adjacency list. [2]

3 In a computer game the position of a security guard is described by the vector, u, [3,5] and is moving in the direction described by vector, v, [−4,4].

The player is standing at the position described by the vector, w, [1,4].

a) Calculate the resulting position of the security guard by adding the vectors u and v. [1]

b) Calculate the vector, x, between the security guard's original position (u) and the player's position (w). [1]

c) Calculate the result of $3w$. [1]

d) Calculate the result of $0.7u + 0.3w$. [2]

e) Explain the significance of the result of part c. [1]

f) Explain why the calculation $0.7u + 0.4w$ would not produce a result with the same significance. [1]

g) Calculate the result of $v \bullet x$. [2]

h) Explain the meaning of the dot product and why finding the dot product of v and x could be useful as part of the game mechanics. [2]

3 Fundamentals of algorithms

Several standard algorithms are covered in this chapter.

For each algorithm, you are expected to be familiar with:
+ the purpose of the algorithm
+ the general steps involved in the algorithm
+ the program code for the algorithm
+ how to hand-trace the algorithm.

You are not expected to memorise the program code for each algorithm, although you should be able to recognise each algorithm if you see it.

> **Making links**
>
> Hand-tracing algorithms is an important concept that appears in every Component 1 exam. More detail on how to tackle trace table problems is covered in Chapter 4. When you are confident with the principles of hand-tracing algorithms it is advised to practise with each of the examples in this chapter.

> **Algorithm** A sequence of instructions that are followed in order to solve a problem.
>
> **Hand-trace** Also known as dry run. Without using a computer, completing a table to record the values of each variable as the program is executed line-by-line.

Graph-traversal

Graph traversal algorithms are designed to find a route from one node of a graph to another.

There are two main approaches to this problem, the breadth first search (BFS) and depth first search (DFS).

In each of the examples below, the algorithm is being used to find a route from node A to node F.

> **Making links**
>
> For more on graphs, see Chapter 2.

Breadth first search

In the breadth first search, the algorithm:
+ removes the first node in the queue
+ inspects this node by adding all adjacent nodes to the queue
+ marks the node as visited.

It repeats this sequence until the required node is found, or all nodes have been visited.

We start by adding the first node (node A in this example) to a queue.

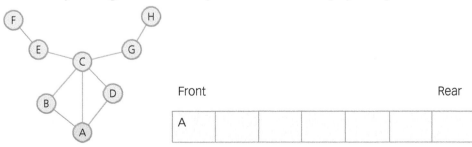

In each step, the item at the front of the queue is removed, and each adjacent node is added to the queue.

In this first step, we remove the first item, A, from the queue and inspect it. The adjacent nodes are B, C and D so these are added to the queue and A is marked as visited:

> **Graph traversal** Inspecting the items stored in a graph data structure.
>
> **Breadth first search (BFS)** Searching a graph by checking every node one step from the starting point, then every node two steps away, etc.
>
> **Depth first search (DFS)** Searching a graph by heading in one direction until you reach a dead end, then stepping back one node at a time.

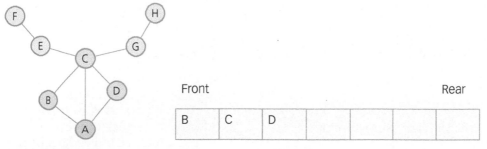

Visited: A

In the next iteration the first item (node B) is removed from the queue and inspected. The only adjacent node to B is C, which is already in the queue. As there are no new adjacent nodes no items are added to the queue. Node B is marked as visited.

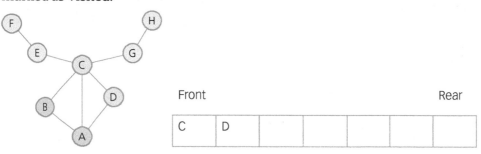

Visited: A, B

Again, the first item in the queue is removed and inspected. In this case it is node C. Node C is adjacent to nodes E and G which are added to the queue. Node D is also adjacent to node C but is already in the queue. Node C is marked as visited.

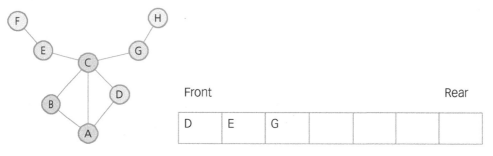

Visited: A, B, C

The first item in the queue, node D, is removed and inspected. There are no new adjacent nodes to node D, and so the queue is unchanged. Node D is marked as visited.

Visited: A, B, C, D

The first item in the queue, node E, is removed and inspected. Node E is inspected next, which has an adjacent node F (the target). F is added to the queue and E is marked as visited.

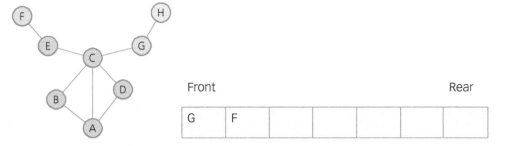

Front   **Rear**

G	F					

Visited: A, B, C, D, E

By the end of the algorithm the nodes have been visited in the order [A,B,C,D,E,G,F,H], however by keeping track of the parent for each node (which node was being interrogated when that node was found) it is possible to identify the shortest route – in this case [A, C, E, F].

This algorithm will always find the shortest path through an unweighted graph, however it may take many steps to do so in a large graph.

A queue is the most appropriate data structure to use as each newly discovered node is added to the rear of the queue and nodes are inspected in the order in which they are found (FIFO).

Now test yourself   TESTED ⬤

1   What data structure should be used in a breadth first search?
2   State **one** potential use for a breadth first search.

Answers available online

Revision activity

Using a section of the London Underground Walking Tube Map (you can find a PDF of this on the Transport for London website, tfl.gov.uk), carry out a breadth first search to find the shortest route between two stations.

Depth first search   REVISED ⬤

In the depth first search a very simplistic description is to traverse the graph in one direction until a dead end is found, at which point the algorithm backtracks until it finds an alternative route it has not tried. This is very similar to the approach most people take in a maze.

In each iteration the top item in the stack is removed and inspected for adjacent nodes which have not yet been visited:
✚ if they exist, then these adjacent nodes are added to the top of the stack
✚ if they don't exist, then the top item in the stack is removed.

In this case the starting node (node A) is added to a stack.

Note

There is more than one way to implement the depth first search, and the following description covers one specific implementation. You may come across slightly different steps, however the overall principle remains the same.

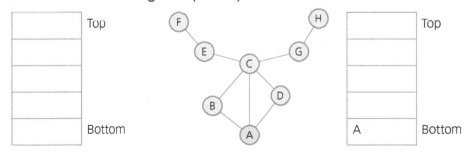

When node A is removed from the stack and inspected, the nodes B, C and D are added.

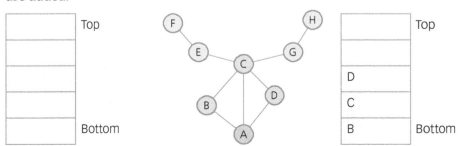

My Revision Notes AQA A-level Computer Science Third Edition

The node at the top of the stack is always inspected first. Node D is not adjacent to any new nodes, and so the stack is unchanged.

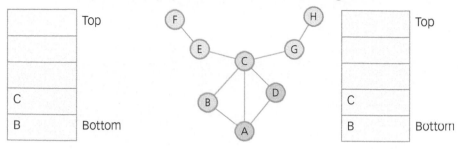

Inspecting node C means that nodes E and G are added to the stack.

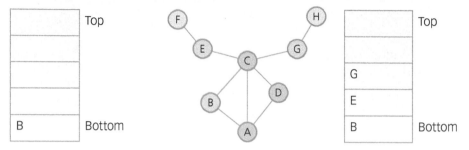

Inspecting node G leads on to node H, which is added to the stack.

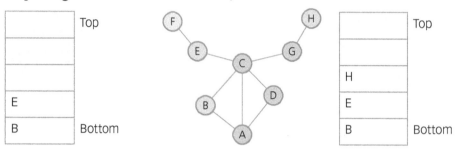

Node H is inspected but does not have any new adjacent nodes, and so the stack is unchanged.

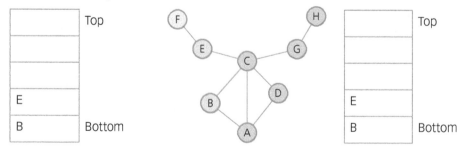

The next node to be inspected is node E, effectively back-tracking from the dead end at node H. Node F is now discovered and added to the stack.

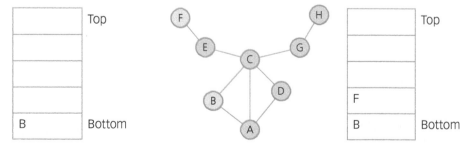

At this point the node has been identified and the route take is described as [A, D, C, E, F].

A stack is the most appropriate data structure to use as each newly discovered node is inspected immediately (LIFO) and the route to this point can be stepped through in reverse (popped) to find a new path.

Check your understanding and progress at www.hoddereducation.co.uk/myrevisionnotesdownloads

This algorithm can be effective at finding a route through a maze more quickly than the BFS because not every route must be explored, though the route may not be the optimal route.

Algorithm	Data Structure to use	Useful for
Breadth First Search (BFS)	Queue	Finding the shortest path between two nodes
Depth First Search (DFS)	Stack	Navigating a maze

Now test yourself

TESTED ○

3 What data structure should be used in a depth first search?

4 State **one** potential use for a depth first search.

Answers available online

Revision activity

Using a section of the London Underground Walking Tube Map, carry out a depth first search to find the shortest route between two stations.

Exam tip

You are not expected to memorise the exact syntax for the BFS and DFS algorithms, though you should be familiar with the principles of the algorithm and be able to describe which algorithm might be chosen in different circumstances.

It is also important to be able to hand-trace both the BFS and DFS algorithms. The pseudo-code algorithm would be provided for this, as well as a trace table to fill in.

Making links

It is important to be familiar with the workings of the algorithms covered in this chapter, and how to hand-trace the algorithm. This chapter focuses on the principles of the algorithms. Hand tracing technique is covered in *Trace tables* in Chapter 4 and the pseudo-code for the breadth first search and depth first search is included in that chapter.

Tree traversal

Tree traversal is carried out using one of three recursive algorithms, all of which look similar.
+ Pre-order tree traversal
+ In-order tree traversal
+ Post-order tree traversal

The difference between the algorithms is in when the node's value is output.

```
// In-Order Traversal
FUNCTION Traverse (node)
    OUTPUT node
    IF node.left THEN
        Traverse(node.left)
    IF node.right THEN
        Traverse(node.right)
ENDFUNCTION
// In-Order Traversal
FUNCTION Traverse (node)
    IF node.left THEN
        Traverse(node.left)
    OUTPUT node
    IF node.right THEN
        Traverse(node.right)
ENDFUNCTION
```

Making links

For more on trees see Chapter 2.

Tree traversal Inspecting the items stored in a tree data structure.

Pre-order tree traversal Inspecting or displaying the value of each node before moving on to other nodes.

In-order tree traversal Inspecting or displaying the value of each node after checking the node on the left but before checking the node on the right.

Post-order tree traversal Inspecting or displaying the value of each node after checking for all child nodes.

```
// Post-Order Traversal

FUNCTION Traverse (node)

    IF node.left THEN

            Traverse(node.left)

    IF node.right THEN

            Traverse(node.right)

    OUTPUT node

ENDFUNCTION
```

Pre-order tree traversal

In pre-order tree traversal the value of the node is always output first, before checking for nodes on the left, and then for nodes on the right.

Because the tree traversal algorithms use a recursive subroutine, each of the left nodes is inspected until there are no more left nodes to be found. At this point the right nodes are inspected.

If there are no nodes left to inspect then the subroutine returns to the previous node.

The order in which nodes are examined can be described using the following technique.

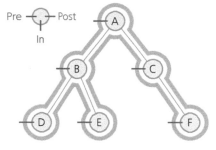

Figure 3.1 Pre-order tree traversal

In Figure 3.1, the green outline shows the order in which the nodes are traversed, starting with Node A and then checking the left node each time until a dead end is reached. The subroutine then goes back a stage and checks the right-hand node.

Using pre-order tree traversal the value of the node is output as soon as that node is first inspected. This can be shown by placing a horizontal bar to the left each time the green outline meets a node.

The output of pre-order tree traversal can be found by following the outline and writing down the value of the node each time it crosses a purple line. With this tree the output would be A, B, D, E, C, F.

The pre-order tree traversal is used when copying a tree, as each node value will be immediately copied to the new tree as soon as it is found, meaning that it is impossible to copy node E, for example, before node B has already been copied.

> **Making links**
>
> A binary search tree is a data structure used to store data that can be quickly searched. The binary search algorithm is explored on page 66.

In-order tree traversal

REVISED

For in-order tree traversal the value of the node is output after the left-hand nodes are inspected, but before the right-hand node is inspected.

This can be represented by using a vertical bar underneath each node. Whenever the outline path crosses a vertical bar, the value from that node should be output.

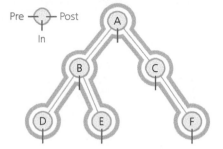

Figure 3.2 In-order tree traversal

The output from the tree in Figure 3.2 would be D, B, E, A, C, F.

In a binary search tree the nodes are arranged so that an in-order tree traversal would output the nodes in the correct order.

Post-order tree traversal

REVISED

For post-order tree traversal the value of the node is output after both the left AND the right nodes have been inspected.

To represent this horizontal bar on the right of each node indicates the point in the subroutine where the value can be output. Each time the green outline passes a brown bar, that value has been processed.

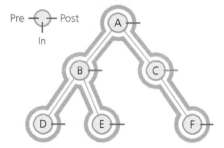

Figure 3.3 Post-order tree traversal

The output from the tree in Figure 3.3 would be D, E, B, F, C, A.

Post-order tree traversal is useful for emptying a tree, as nodes with children cannot be destroyed until the child nodes have already been destroyed.

Post-order tree traversal is also used for converting from infix notation to postfix notation.

> **Making links**
>
> Infix notation is how people typically write mathematical equations. Postfix notation is an alternative format that is easier and faster for a computer to process. Both notations are described in more detail later in this chapter.

Each method of traversal has a different effect on the order in which the items are displayed.

	Uses	Mathematical expressions
Pre-order	Copying a tree	Prefix
In-order	Outputting the contents of a binary search tree in ascending order	Infix
Post-order	Emptying a tree Converting from infix to postfix notation (see next section)	Postfix (reverse Polish notation)

Reverse Polish notation

Mathematical expressions can be expressed using a number of different notations.

Typically, people are used to writing mathematical expressions using infix notation. Here the operations are written in between their operands; for example, (2 – 5) x 7.

Postfix, or reverse Polish notation (RPN) looks slightly different because the operations are written after their operands; for example, 2 5 – 7 x.

Reverse Polish notation is useful for processing because:
✦ there is no need for parentheses/brackets
✦ the processing can be carried out using a stack.

When processing RPN using a stack, each value is added to the stack until an operator is found. At this point two items are popped from the stack, the answer calculated and then pushed back onto the stack.

> **Infix notation** A method of writing mathematical or logical expressions with operators placed between operands; for example, 2 + 2.
>
> **Postfix / Reverse Polish notation** A method of writing mathematical or logical expressions in which the operators appear after their operands; for example, 2 2 +.
>
> **Operation** A function to be applied; for example, +, -, AND, OR.
>
> **Operand** A value or object that is to be operated on.

Worked example

In RPN, the following calculation 2 5 – 7 x is performed, using a stack, as follows:

2	5	–	7	x
2 pushed	5 pushed	Operator found. Pop values and perform calculation.	Result pushed	7 pushed	Operator found. Pop values and perform calculation.	Result pushed

Transforming between infix and postfix/reverse Polish notation can be carried out by inspection (that is, by looking at the expression and working out the answer in your head).

The transformation can also be carried out using a tree.

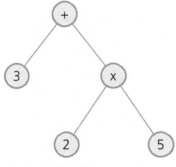

Figure 3.4 A binary tree representing a mathematical expression

Using in-order tree traversal on Figure 3.4 gives the result 3 + 2 x 5

Remembering to apply BIDMAS rules to infix notation, this gives 3 + 10 = 13

Using post-order tree traversal on Figure 3.4 gives the result 3 2 5 x +

When the first operator is found this will be applied to the two preceding values, giving 3 10 + = 13

Revision activity

✦ Practise writing infix notation expressions using a binary tree and then using post-order tree traversal to convert them into RPN.
✦ Draw out and step-through the process of using a stack to evaluate, or solve, RPN expressions.

Exam tip

Make sure you are confident with converting between infix notation and reverse Polish notation by inspection as well as understanding how trees can be used to perform the translation algorithmically.

Now test yourself

TESTED

9 Transform each of the following infix expressions into reverse Polish notation.
   a 3 + 7
   b 12 – 3 + 9
   c 4 x 12 + 6
   d (7 – 3) ÷ 2
10 Transform each of the following reverse Polish expressions into infix notation.
   a 12 6 –
   b 15 2 x 6 +
   c 3 7 2 x –
11 Give two advantages for using reverse Polish notation.

Answers available online

Searching algorithms

Linear search

The linear search is a very inefficient but simple algorithm for finding an item in an array of items.

The basic aim of the algorithm is to check each item in an array, one-by-one, from start to finish.

```
FOR i ← 0 to Length(Items)

    IF Items[i] = Target

        OUTPUT "Found"

    ENDIF

ENDFOR
```

The linear search is very simple to program and can be effective for very small lists. It is also useful if the list is unordered, however it is extremely inefficient for large lists.

> **Linear search** A searching algorithm in which each item is checked one-by-one.

Making links

The efficiency of algorithms is an important consideration when deciding how to solve a problem. This is measured using time-wise complexity and space-wise complexity, both of which are discussed in *Comparing algorithms* in Chapter 4.

Exam tip

You are expected to be very familiar with the linear search and you should be confident to program one from scratch in the Component 1 exam.

Time-wise complexity is a measure of how efficient an algorithm is in terms of time. It is worth trying to remember the time-wise complexity for each of the algorithms in the next sections.

Algorithm	Time-wise Complexity
Linear search	$O(n)$

Binary search

The binary search is an example of a 'divide and conquer' approach to searching.

Given a sorted array of items the algorithm will check the middle item. Because the list is sorted, this means that half of the array can then be discarded, halving the possible number of values to search each time.

> **Binary search** A searching algorithm in which the middle item is checked and half of the list is discarded.

The implementation of a binary search uses pointers to mark the Start, End and Midpoint of the array, Mid, calculating the midpoint by adding the Start and End values and halving them.

```
Mid = (Start + End) / 2
```

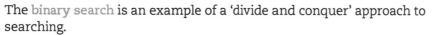

Start			Mid			End
[0]	[1]	[2]	[3]	[4]	[5]	[6]

Start	0
End	6
Mid	3

Where there are an even number of items to choose from the algorithm can be programmed to use the item on the left, or the item on the right. Using integer division will mean that the item on the left is chosen in this case.

```
Mid = (Start + End) // 2
```

Start		Mid		End	
[0]	[1]	[2]	[3]	[4]	[5]

Start	0
End	5
Mid	2

It is important to remember that the midpoint value should be discarded if it does not match, and so the full implementation may look like this:

```
Start ← 0
End ← Length(Items) - 1
Mid ← (Start + End) // 2
WHILE Start <= End AND Items[Mid] != Target
    IF Items[Mid] < Target THEN
            Start ← Mid + 1
    ELSE
            End ← Mid - 1
    ENDIF
    Mid ← (Start + End) // 2
ENDWHILE
IF Items[Mid] = Target THEN
    OUTPUT "Item found"
ELSE
    OUTPUT "Item not found"
ENDIF
```

> **Integer division** A division operation in which any fractional part is discarded, equivalent to rounding down to the nearest whole number.

The binary search is considered to be very efficient. It is generally much quicker than the linear search for large, sorted lists. However, it cannot be carried out on an unsorted list.

Algorithm	Time-wise Complexity
Binary search	$O(\log n)$

> **Making links**
>
> Time-wise complexity is explored in more detail in *Comparing algorithms* in Chapter 4.

> **Exam tip**
>
> You are expected to be very familiar with the binary search and you should be confident to program one from scratch in the Component 1 exam.

Binary tree search

A binary tree search uses the same principles as a binary search to find an item held in a binary tree.

Because each item is added to a tree in order, a recursive algorithm can be used to travel through the tree, moving through the left or right node depending on the target value.

An example implementation might look like this:

```
FUNCTION BinaryTreeSearch (Node)

    IF Node.Value = Target THEN

            Return True

    ELSEIF Node.Value > Target AND Exists(Node.Left) THEN

            Return BinaryTreeSearch(Node.Left)

    ELSEIF Node.Value < Target AND Exists(Node.Right) THEN

            Return BinaryTreeSearch(Node.Right)

    ELSE

            Return False

    ENDIF

ENDFUNCTION
```

> **Binary tree search** A searching algorithm in which a binary tree is traversed.
>
> **Binary tree** A tree in which each node can have no more than two child nodes, each placed to the left or right of the preceding node so that the tree is always in order.

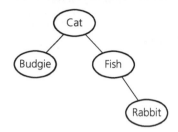

Figure 3.5 A binary tree

And a trace table might look like this:

Target	Call	Node	Value returned
Dog	1	Cat	
	2	Fish	
	3	Dog	True
	2	Fish	True
	1	Cat	True

Algorithm	Time-wise Complexity
Binary tree search	$O(\log n)$

Binary search trees are an efficient method of searching because they can remove large sections of the possible values at each step, much like the more traditional binary search.

> **Making links**
>
> Time-wise complexity is explored in more detail in *Comparing algorithms* in Chapter 4.
>
> Hand-tracing algorithms is an important concept that appears in every Component 1 exam. More detail on how to tackle trace table problems is covered in *Trace tables* in Chapter 4.

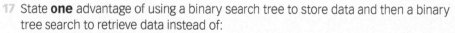

17 State **one** advantage of using a binary search tree to store data and then a binary tree search to retrieve data instead of:

a   an array and a linear search

b   an array and a binary search.

Answers available online

Revision activity

Create a binary search tree using any data you like (such as film names or book titles) and hand trace the steps in searching for specific items.

Sorting algorithms

Bubble sort

The bubble sort is a relatively simple, but very inefficient sorting algorithm.

In the first pass, each item is compared to its immediate neighbour and the value are swapped if necessary. In this way, the highest value bubbles to the end of the list each time.

If there are n items in the list, there are (n-1) comparisons in each pass, so in a list of six items there are five comparisons.

Bubble sort A sorting algorithm in which pairs of items are sorted, causing the largest item to bubble up to the top of the list.

Pass Travelling through a list from start to finish exactly once.

[0]	[1]	[2]	[3]	[4]	[5]	
9	7	3	12	4	8	9 and 7 are compared and swapped
7	9	3	12	4	8	9 and 3 are compared and swapped
7	3	9	12	4	8	9 and 12 are compared and not swapped
7	3	9	12	4	8	12 and 4 are compared and swapped
7	3	9	4	12	8	12 and 8 are compared and swapped
7	3	9	4	8	12	The first pass is completed

The same algorithm is then repeated (n-1) times; that is, there are (n-1) passes because, in the worst case scenario (where the last number in the list is the smallest value), the value will be moved down one place each time.

```
FOR i ← 0 to n - 1 //This loop is for each pass

    // Complete one pass:

    FOR j ← 0 to n - 1 //This loop is for each comparison

        IF Items[j] > Items[j+1] THEN

            Temp ← Items[j]

            Items[j] ← Items[j+1]

            Items[j+1] ← Temp

        ENDIF

    ENDFOR

ENDFOR
```

Exam tip

You are expected to be very familiar with the bubble sort and you should be confident to program one from scratch in the Component 1 exam.

There are two main methods to improve the efficiency of the bubble sort.
1. Record the number of swaps completed in each pass. If 0 swaps were made then the list must be in order and the algorithm can be stopped.
2. For each pass (outer loop), reduce the number of comparisons by 1. This is because the highest value is guaranteed to have bubbled to the end of the list each time, and so on the second pass it is not necessary to make the final comparison. On the third pass it is not necessary to make the final two comparisons, and so on.

For a large list, or a list that is nearly sorted, these improvements can have a dramatic impact on the running time of the algorithm.

The bubble sort is still considered to be very inefficient in most cases and is rarely used in industry.

The bubble sort can be suitable for a list that is nearly sorted.

Making links

Time-wise complexity is explored in more detail in *Comparing algorithms* in Chapter 4.

Algorithm	Time-wise Complexity
Bubble sort	$O(n^2)$

Now test yourself
TESTED ◯

18 State the number of comparisons needed to run through one pass of the bubble sort for a list of 10 items.

19 Suggest **two** methods for improving the efficiency of the standard bubble sort.

Answers available online

Revision activity

✦ Take a physical collection (such as CDs, DVDs, books) and practise carrying out a bubble sort in real life.

✦ Practise programming the basic bubble sort from scratch.

✦ Improve your basic implementation by reducing the number of steps in the inner loop by 1 each time and by using a flag to check whether any swaps were made during that pass.

✦ Hand-trace the bubble sort with some sample values and then use your programming platform's debugging tool to check your accuracy.

Merge sort

REVISED ◯

The merge sort is significantly more efficient than the bubble sort, though it is also significantly more complex.

✦ A list is broken in half, and in half again until we have a series of single elements.

✦ The elements are placed into pairs and each pair is sorted.

✦ Each group of two pairs is merged into a sorted group of four.

✦ Each group of two fours is merged into a sorted group of eight.

✦ Repeat as necessary until the list is complete.

Merge sort A sorting algorithm in which items are split into single items and then merged into sorted pairs, fours, eights and so on.

| 3 | 7 | 12 | 9 | 4 | 8 | 6 | 2 |

| 3 | 7 | 12 | 9 | | 4 | 8 | 6 | 2 |

| 3 | 7 | | 12 | 9 | | 4 | 8 | | 6 | 2 |

| 3 | | 7 | | 12 | | 9 | | 4 | | 8 | | 6 | | 2 |

| 3 | 7 | | 9 | 12 | | 4 | 8 | | 2 | 6 |

| 3 | 7 | 9 | 12 | | 2 | 4 | 6 | 8 |

| 2 | 3 | 4 | 6 | 7 | 8 | 9 | 12 |

Making links

The nature of this solution, repeatedly breaking down and then merging lists, means that a **recursive** solution is an ideal way of tackling this problem. Recursion is introduced in Chapter 1.

Recursive An algorithm that uses a sub-routine which calls itself.

When merging two lists, only the top two values need to be compared each time as each list is already guaranteed to be in order.

This reduces the overall number of steps required and means that the algorithm is much more efficient than the bubble sort in most cases.

The merge sort also has a fixed number of steps, no matter how ordered or unordered the list may be. As a result, some lists that are nearly in order can be sorted more quickly using a bubble sort, though this is rare.

Making links

Time-wise complexity is explored in more detail in *Comparing algorithms* in Chapter 4.

Check your understanding and progress at **www.hoddereducation.co.uk/myrevisionnotesdownloads**

Algorithm	Time-wise Complexity
Merge sort	O($n \log n$)

Note

Though not covered in this specification, there are many other sorting algorithms. These include the quick sort, heap sort, insertion sort and shell sort. An investigation into the efficiency of different sorting algorithms could make for an interesting NEA programming project.

Exam tip

You may be asked to trace the merge sort, or to demonstrate your understanding of how the merge sort works. You are unlikely to be asked to program a merge sort from scratch so focus your revision on understanding the algorithm rather than programming it from memory.

Algorithm	Time-wise Complexity
Linear search	O(v)
Binary search	O($\log n$)
Binary tree search	O($\log n$)
Bubble sort	O(n^2)
Merge sort	O($n \log n$)

Now test yourself TESTED ◯

20 Give **two** situations in which the merge sort would be more suitable than the bubble sort.

21 Give **one** situation in which the bubble sort would be more suitable than the merge sort.

22 Which sorting algorithm always has a fixed number of steps?

Answers available online

Revision activity

Take a physical collection (such as CDs, DVDs, books) and practise carrying out a merge sort in real life.

Making links

As discussed, time-wise complexity is a measure of how efficient an algorithm is in terms of time and is explored in more detail in *Comparing algorithms* in Chapter 4. However, it is worth trying to remember the time-wise complexity for each of these algorithms:

Optimisation algorithms

Dijkstra's shortest path algorithm

REVISED ◯

Dijkstra's shortest path algorithm is a graph traversal algorithm that will find the shortest route from a given starting node to every other node on the graph. It is very efficient for route finding across weighted graphs, though a breadth first search is more efficient for unweighted graphs.

The trace table for Dijkstra's algorithm provides the shortest overall distance to each node in the graph and the previous node to travel from. This means that the quickest path to different nodes from the starting node can be found quickly, without the need to carry out the algorithm again.

Shortest path The route between two nodes on a graph that incurs the least cost. In an unweighted graph the cost for each path can be assumed to be 1.

My Revision Notes AQA A-level Computer Science Third Edition

Initially the distance from the start node to each node is set to ∞ (infinity). Then the algorithm works as follows:

+ For every node attached to the current node:
    + add the distance from this closest unvisited node to the current node, and add it to the distance from the current node to the start node – this is the distance of the unvisited node to the start node
    + if this calculated distance is less than the current distance between the start node and unvisited node, the value is updated – this is how the shortest route is calculated
    + note the current node as the previous 'parent' node for the unvisited node
    + repeat until all nodes attached to the current node have distances recorded.
+ Mark the current node as visited.
+ Select a new current node, which is the closest unvisited node, and repeat all the steps above.
+ Repeat until the target is reached.

Worked example

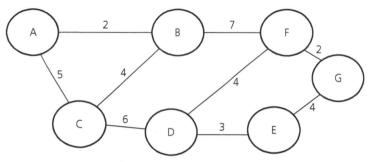

Figure 3.6 An example graph

Applying Dijkstra's algorithm to Figure 3.6, starting from Node A, would produce the following results:

	A	B	C	D	E	F	G
Shortest distance	0	2	5	11	14	9	11
Previous node	-	A	A	C	C	B	F

Once Dijkstra's algorithm has produced a result, the shortest route from node A to any other node can be found by working backwards, using the 'previous node'.
+ The shortest route to G ends by moving to node G from node F.
+ Node F is reached from node B.
+ Node B is reached from node A.

Therefore, the shortest path is A–B–F–G.

Making links

Hand-tracing algorithms is an important concept that is assessed in every Component 1 exam. More detail on how to tackle trace table problems is covered in Chapter 4. When you are confident with the principles of hand-tracing algorithms it is advised to practise with each of the examples in this chapter.

Now test yourself

TESTED ⬤

23 Explain the purpose of Dijkstra's algorithm.
24 State what **two** values must be stored for each node following the application of Dijkstra's algorithm.

Answers available online

Exam tip

It is not necessary to remember each and every step in Dijkstra's shortest path algorithm, but understanding how the algorithm works makes it simpler to complete a trace table. You should make sure you are confident identifying the shortest path to a given node once the trace is complete.

Check your understanding and progress at **www.hoddereducation.co.uk/myrevisionnotesdownloads**

Revision activity

Using a section of the London Underground Walking Tube Map, carry out Dijkstra's shortest path algorithm to find the shortest route from one station to all other stations in that section.

Summary

+ Graph traversal algorithms are used to find a path from one node to another in a graph
+ The breadth first search (BFS) scans all of the nodes one step away from the start point, then all the nodes two steps away, and so on
+ The breadth first search uses a queue data structure and is used to find the shortest path between two nodes of an unweighted graph
+ The depth first search (DFS) continues in one direction until it reaches a dead end and then steps backwards until it finds a new, unused path
+ The depth first search uses a stack data structure and is used to find a route through a maze
+ Tree traversal algorithms are used to interrogate each node in a tree
+ The three main tree traversal algorithms look very similar, with only the position of the print statement moving
+ Pre-order tree traversal is used for copying a tree
+ In-order tree traversal is used to output a sorted list of values from a binary search tree and for outputting an infix notation expression
+ Post-order tree traversal is used for emptying a tree and for outputting a reverse Polish notation expression
+ Operators are terms such +, −, AND, OR
+ Operands are the values on which operators act, such as numbers (for example, 3, 81.2) or variables (for example, x)
+ Infix expressions place the operator inbetween its operands
+ Reverse Polish notation (RPN) or outfix expressions place the operator after its operands
+ RPN expressions do not need to use brackets and can be evaluated using a stack

+ RPN is used in interpreters based on a stack; for example, Postscript and bytecode
+ The linear search steps through each item from a list in a line, and is very inefficient, with a time-wise complexity $O(n)$
+ The binary search checks the middle item from a list and discards half of the values each step, making it much more efficient, with a time-wise complexity $O(\log n)$
+ The binary search can only be applied to an ordered list
+ The binary tree search discards an entire branch each step, making the search quick and efficient, with a time-wise complexity $O(\log n)$
+ The bubble sort involves swapping pairs of values so that the largest value will bubble up to the end each pass
+ The bubble sort can be improved by reducing the number of comparisons in each step by 1 and by halting if no swaps are made in a full pass
+ The bubble sort has a time-wise complexity $O(n^2)$
+ The merge sort involves splitting a list into individual items and then continually merging them into sorted lists of 2, 4, 8, … items, comparing only the front-most items in each case
+ The merge sort is much more efficient than the bubble sort for large, unsorted lists, with a time-wise complexity $O(n \log n)$
+ Dijkstra's shortest path algorithm is used to find the shortest route from one node to any other node in that graph
+ Dijkstra's algorithm is used for route finding across weighted graphs

Exam practice

1   This graph represents train routes between different towns, and the distance between each station in miles. Dave lives in town A and wants to travel to town G.

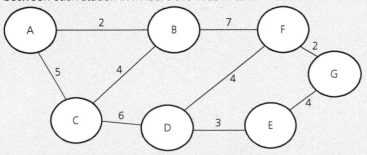

a) Dave has the choice of using a breadth first search or a depth first search. State the name of the graph traversal algorithm that would be most suitable to find the shortest path between two nodes. [1]

b) State what data structure would be most suitable to be used in the algorithm identified in Question 1a), justifying your choice. [2]

c) Give a suitable use for the algorithm that was not chosen in Question part a). [1]

d) Dave is advised to used Dijsktra's shortest path algorithm since he travels by train a lot. Explain why using Dijkstra's algorithm will save time overall.   [2]

2 This array, Cars, contains the names of car manufacturers.

[0]	[1]	[2]	[3]	[4]	[5]
AMG	BMW	Corvette	Ferrari	McLaren	Porsche

Below is a pseudo-code algorithm for a search algorithm.

```
Start ← 0
End ← Length(Cars) – 1
Mid ← (Start + End) // 2
WHILE Start <= End AND Cars[Mid] != Target
   IF Cars[Mid] < Target THEN
     Start ← Mid + 1
   ELSE
     End ← Mid – 1
   ENDIF
   Mid ← (Start + End) // 2
ENDWHILE
IF Cars[Mid] = Target THEN
   OUTPUT "Car found"
ELSE
   OUTPUT "Car not found"
ENDIF
```

a) Copy and complete the trace table below by following the given algorithm.   [3]

Target	Start	End	Mid	Cars[Mid]	Output
Porsche	0	5			

b) Copy and complete the trace table below by following the given algorithm.   [4]

Target	Start	End	Mid	Cars[Mid]	Output
Aston Martin	0	5			

c) State the name for the algorithm shown.   [1]

d) State **one** feature of the list that makes it possible to use this algorithm.   [1]

e) Describe **one** situation in which a linear search would be more appropriate.   [1]

3 This list of city names has been stored in an unsorted array.

Newcastle   Berlin   Paris   Barcelona   London   Amsterdam

Maariyah has been asked to sort the list of names in alphabetical order and has access to a bubble sort algorithm and a merge sort algorithm.

a) State which of the two available algorithms is typically most efficient.   [1]

b) Describe the situation where the other algorithm would be suitable.   [1]

c) Maariyah decides to use the bubble sort.
Explain **one** method she could use to improve its efficiency and how it would help.   [2]

d) Show the results of the bubble sort algorithm on the list above after one pass.   [2]

4 Theory of computation

Abstraction and automation

Problem-solving

REVISED

The ability to solve logic problems is an important part of being a good programmer, and logic puzzles can take many forms.

> **Exam tip**
>
> Any form of logic puzzle could be used in an exam paper and past examples include murder mystery puzzles, riddles and even sudoku style puzzles.

Logic problem A puzzle which is intended to be solved using logical reasoning.

Syllogism An argument that uses logical reasoning.

Logical syllogisms are a test of logical understanding in which two statements are made and logical deductions must be made. The logical deductions can be true, false, or uncertain. To help avoid any real-world bias the statements are usually nonsensical.

> **Worked example**
>
> Statements:
> + All elephants are green.
> + Some elephants are big.
>
> Proposed deduction:
> + All big things are green.
>
> Response:
>
> The deduction is uncertain (or does not follow) because we can't know if there are other big things that are not elephants.

> **Exam tip**
>
> Try looking online for puzzles, riddles and logic problems to help prepare for this topic, which is often covered in the first question in Component 1.

> **Now test yourself** TESTED
>
> 1 All sweets are blue. All sweets are small. Which of these statements follows?
>   A All small things are blue.
>   B All blue things are sweets.
>   C Some blue things are small.
> 2 A farmer is travelling with a wolf, a goat and a cabbage. If left alone the wolf will eat the goat and the goat will eat the cabbage. The farmer must cross a river in a boat, but can only take one companion at a time. How can the farmer get all three across?
>
> **Answers available online**

> **Revision activity**
>
> Search the internet for logic puzzles such as:
> + sudokus
> + logic problems
> + syllogisms
>
> and practise solving them.

Following and writing algorithms

REVISED

Understanding algorithms

An algorithm is a sequence of steps that can be followed in order to complete a task. An algorithm always terminates (in other words, it stops).

Algorithms can be represented using pseudo-code, which is a form of program code but is not written in any particular programming language.

Pseudo-code is intended to be read and understood by programmers, who can then translate the intentions of the program designer into a working program in a specific language.

This is particularly relevant to the Component 1 exam as students in different centres will be programming using different programming languages.

Algorithm A sequence of steps that should be carried out in order.

Pseudo-code A simplified notation similar to program code, used in program design.

Pseudo-code doesn't always have strict rules about the exact syntax that is used, although AQA questions are written using a consistent format.

It is important to be familiar with reading and understanding each of the following programming constructs in pseudo-code:

Sequence	The concept that the instructions are carried out in the order that they are written.
Assignment	The concept that a value, pointer, or the result of a process can be assigned to a variable; for example: `Total ← Total + ExtraValue`

Selection	The concept that a decision over whether to execute a particular part of the program can be made based on a condition; for example:
	
	`IF Total < 100 THEN`
	
	`...`
	
	`ENDIF`

Iteration	That concept that a section of code can be repeated; for example:
	
	`FOR i ← 0 to 5`
	
	`...`
	
	`ENDFOR`

Sequence Executing instructions in the order they are written.

Assignment Changing the value stored in a variable.

Selection Using conditions to decide whether to execute part of a program.

Iteration Repeating or looping through a section of code.

It is important that you can read an algorithm represented in pseudo-code. It is possible that you will be given a pseudo-code algorithm in Section B which you will be asked to implement in your chosen programming language, particularly if you are sitting the AS-level examination. However, at A-level it is more common that you will be given an explanation of an algorithm rather than pseudo-code, which makes this task more challenging.

Revision activity

Look through past papers for examples of pseudo-code and implement these in your chosen programming language.

Exam tip

If you are asked to implement a pseudo-code algorithm it is very important to use the variable identifiers given in the program, and to make sure that any prompts are written exactly as they appear in the exam paper.

Trace tables

One way in which your ability to read and understand algorithms is assessed is using a trace table to hand-trace an algorithm.

In these questions a pseudo-code algorithm is provided and the task is to fill in a table showing how the values of the variables in the program change.

The key advice for completing trace tables is:
+ use your finger to record where you are up to in the algorithm at all times
+ write the values of the variables as they change from left to right, moving to a new line when necessary
+ only write down a value when that variable changes.

Trace table A table for recording the values of variables as a program runs.

Hand-trace Simulating the execution of an algorithm without running it, using a trace table to record the state of the program after each instruction.

For example, hand-tracing the algorithm below using the following list of values:

`List`

[0]	[1]	[2]	[3]	[4]
"Apple"	"Banana"	"Grape"	"Orange"	"Pear"

`Target ← Banana`

`Start ← 0`

`End ← Length(Items) - 1`

```
Mid ← (Start + End) // 2
WHILE Start <= End AND Items[Mid] != Target
    IF Items[Mid] < Target THEN
        Start ← Mid + 1
    ELSE
        End ← Mid - 1
    ENDIF
    Mid ← (Start + End) // 2
ENDWHILE
```

Target	Start	End	Mid	Items[Mid]
"Banana"	0	4	2	"Grape"
		1	0	"Apple"
	1		1	"Banana"

Because you should always read left to right through the table, the final change to the value of Start takes place on a new line, and it is not necessary to replace the value of End.

It is also common to be asked to identify the purpose of an algorithm.

More complex algorithms lead to more complex trace tables and it is common for some data to be filled in, and those boxes greyed out, in order to help students check that their progress through the trace table is correct.

More complex trace tables often refer to the standard algorithms discussed in Chapter 3. Common examples include the breadth first search and depth first search.

Breadth first traversal

Figure 4.1 is an example of a graph. The pseudo-code algorithm for a breadth first traversal of the graph is shown underneath.

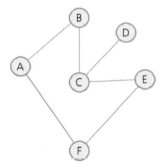

Figure 4.1

```
PROCEDURE Breadth(Start, Target)

    Queue.Enqueue(Start)

    Discovered[Start] ← True

    Complete ← False

    DO

        Current ← Queue.Deqeue()

        FOR each node Temp adjacent to Current DO

            IF Discovered[Temp] = False AND
Complete = False THEN

                Queue.Enqueue(Temp)

                Discovered[Temp] ← True

                Parent[Temp] ← Current

                IF Temp = Target THEN

                    Complete ← True

                ENDIF

            ENDIF

        ENDFOR

    WHILE Queue Not Empty AND Complete = False

ENDPROCEDURE
```

The task is to trace the algorithm to show how the graph is traversed when given the call `Breadth(A,E)`.

> **Note**
>
> This particular algorithm is designed for an unweighted graph.

> **Making links**
>
> For a full and detailed explanation of how to complete this trace table see:
>
> www.hoddereducation.co.uk/myrevisionnotesdownloads

The full trace table is shown below.

Queue		Start	Target	Discovered						Complete	Current	Temp	Parent					
Front	Back			A	B	C	D	E	F				A	B	C	D	E	F
		A	C	F	F	F	F	F	F				-	-	-	-	-	-
A				T						F								
-											A							
												B						
B					T									A				
												F						
B	F								T									A
F											B							
												A						
												C						
F	C					T									B			
											T							

Working backwards from node C we can see that the parent node is node B, and from node B the parent node is node A. Therefore the route found is A→ B → C.

Depth first traversal

Figure 4.2 shows another example algorithm, this time for a depth first traversal of the same graph.

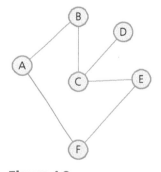

Figure 4.2

```
PROCEDURE Depth(Current,Target)

    Stack ← [Empty]

    Discovered ← [False]

    Stack.Push(Start)

    DO

            Current ← Stack.Pop()

            IF Not Discovered[Current] THEN

                    Discovered[Current] ← True

                    FOR each node Temp adjacent to Current
AND not in Stack DO

                            IF Not Discovered[Temp] DO

                                    Stack.Push(Temp)

                            ENDIF

                    ENDFOR

            ENDIF

    WHILE Stack is Not Empty And Current != Target

ENDPROCEDURE
```

The task is to trace the algorithm to show how the graph is traversed when given the call Depth(A,C).

The first three lines of the algorithm have already been completed and the initial state of the program has been highlighted in grey in order to indicate that no changes should be made to those cells. A typical exam question might include the values of variables Current and Target in order to support students in ensuring they are carrying out the algorithm correctly.

> **Note**
>
> This particular algorithm is designed for an unweighted graph.

Current	Target	Stack		Discovered						Temp
		Bottom	Top	A	B	C	D	E	F	
A	C		A	F	F	F	F	F	F	
A			-							
			B							
			BF							
F			B							T
			BA							
			BAE							
E			BA						T	
			BAC							
			BACF							
F			BAC							
C			BA			T				
			BAD							
			BADE							

> **Making links**
>
> For a full and detailed explanation of how to complete this trace table see:
>
> www.hoddereducation.co.uk/myrevisionnotesdownloads

Now test yourself TESTED

3 Look at the graph (Figure 4.3) and the pseudo-code underneath.

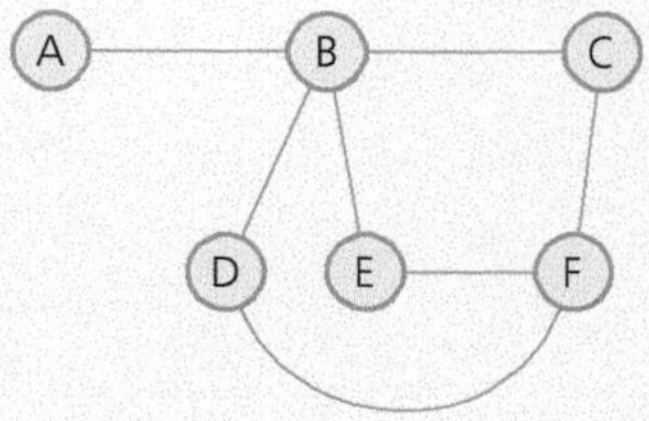

Figure 4.3

```
PROCEDURE Breadth(Start, Target)
    Queue.Enqueue(Start)
    Discovered[Start] ← True
    Complete ← False
    DO
        Current ← Queue.Deqeue()
        FOR each node Temp adjacent to Current DO
            IF Discovered[Temp] = False AND Complete = False THEN
                Queue.Enqueue(Temp)
                Discovered[Temp] ← True
                Parent[Temp] ← Current
                IF Temp = Target THEN
                    Complete ← True
                ENDIF
            ENDIF
        ENDFOR
    WHILE Queue Not Empty AND Complete = False
ENDPROCEDURE
```

a Copy and complete this trace table to show the steps involved in following the breadth first search. The function call is `ShortestPath(A,E)`.

Queue		Start	Target	Discovered						Complete	Current	Temp	Parent					
Front	Back			A	B	C	D	E	F				A	B	C	D	E	F
		A	E	F	F	F	F	F	F				-	-	-	-	-	-
A																		
B																		
C																		
C D																		
C D E																		

b Copy and complete the trace table below to show the steps involved in following the depth first search. The function call is `DFS(A,E)`.

```
PROCEDURE Depth(Start,Target)
    Stack <- [Empty]
    Discovered <- [False]
    Stack.Push(Start)
    DO
        Current <- Stack.Pop()
        IF Not Discovered[Current] THEN
```

```
                    Discovered[Current] <- True
            FOR each node Temp adjacent to Current AND not in Stack DO
                    IF Not Discovered[Temp] DO
                            Stack.Push(Temp)
                    ENDIF
            ENDFOR
        ENDIF
    WHILE Stack is Not Empty And Current != Target
ENDPROCEDURE
```

Current	Target	Stack		Discovered						Temp
		Bottom	Top	A	B	C	D	E	F	
A	E			F	F	F	F	F	F	
A										
B										
E										

Answers available online

Trace tables with recursion

When tracing recursive algorithms it is usual to have a column for the call number. Previous calls are then repeated when data is returned and new calls to the same subroutine are given new, unique numbers.

In the example below, an algorithm has been written to traverse the binary tree shown in Figure 4.4.

An example implementation might look like this:

```
FUNCTION BinaryTreeSearch (Node)

    IF Node.Value = Target THEN

        Return True

    IF Node.Value > Target AND Exists(Node.Left) THEN

        Return BinaryTreeSearch(Node.Left)

    ELSEIF Node.Value < Target AND Exists(Node.Right)
THEN

        Return BinaryTreeSearch(Node.Right)

    ELSE
```

> **Recursive** An algorithm which calls itself.

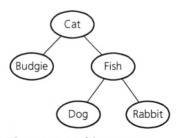

Figure 4.4 A binary tree

My Revision Notes AQA A-level Computer Science Third Edition

```
            Return False

        ENDIF

    ENDFUNCTION
```

It can be helpful to see the sequence of a recursive algorithm, as follows:

Call 1 – Node 'Cat'	Call 2 – Node 'Fish'	Call 3 – Node 'Rabbit'

`FUNCTION BinaryTreeSearch`
`(Node)`
`        IF Node.Value = Target`
`THEN`
`                Return True`
`        IF Node.Value > Target`
`AND Exists(Node.Left) THEN`
`                Return`
`BinaryTreeSearch(Node.Left)`
`        ELSEIF Node.Value <`
`Target AND Exists(Node.Right)`
`THEN`
`                Return`
`BinaryTreeSearch(Node.Right)`		

	`FUNCTION BinaryTreeSearch`
	`(Node)`
	`        IF Node.Value = Target`
	`THEN`
	`                Return True`
	`        IF Node.Value > Target`
	`AND Exists(Node.Left) THEN`
	`                Return`
	`BinaryTreeSearch(Node.Left)`
	`        ELSEIF Node.Value <`
	`Target AND Exists(Node.Right)`
	`THEN`
	`                Return`
	`BinaryTreeSearch(Node.Right)`	

		`FUNCTION BinaryTreeSearch`
		`(Node)`
		`        IF Node.Value = Target`
		`THEN`
		`        Return True`
		
		`IF Node.Value > Target AND`
		`Exists(Node.Left) THEN`
		`                Return`
		`BinaryTreeSearch(Node.Left)`
		`        ELSEIF Node.Value <`
		`Target AND Exists(Node.Right)`
		`THEN`
		`                Return`
		`BinaryTreeSearch(Node.Right)`
		`        ELSE`
		`                Return False`
		
		`ENDIF`
		`ENDFUNCTION`

	`ELSE`
	`                Return False`
	`        ENDIF`
	`ENDFUNCTION`	

Check your understanding and progress at **www.hoddereducation.co.uk/myrevisionnotesdownloads**

```
        ELSE
                Return False
            ENDIF
ENDFUNCTION
```

If the target was 'Rabbit' then the trace table would look like this:

Target	Call	Node	Value returned
Dog	1	Cat	
	2	Fish	
	3	Rabbit	True
	2	Fish	True
	1	Cat	True

Worked example

Here is an example of another pseudo-code algorithm and its final trace table.

```
    FUNCTION Fact(x)

        IF x < 2 THEN

          RETURN 1

        ELSE

          RETURN x * Fact(x - 1)

        ENDIF

    ENDFUNCTION
```

Call	x	Return
1	4	
2	3	
3	2	
4	1	1
3	2	2
2	3	6
1	4	24

The final result indicates that 4! = 24, which is correct.

Worked example

A more complex example might include more than one recursive call. For example:

```
    FUNCTION Fib (int x)

        IF x < 2 THEN

          RETURN 1

        ELSE

          RETURN Fib(x-1) + Fib(x-2)

        ENDIF

    ENDFUNCTION
```

As with the non-recursive trace tables, it is common to be provided with pre-completed values highlighted in order to help you check that you are completing the table correctly.

Call	x	Fib(x-1)	Fib(x-2)	Return
1	3			
2	2			
3	1			1
2	2	1		
4	0			1
2	2	1	1	2
1	3	2		
5	1			1
1	3	2	1	3

A full work through of these trace tables is provided online.

Making links

For a full and detailed explanation of how to complete this trace table see:

www.hoddereducation.co.uk/myrevisionnotesdownloads

For more on recursive algorithms, including general case and base case, see Chapter 1.

Now test yourself TESTED

4 Complete the trace table below by hand-tracing the algorithm, from the **FUNCTION** Fact (X) algorithm in the first Worked example above, when the call Fact(5) is made.

Call	x	Return
1	5	
2		
3		
4		
5		
4		
3		
2		
1		

5 Complete the trace table below by hand-tracing the algorithm, from the **FUNCTION** Fib (X) algorithm in the second Worked example above, when the call Fib(4) is made.

Call	x	Fib(x-1)	Fib(x-2)	Return
1	4			
2				
3				
4				
3				
5				
3				
2				

Check your understanding and progress at **www.hoddereducation.co.uk/myrevisionnotesdownloads**

Call	x	Fib(x-1)	Fib(x-2)	Return
6				
2				
1				
7				
8				
7				
9				
7				
1				

Answers available online

Revision activity

+ Find pseudo-code algorithms for each of the key algorithms in Chapter 3 and hand-trace them, using your own lists as inputs.
+ Practise tracing recursive algorithms in particular, including tree-traversal and factorial algorithms.

Making links

Tree traversal algorithms are covered in Chapter 3

Factorials are covered later in this chapter (See *Maths for understanding Big-O notation*).

Abstraction

REVISED ○

Abstraction is a method of reducing the complexity of a problem.

This makes the problem easier to understand, and easier to solve.

There are a number of different techniques, each discussed below.

Abstraction Making a problem simpler by removing or hiding features.

Representational abstraction

In order to design a solution to a real-world problem it is necessary to remove any features or details that are unnecessary.

A famous example of this is the London Underground Tube Map, in which geographical features are hidden and the resulting map is not drawn to scale in order to make it easier for commuters to understand and navigate.

Note

It is important to be able to identify and describe each technique in an exam question, but it is also very useful to be able to use and apply your understanding – particularly as part of the NEA programming project.

Generalisation

Another method of abstraction involves identifying the key features or characteristics of a problem in order to identify the type of problem.

When trying to navigate the London Underground, for example, the problem can be identified as a graphing problem, with stations as nodes and tube lines as edges.

Information hiding

REVISED ○

When designing a solution it is helpful to hide any details that that do not need to be accessed by other parts of the program.

In procedural-oriented programming this can be carried out by using local variables which are not accessed by other subroutines.

In object-oriented programming this can be carried out by declaring attributes and methods as private in order to hide them from other objects

Procedural abstraction

REVISED

In order to avoid repeatedly typing very similar code to carry out tasks that rely on the same method over and over again, it is good practice to use a subroutine to abstract the process.

Procedural abstraction describes a method of ensuring that subroutines are as generalised and re-usable as possible. For example, a subroutine called add One To Users Score is extremely specific, however a subroutine called add Two Numbers can be re-used in a wider range of scenarios.

Best practice in procedural abstraction is to separate the user interface (prompts and responses) and the processing of data into separate subroutines, and to use generic identifiers for both the subroutine names and the variables used. For example, DisplayGreeting(Greeting) is poorly designed, whereas DisplayMessage(Message) is more re-usable.

Functional abstraction

REVISED

Functional abstraction aims to hide the complexity of a specific algorithm, or how a part of the program works, using a subroutine. A programmer can then call that subroutine without needing to know exactly how it functions.

A good example is a method to print a message to the screen. This is actually a very complex process that involves re-drawing the screen with the new data. However it is often the very first program written by new programmers and the complexity is almost completely hidden from the programmer by putting the code inside a procedure called print.

When a programmer wants to carry out this very complex procedure, they can simply call print (for example, print("Hello World")) - the need to understand the detail of how the message is printed is avoided.

Data abstraction

REVISED

In data abstraction, because the details of how the data are actually stored in a computer are hidden, it is possible to create structures that behave in a particular way.

It is straightforward to understand how structures such as stacks, queues, graphs and trees work at a conceptual level. However, these structures are not really stored in the computer as stacks, queues, graphs or trees.

For instance:
+ Implementing a circular queue can be achieved using a one-dimensional array and two pointers.
+ Once implemented, a programmer can then interact with this circular queue using subroutines such as enqueue, dequeue and peek.
+ However, the programmer does not need to be concerned with the way that the data is actually stored within the array – they just need to know how to use the enqueue, dequeue and peek subroutines.

Problem abstraction/reduction

REVISED

Problem abstraction involves removing unnecessary detail from the problem in order to reduce the problem to one that has already been solved.

One example might be that the owner of a chain of shops may want to visit each of their stores in order to award a prize for the employee of the month at each location.

By removing the unnecessary detail of the purpose of the visit, this can be identified as an example of the travelling salesman problem, for which a number of potential solutions already exist.

Check your understanding and progress at **www.hoddereducation.co.uk/myrevisionnotesdownloads**

Decomposition

REVISED

Decomposition is the process of taking a large problem and breaking it down into smaller and smaller sub-problems until each sub-problem covers exactly one task.

A programmer can then create a subroutine for each task in order to create a complete solution.

This technique doesn't necessarily reduce the overall level of complexity, but is intended to provide a method of breaking the problem into more manageable chunks.

> **Decomposition** Breaking a problem into smaller sub-problems.

Composition

REVISED

Composition refers to the concept of combining features together.

One example is using a subroutine which calls another subroutine. For example, a subroutine to start a game of cards may be composed of subroutines to shuffle the deck and then deal the cards to the players.

Another example is the concept of combining data objects. For example, a binary tree data structure can be composed of three one-dimensional arrays; one containing the values for each node, one containing the index for the left branch and one containing the index for the right branch.

> **Composition** Combining parts of a solution together to create a solution made of component parts.

Automation

REVISED

Automation is the overall goal of applying some or all of the abstraction methods discussed above.

In order to solve a problem, it is necessary to:
+ design an algorithm to solve the problem
+ implement the data structures to store the data that must be stored
+ implement the algorithms using program code
+ execute the code.

By completing these four steps it is possible to automate processes and to model real-world problems and scenarios in a meaningful and useful way.

> **Automation** Designing, implementing and executing a solution to solve a problem automatically.

Now test yourself

TESTED

6　Describe the difference between procedural and functional abstraction.

7　State which method of abstraction is used to remove unnecessary aspects of the problem.

8　Explain the difference between problem abstraction and generalisation.

9　What type of abstraction is used to allow the creation of stacks and queues using an array and some pointers?

10　List the four steps involved in automation.

Answers available online

Regular languages

Finite state machines (FSM) with and without output

REVISED

A finite state machine can be used to represent potential states within a system in order to help the programmer understand the task more clearly.

For this use, each state represents a real-world state. For instance, in a computer program that controls a lift the states might be:

> **Finite state machine (FSM)** A computational model which has a fixed number of potential states.

+ stopped at a floor
+ travelling up
+ travelling down
+ overloaded.

Another use for a finite state machine is to check whether a particular series of inputs is acceptable.

State Transition Diagrams – no output

Finite state machines are often represented as a state transition diagram.

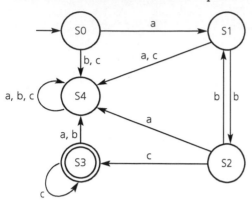

Figure 4.5 A state transition diagram for a finite state machine with no outputs

The state transition diagram above shows the following features.
+ Each circle represents a state.
+ Each arrow represents a transition.
+ Each label represents an input.

The FSM starts at state S0 – indicated by the arrow.

State S3, with two concentric circles, is the accepting state.

State S4, with no way to transition out, is a trap state.

An acceptable input would end at S3, because this is the accepting state. This diagram is used to check whether a series of inputs is valid or not; for example:
+ a is not acceptable because it ends at S1
+ b is not acceptable because it ends at S4
+ aa is not acceptable because it ends at S4
+ abc is acceptable because it ends at S3
+ abcc, abccc, abcccc, etc. are all acceptable
+ abca is not acceptable because it ends at S4

The finite state machine can also be represented as a state transition table, with each row indicating the starting state, input and next state.

Part of a state transition table to represent the same finite state machine is shown below:

Starting State	Input	Next State
S0	a	S1
S0	b	S4
S0	c	S4
S1	a	S4
S1	b	S2
S1	c	S4
…	…	…

> **State transition diagram**
> A diagram showing the states, inputs and transitions in a FSM.

> **State transition table**
> A table showing the states, inputs and transitions in a FSM.

Check your understanding and progress at **www.hoddereducation.co.uk/myrevisionnotesdownloads**

Revision activity

Create state transition diagrams for everyday devices, such as hairdryers and ovens.

State transition diagrams – with output

The finite state machines with outputs that you will see are also called Mealy machines. These are similar to the previous example, except that the labels on the transitions show both an input and an output.

Mealy machine A finite state machine in which each input has a corresponding output as well as a transition between states.

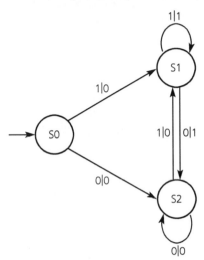

Figure 4.6 A state transition diagram showing a Mealy machine

The first value in the label for a transition is the input, and the second is the output.

Starting at state S0, an input of 1 will give an output of 0.

This finite state machine does not have an accepting state, as its purpose is not to validate an input, but to display an output based on its input.

In this particular case an input of 0110, reading from left to right, would give an output of 0011.

The purpose of this finite state machine is to carry out a right logical shift.

Mealy machines can also be described using a state transition table, with an extra column indicating the output.

Exam tip

It is very important to read the question very carefully. In the example above, reading the input from right to left would give a different answer – the output 1100, carrying out a left logical shift. You need to pay careful attention to these details in the question.

Starting state	Input	Output	Next state
S0	0	0	S2
S0	1	0	S1
S1	0	1	S2
S1	1	1	S1
S2	0	0	S2
S2	1	0	S1

Revision activity

Create state transition diagrams to demonstrate binary operations such as left shifts, right shifts, and twos complement conversion.

85

Maths for regular expressions

In order to better understand regular expressions, it is important to understand some relevant mathematical principles relating to set theory.

You should not be assessed specifically on this mathematical understanding, but it will form part of the basis for the regular expressions topic.

A set is an unordered collection of values, with no duplicates.

    A = {1, 2, 3, 4, 5}

A set can also be described using a set of rules, known as set comprehension or set-builder notation.

These symbols are used in set comprehension:

		'such that'
$\in$	'is a member of'
$\wedge$	logical operator for 'and'
$\leq, \geq, <>$	logical operators for inequalities

Here is the set comprehension for A:

    A = { x | x ∈ ℕ ∧ x ≥ 1}

This translates as: A is the set of x, such that x is a member of the set of natural numbers and x is greater than or equal to 1.

An empty set can be described using {} or Ø.

A compact representation of a set can be listed without needing to specify x.

A = { anbn | n > 0 ∧ n < 4 } would give the set {ab, aabb, aaabbb}

> **Now test yourself**
> TESTED
>
> 16 Which one of these statements is true?
>   a Sets must be written in order.
>   b Sets cannot contain duplicate values.
>   c Sets cannot be empty.
> 17 What values would be in each of the following sets?
>   a A = { x | x ∈ ℤ ∧ x < 3 ∧ x > -2 }
>   b B = { x | x ∈ ℕ ∧ x/2 < 2 }
>   c C = { bna2bn | n ≥ 1 ∧ n ≤ 3 }
>
> **Answers available online**

Categorising sets

A countable set is any set with the same number of elements as some subset of the natural numbers. For example, a set with 72 elements is countable.

Some sets are finite sets – they have a fixed number of values and their elements can be counted off in a similar way to an index in an array (for example, 1st element, 2nd element, 3rd element, and so on).

The number of values in a set is referred to as its cardinality.

Some sets are infinite sets, and will carry on forever.
+ Some infinite sets are countable sets; for example, the set of natural numbers – these can be called countably infinite sets.
+ Some infinite sets are not countable sets; e.g., the set of real numbers.

The Cartesian product of two sets (written A x B) contains the set of ordered pairs of values in A and B.

A x B = { (a,b) | a ∈ A ∧ b ∈ B}

A = {1, 2} and B = {4, 5, 6}

A x B = { (1, 4), (1, 5), (1, 6), (2, 4), (2, 5), (2, 6) }

Check your understanding and progress at **www.hoddereducation.co.uk/myrevisionnotesdownloads**

Set theory A branch of mathematical logic in which sets are collections of objects.

Set comprehension A collection of rules to define which values are in a set.

Making links

Set theory, and particularly the sets of ℕ (natural numbers), ℤ (integers), ℚ (rational numbers) and ℝ (real numbers), are essential to understanding the maths that underpins regular expressions. This topic is explained in more detail in Chapter 5.

Countable set A set with the same number of values as a subset of the natural numbers ℕ.

Finite set A set with a fixed number of values.

Infinite sets A set whose values will go on forever.

Countably infinite sets A set whose values will go on forever, but can still be counted (for example, ℕ).

Cardinality The number of values in a finite set.

Cartesian product The set of ordered pairs of values from both sets.

A subset is made up of some elements of the main set. The main set is sometimes called the superset.

Subsets can be described in one of these three ways:

✚ A ⊆ B means 'A is a subset of B'.

This means that everything in A is also in B. They may or may not be equal. For example:

{0,1} ⊆ {0,1,2} and {0,1,2} ⊆ {0,1,2}

✚ A ⊂ B means 'A is a proper subset of B'.

This means that everything in A is also in B, but they are not equal. There is at least one other value in B.

{0,1} ⊂ {0,1,2}

✚ A = B means 'A is identical to B'.

{0,1,2} = {0,1,2}

Exam tip

Remember that the sign for a subset, ⊆, incorporates an underscore in the same way as the 'greater than or equals' symbol, ≥. This indicates that the subset can be equal to its superset.

The symbol for a proper subset, ⊂, does not incorporate an underscore and cannot be the same as its superset.

Now test yourself   TESTED ⬤

18 State whether each of these sets is finite, infinite or countably infinite
  a A = { x | x ∈ ℕ }
  b B = { x | x ∈ ℝ ∧ x > 0 ∧ x < 10}
  c C = { x | x ∈ ℤ ∧ x > 0 ∧ x < 10}

19 What symbol is used to represent a subset?

20 What symbol is used to represent a proper subset?

21 A = {r, s, t}, B = {q}, C = {r, t, s}
  a State whether C is a subset of A and explain why
  b State whether C is a proper subset of A and explain why
  c Write down the Cartesian product of A x B

Answers available online

Set operations

For each example, A = {1, 2, 3} and B = {3, 4, 5}.

✚ Membership of a set indicates that a value is in that set.

1 is a member of A.

✚ Union (represented as ∪) means joining both sets together and including all elements, see Figure 4.7.

The ∪ symbol is similar to the logical ∨ symbol, indicating OR.

A ∪ B = {1, 2, 3, 4, 5}

✚ Intersection (represented as ∩) means joining both sets together and including only those elements common to both, see Figure 4.8.

The ∩ symbol is similar to the logical ∧ symbol, indicating AND.

A ∩ B = {3}

✚ Difference (represented as ϴ, Δ or \) means joining both sets together and including only those elements that are not common to both, see Figure 4.9.

A \ B = {1, 2, 4, 5}

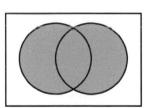

Figure 4.7

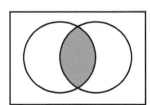

Figure 4.8

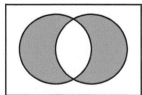

Figure 4.9

Now test yourself   TESTED ⬤

22 A = {r, s, t} and B = {p, q, r, s}
List the values in the following sets.
  a A ∩ B
  b A ∪ B
  c A \ B

Answers available online

Regular expressions

Regular expressions are a way of describing a set. They are also used to describe particular types of languages. They can be extremely useful to identify items that meet certain criteria; for example, for validation checks.

> **Regular expression** A sequence of characters used to describe a pattern. Used in searching and validation.

Symbols used in regular expressions include:

+ | meaning 'or'; for example, a | b

   The set of valid inputs would be {a, b}

+ + meaning '1 or more'; for example, ab+

   The set of valid inputs would include {ab, abb, abbb, abbbb, ...}

+ * meaning '0 or more'; for example, ab*

   The set of valid inputs would include {a, ab, abb, abbb, ...}

+ ? meaning '0 or 1'; for example, ab?

   The set of valid inputs would be {a, ab}

Regular expressions can be represented using finite state machines, and it is common for questions to appear in which a finite state machine should be described as a regular expression.

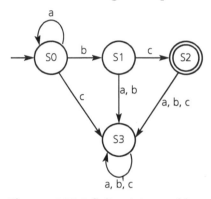

Figure 4.10 A finite state machine

In this machine the acceptable inputs include 0 or more 'a' values followed by a single 'b' and a single 'c'. Any other inputs would be sent to the trap state.

Therefore, the acceptable inputs would be written as: a*bc

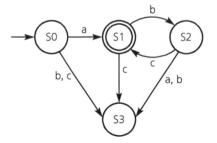

Figure 4.11 A finite state machine

In this finite state machine the accepting state can be reached by inputting 'a' followed by 0 or more repetitions of 'bc'.

This would be written as a(bc)*

Regular languages

A formal language is made up of words that contain letters from the alphabet and where those words fit a set of rules.

A regular language is a formal language that can be represented using a regular expression. If the language cannot be represented using a regular expression then it is not a regular language.

A regular language can also be represented using a finite state machine.

Check your understanding and progress at **www.hoddereducation.co.uk/myrevisionnotesdownloads**

Context-free languages

Backus–Naur form (BNF) and syntax diagrams

REVISED ⬤

Backus–Naur form

Backus–Naur form (BNF) is a method of describing syntax rules.

In BNF, each type of value is described as containing values from a set.

Each individual production rule is replaced with (::=) certain values. The symbol ::= can be read 'is defined as'.

Values in <angle brackets> must be further broken down and defined until all values are made up of terminal values (that is, values that cannot be broken down any further). The symbol | means 'or'.

In the example below, spaces are represented with an underscore.

For example, the syntax rules for entering a name could be defined as follows:

```
<fullname> ::= <title> _ <name>

<title> ::= MR | MISS | MRS | MS

<name> ::= <word> | <name> _ <word>

<word> ::= <letter> | <word> _ <letter>

<letter> ::= A | B | C | D | E | F | G | H | I | J | K
           | L | M | N | O | P | Q | R | S | T | U | V
           | W | X | Y | Z
```

> **Backus–Naur form (BNF)**
> A notation used to describe
> the syntax of a language.
>
> **Syntax** The set of rules for
> a given language.
>
> **Production rule** The set
> of acceptable inputs for a
> given symbol.
>
> **Terminal** A single value
> that cannot be broken down
> into smaller parts.

Line 1 – the set fullname is defined as a value from the set title followed by a value from the set name.

Line 2 – the set title is defined as a value from the set of terminal values MR or MISS or MRS or MS.

Line 3 - the set name is defined as either a value from the set word or as a value from the set name followed by a value from the set word.

Line 4 – the set word is defined as either a value from the set letter or as a value from the set word followed by a value from the set letter.

Line 5 – the set letter is defined as a value from the set of terminal values A or B or C ... through to Z.

Recursion is used in lines 3 and 4. To see how this works consider the set word contains 'DAVE'.

+ Line 4 says if a word is not defined as a single letter then it is defined as a word followed by a letter.
+ This would replace the word 'DAVE' with the word 'DAV' followed by the letter E.
+ The new word 'DAV' is replaced with the word 'DA' followed by the letter 'V'.
+ The new word 'DA' is replaced with the word 'D' followed by the letter 'A'.
+ Finally, the word 'D' is replaced with the a value from the set letter, which contains the terminal value 'D'.

The set might contain other values which need to be defined. For example, a fullname is made up of further sets title and name. The set might be defined as containing one of a series of terminal values which do not need to be defined.

For example, acceptable titles include Mr, Miss, Mrs and Ms.

The set might use recursion to allow for values that can be of variable length. For example, a name is made up of a word, or a name followed by a word.

'Dave' is a word, and so can be accepted as a name.

'Dave Andrew' is a name followed by a word, and so can be accepted as a name.

'Dave Andrew Smith' is a name followed by a word, and so can be accepted as a name.

Exam tip

When asked in an exam, BNF definitions that do not use recursion can be described using a regular expression (such as fullname, title and letter in the previous example). BNF definitions that do use recursion cannot be described using a regular expression (such as name and word in the previous example). This is a simplification of the real world but provides the expected answer for A-level exam requirements.

Syntax diagrams

Syntax diagrams are an alternative way to represent BNF.

Definitions that contain terminals tend to be quite straightforward, demonstrating each possible value. For instance, a digit can be described as:

Syntax diagram A diagram used to describe BNF graphically.

```
Digit ::= 0 | 1 | 2 | 3 | 4 | 5 | 6 | 7 | 8 | 9
```

Digit

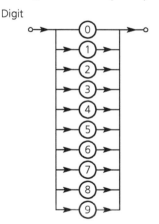

Figure 4.12 A syntax diagram for a digit

Definitions that contain recursion are drawn using a loop, so that an integer can be described as:

```
Integer ::= <digit> | <digit><integer>
```

Integer

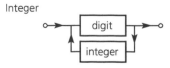

Figure 4.13 A syntax diagram for an integer

Check your understanding and progress at **www.hoddereducation.co.uk/myrevisionnotesdownloads**

Now test yourself

The rules for a name are given using the following syntax rules:

```
<name> ::= <word> | <word> _ <name>

<word> ::= <letter> | <letter> _ <word>

<letter> ::= A|B|C|D|E|F|G|H|...
```

27 Give **one** example of a terminal value in this syntax.

28 Explain why the rule for a name cannot be described using a regular expression.

29 Represent the production rule for a word using a syntax diagram.

Answers available online

Revision activity

✚ Identify patterns and rules in constructions such as postcodes and addresses, and try to represent these using BNF.

✚ For each production rule, create the equivalent syntax diagram.

Classification of algorithms

Comparing algorithms

It is important to be able to compare the efficiency of different algorithms in order to identify which is the best solution for each particular problem

As the size of the data to be processed grows, the efficiency of the algorithm becomes much more important. Sorting a list of 10 values with an inefficient algorithm may not cause a problem, but when sorting a list of 100 000 values it is much more important to choose wisely.

The efficiency of an algorithm can be described by looking at two main aspects:
✚ Time-wise complexity: Algorithms that have a lot of steps or comparisons will take longer to compute for large data sets.
✚ Space-wise complexity: Algorithms that store a lot of temporary values while the processes take place will take up a lot of memory.

An ideal algorithm will be efficient in terms of both time to execute and space needed for memory.

However, depending on the particular situation, sometimes it might be more important to:
✚ choose an algorithm which is time-efficient even if it uses a lot of memory to store values temporarily during execution
✚ choose an algorithm which is space-efficient even if it might take longer to carry out the instructions.

> **Efficiency** Being able to complete a task with the least use of time or memory.
>
> **Time-wise complexity** A measure of how much time, or how many steps, will be required to complete an algorithm.
>
> **Space-wise complexity** A measure of how much memory will be required to complete an algorithm.

Note

Recursive algorithms are often considered to be elegant solutions as they can be described using few lines of code. They are typically inefficient however, particularly space-wise, as the local variables for each call need to be stored while any further calls are running.

Now test yourself

30 What is the key consideration in time-wise complexity?

31 What is the key consideration in space-wise complexity?

32 Why might a time-efficient algorithm not always the best choice?

Answers available online

Maths for understanding Big-O notation

In order to understand Big-O notation it is important to understand some underlying mathematical concepts.

Functions

A function is a method of mapping one set of values to another.

For example, the function $y = 2x$ maps each value of x to a new value, y.

x
−3
−2
−1
0
1
2
3

$y = 2x$

y
−6
−4
−2
0
2
4
6

Figure 4.14 A mapping function

> **Making links**
>
> The issues surrounding function terminology, including domains, co-domains and sets, is typically only assessed in questions relating to functional programming. Functional programming is covered in detail in Chapter 12.

The input values are referred to as the domain, and the output values are referred to as the co-domain.

If the domain (input values) is made of integers (natural numbers) and the co-domain is also made of integers then this can be described using the format $\mathbb{Z} \to \mathbb{Z}$.

Consider each of the following graphs.

+ The graph of $y = 3$ represents a constant function.

  The value of y is constant and does not go up as x changes

+ The graph of $y = 2x$ represents a linear function.

  The value of y goes up in a straight line – so if x doubles, so does y.

+ The graph of $y = 2x^2$ represents a polynomial function.

  The value of x is raised by a power. Other examples include graphs with x^3, x^4 and so on.

+ The graph of $y = 2^x$ represents an exponential function.

  A value is raised by the power of x. Whenever x is used as a power the value of y will go up increasingly quickly.

+ The graph of $y = \log_2 x$ represents a logarithmic function.

  The value of y goes up very slowly. Using $y = \log_2 x$ is the opposite of using 2^x.

+ The graph of $y = x!$ represents a factorial function.

  The value of y goes up extraordinarily quickly.

> **Linear** Rising in a straight line; for example, the graph of $y = 2x$.
>
> **Polynomial** An expression involving powers; for example, $y = 2x^2$.
>
> **Exponential** An expression where the variable is used as an exponent, or power; for example, $y = 2^x$.
>
> **Logarithmic** The opposite of exponential. If $y = 2^x$, then $x = \log_2 y$.

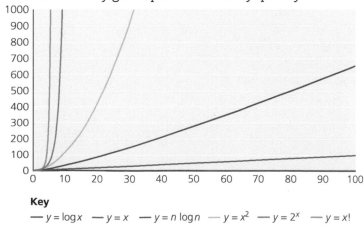

Key

— $y = \log x$ — $y = x$ — $y = n \log n$ — $y = x^2$ — $y = 2^x$ — $y = x!$

Figure 4.15 A graph representing different types of function

Check your understanding and progress at **www.hoddereducation.co.uk/myrevisionnotesdownloads**

To better understand the meaning of a logarithm, consider this table showing powers of 2; that is, the first few values of $y = 2^x$:

2^0	2^1	2^2	2^3	2^4	2^5	2^6	2^7	2^8
1	2	4	8	16	32	64	128	256

Applying a logarithm to the same base is the inverse of raising to a power; in other words:

$\log_2(2^x) = x$

This can be see if we consider the following values of $y = \log_2 x$:

$\log_2 1$	$\log_2 2$	$\log_2 4$	$\log_2 8$	$\log_2 16$	$\log_2 32$	$\log_2 64$	$\log_2 128$	$\log_2 256$
0	1	2	3	4	5	6	7	8

Factorials and permutations

It is also important to be familiar with the concept of a factorial.

$n!$ (pronounced 'n factorial') multiplies all of the positive integers up to and including n. For example:

$5! = 5 \times 4 \times 3 \times 2 \times 1$

$6! = 6 \times 5 \times 4 \times 3 \times 2 \times 1$

The graph of $n!$ grows more rapidly than an exponential function.

A factorial is used to describe the maximum number of permutations of a set of values.

For example, if I want to visit cities A, B and C in any order then I could use any of the following permutations:

{A,B,C}, {A,C,B}, {B,A,C}, {B,C,A}, {C,A,B}, {C,B,A}

If there are three values in the set, then there are 3! (= 6) possible permutations.

If there are four values in the set, then there are 4! (= 24) possible permutations.

Order of complexity

Time-wise efficiency is described using Big-O notation.

This is used to put the time efficiency of different algorithms into some sort of order, and uses the notation O(n), where n is the number of steps and different terms are used inside the brackets for each order of complexity.

Constant time

Finding the first item in a list, or jumping straight to a value at a given index, always takes exactly one step.

The time-wise complexity for an algorithm that always takes the same number of steps, no matter how big the list, is described using the time-wise complexity O(1) for one step, O(2) for two steps, O(3) for three steps, and so on – though O(1) is much more likely.

Logarithmic time

A binary search of n values will usually take very little time because the possible list of remaining values is halved each time. This halving at each step means that the maximum possible number of steps taken to find the right item goes up on a logarithmic scale.

We can, therefore, state that the time-wise complexity of the binary search is O($n \log n$).

> **Factorial** The product of all positive integers less than or equal to a given integer.
>
> **Permutation** One of the different ways that a set can be arranged.

Now test yourself

33 Give an example of a linear function.

34 What type of function is the graph of $y = 2x^3$?

35 Which graph rises most steeply – an exponential function or a logarithmic function?

36 What type of function is $y = 1$?

Answers available online

TESTED

Linear time

In the worst case, a linear search of n items will take n steps. If the item is the last one in the list then every item much be checked before it is found.

We can therefore state that the time-wise complexity of the linear search is $O(n)$.

Loglinear ($n \log n$) time

The merge sort is a very efficient algorithm which, much like the binary search, involves splitting lists in half repeatedly. Sorting is always a more complex task than search, and so the time-wise complexity is not quite as small.

The time-wise complexity of the merge sort is $O(n \log n)$.

Polynomial time

To sort a list of n values using the bubble sort, each pass would require $(n-1)$ comparisons.

To fully sort the list it will be necessary to complete $(n-1)$ passes. The total steps would therefore be $(n-1) \times (n-1)$.

However, for a large list, $n \approx n-1$ (that is, n is almost equal to $(n-1)$)

So, $(n-1)(n-1) \approx n^2$

We can, therefore, state that the time-wise complexity of the bubble sort is $O(n^2)$.

Other algorithms that can be expressed as $O(n^2)$ time-wise complexity include the insertion sort and selection sort.

Exponential time

The time-wise complexity for an algorithm that uses exponential time will be written as $O(k^n)$, where k is a constant and the value is raised to the power of n.

An example could be trying every possible value of a passcode. If a passcode uses four digits then there are 10^4 possible values to try. If the passcode uses six digits then there are 10^6 possible values.

Factorial time

Factorial time is even worse than exponential time. The travelling salesman problem is an example of a problem that has a time-wise complexity of $O(n!)$.

To make it easier to remember these time complexities, and examples of each, consider this graph:

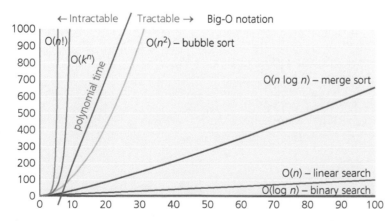

Figure 4.16 A graph showing the time complexities for different algorithms

> **Notes**
>
> The term loglinear is not often used – simply writing $n \log n$ is more common.
>
> Polynomial time refers to time-wise complexity where n is raised to a power; for example, $O(n^2)$, $O(n^3)$, $O(n^4)$, and so on.

> **Exam tip**
>
> Remember that searching is always simpler than sorting, and for each topic there is a good algorithm and a bad algorithm. The good search and the good sort techniques can both be described using logarithms because they use divide and conquer techniques. The bad search and the bad sort both involve going through every item in the list, and so scale up with n (rather than $\log n$).

Limits of computation   REVISED ⬤

Although many problems can be solved with enough time and enough memory, it is important to consider the physical constraints of computing hardware.

A time-efficient algorithm that uses a large amount of memory may not be able to function effectively once all available RAM is used.

Similarly, while CPUs run at enormously high frequencies, time-complex algorithms may still take longer than is reasonable to carry out their processing.

As such, even if a problem can be computed in theory, hardware limits may mean that it is not possible to compute it in a practical setting.

Classification of algorithmic problems   REVISED ⬤

Problems that can be solved in polynomial or less time are considered to be tractable. This means that they can be solved in a reasonable amount of time.

Problems that cannot be solved in polynomial or less time (for example, exponential or factorial time) are considered to be intractable. This means that they cannot be solved in a reasonable amount of time. See Figure 4.15.

> **Tractable** A problem which can be completed in a reasonable amount of time (polynomial time or less).
>
> **Intractable** A problem which can be solved, but not in a reasonable amount of time (worse than polynomial).
>
> **Heuristic** An approach to solving intractable problems in a reasonable amount of time by accepting an imperfect solution.

> **Exam tip**
>
> Exam questions often ask you to explain what is meant by the term *intractable*. It is vital to point out that intractable problems **can be solved**, but **not in a reasonable amount of time**. Both parts of the statement are required, and it is important to emphasise that intractable problems can be computed.

In order to solve intractable problems, heuristic methods are often used.

These include:
+ reducing the complexity of the problem
+ relaxing some of the constraints on the problem
+ using an algorithm that uses a best-guess or estimate based on experience
+ accepting a close-to-optimal solution.

> **Exam tip**
>
> Make sure you memorise these examples of heuristic algorithms as this topic comes up often.

> **Note**
>
> Though not covered on the specification, Prim's and Kruskal's algorithms are interesting examples of heuristic solutions and could form part of an interesting NEA project.

> **Revision activity**
>
> Investigate problems such as the travelling salesman problem, the bin-packing problem and the knapsack problem to see examples of intractable problems.

Computable and non-computable problems

Many problems are computable, even if they can't always be completed efficiently.

Some problems are non-computable. That means that they simply cannot be solved using a computer.

> **Computable** A problem that can be solved with a computer.

Halting problem

The halting problem is: given a computer program and an input, is it possible to determine whether that program would loop forever or would eventually stop, without running it?

A mathematical proof shows that an algorithm to solve the halting problem cannot exist.

> **Note**
>
> The proof for the halting problem is not required for A-level computer science, but it involves demonstrating that a successful solution would create a paradox, which is therefore impossible.

> **Non-computable** A problem that cannot be solved by a computer.
>
> **Halting problem** A specific example of a non-computable problem that proves that some problems are non-computable.

The significance of the halting problem is that it demonstrates that there are some problems that cannot be solved using a computer.

> **Now test yourself**
>
>
> 45 What is a *non-computable problem*?
> 46 Explain what is meant by the *halting problem*.
> 47 Explain why the halting problem is significant.
>
> **Answers available online**

A model of computation

Turing machine

A Turing machine is a theoretical computing device with a single, fixed program that is made up of:
+ a finite set of states
+ a finite alphabet of symbols
+ an infinite length of tape, with marked off squares
+ a read-write head that can travel across the tape, one square at a time.

Because a Turing machine uses a finite set of states, it can be described using a finite state machine (FSM), either using a state transition diagram or a state transition table.

An FSM should have one state as the starting state.

Any states with no outgoing transitions are called halting states.

Empty states can be recorded using a number of symbols, but it is typical for AQA to use the # symbol.

Each transition is labelled with an input, output and an arrow indicating the movement of the read-write head.

An example of Turing machine is described below using a state transition diagram.

> **Turing machine** A model of computation with a single program which manipulates symbols on a strip of tape.
>
> **Starting state** The state a Turing machine is in when it starts its program.
>
> **Halting state** A state with no outgoing transitions, and so the Turing machine will stop.

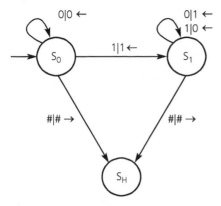

Figure 4.17 A state transition diagram representing the operation of a Turing machine

The diagram in Figure 4.16 could be shown using this state transition table:

Starting state	Input	Next state	Output	Movement
S_0	0	S_0	0	←
S_0	1	S_1	1	←
S_0	#	S_H	#	→
S_1	0	S_1	1	←
S_1	1	S_1	0	←
S_1	#	S_H	#	→

An alternative format that could be used is a transition function. It shows the starting state and input, followed by the next state, output and movement.

δ (delta) means 'change'. The first transition function reads: 'The change if the state is 0 and the input is 0 is that the state should be set to 0, the output set to 0 and the read-write head should move left'.

δ $(S_0,0)$	=	$(S_0, 0, ←)$		δ $(S_1,0)$	=	$(S_1, 1, ←)$
δ $(S_0,1)$	=	$(S_1, 1, ←)$		δ $(S_1,1)$	=	$(S_1, 0, ←)$
δ $(S_0, \#)$	=	$(S_H, \#, ←)$		δ $(S_1, \#)$	=	$(S_H, \#, →)$

The tape for the Turing machine is shown below, with an asterisk showing the current position or the read-write head.

…	#	0	1	1	0*	…		S_0

When the first value is read, the Turing machine is in State 0 and the input is 0.

Reading the transition function for this situation, the state should remain as State 0, the output 0 should be written to the tape and the read-write head should move to the left.

This leads to the result below:

…	#	0	1	1*	0	…		S_0

When the next value is read, the Turing machine is in State 0 – and the input is 1.

Reading the transition function for this situation, the state should be set to State 1, the output 1 should be written to the tape and read-write head should move to the left.

This leads to the result below:

...	#	0	1*	1	0	...		S_1

Following the algorithm described by the state transition diagram or by transition functions produces the following completed trace table:

...	#	0	1	1	0*	...		S_0
...	#	0	1	1*	0	...		S_0
...	#	0	1*	1	0	...		S_1
...	#	0*	0	1	0	...		S_1
...	#*	1	0	1	0	...		S_1
...	#	1*	0	1	0	...		S_H

The purpose of this Turing machine is to calculate the twos complement of a binary number.

Revision activity

+ Try creating your own Turing machine to carry out bit-wise operations such as twos complement, left shifts and right shifts.
+ Find examples of simple Turing machines online and hand-trace them using your own inputs.

Universal Turing machines

It is possible to describe an algorithm for any computable problem using a Turing machine. However, each Turing machine can only solve one problem because the program is fixed.

A universal Turing machine (UTM) is a Turing machine which can read in the description of another Turing machine and its tape in order to simulate that Turing machine.

The UTM will then carry out the operations on the tape exactly as the other Turing machine does. In other words, it can simulate any other Turing machine.

Because the UTM stores both the description of the Turing machine and its tape on the UTM's tape, the UTM acts as an interpreter.

As any single computable problem can be computed by a Turing machine, therefore every possible computable problem can, in theory, be computed on a UTM.

A UTM was the theoretical conception of a modern computer, proposed by computer scientist and mathematician Alan Turing in the 1930s. As a hypothetical machine it can be considered more powerful than any real computer due to the infinite tape, which effectively provides the UTM with an infinite amount of memory.

Universal Turing machine (UTM) A Turing machine that takes the description of another Turing machine and its tape as inputs. It can simulate any conceivable Turing machine.

Note

Exam questions will only be asked about Turing machines that have one tape that is infinite in one direction.

Check your understanding and progress at **www.hoddereducation.co.uk/myrevisionnotesdownloads**

Summary

+ Logic problems can be solved using logical deductions
+ An algorithm is a series of steps to complete a task, that always terminates
+ Algorithms written in pseudo-code solve problems using the standard programming constructs: sequence, assignment, selection, iteration
+ Algorithms can be hand-traced by completing a trace table
+ In recursive algorithms, trace tables should include the call number
+ It is important to be able to convert the description of an algorithm, whether in English or pseudo-code, into program code in your chosen language
+ Where they are provided, always make sure to use the exact variable names and prompts as they appear in the exam paper
+ Abstraction is a technique for simplifying a problem by removing or hiding complexity and includes: representational abstraction, generalisation, information hiding, procedural abstraction, functional abstraction, data abstraction and problem abstraction/reduction
+ Decomposition is the technique of breaking a problem into increasingly small sub-problems
+ Composition is the technique of combining individual subroutines to create compound subroutines that solve larger problems
+ Automation is the technique of designing, implementing, and executing solutions to complex problems
+ A finite state machine is a model of a system that can be described using a fixed number of states
+ Each time an input is provided to a finite state machine there will be a transition to a new state
+ A Mealy machine is a finite state machine where each input provides a specific output as well as a transition between states
+ Finite state machines can be described using state transition diagrams and state transition tables
+ A set is an unordered list of values, with no duplicates
+ Sets can be described using set comprehension symbols; for example:

   $A = \{ x \mid x \in \cup \wedge x \geq 1 \}$

+ Sets can also be described using compact representation; for example:

   $\{ anbn \mid n > 0 \wedge n < 4 \}$

+ The cardinality of a set refers to the number of elements within it
+ Some sets are finite, and some are infinite
+ The elements within countably infinite sets can be counted off by the natural numbers
+ The Cartesian product of two sets contains the set of all ordered pairs from those sets
+ All values in a subset also belong in the superset
+ All values in a proper subset belong in the superset, but this doesn't contain all of the values from the superset
+ The union of two sets includes all values from both sets combined
+ The intersection of two sets only contains those values in both sets
+ The difference of two sets contains only the values that are in one set, but not both

+ A regular expression is a notation used to describe a set
+ Regular expressions are used in searching and validation
+ The symbols *, +, ?, and | are used in regular expressions and have specific meanings
+ Regular expressions can also be represented using a finite state machine, and vice versa
+ It is possible to be asked to represent a finite state machine as a regular expression, and vice versa
+ A language is classed as a regular language if it can be represented as a regular expression
+ The syntax rules of a language can be checked using Backus–Naur form or syntax diagrams
+ Rules in BNF that do not use recursion can be represented using a regular expression
+ If BNF uses recursion, then it can represent languages that cannot be represented using regular expressions
+ The efficiency of algorithms can be described time-wise and space-wise
+ Functions map one set of values (the domain) to another set of values (co-domain)
+ The number of permutations of a set of n objects is $n!$ (where, for example, $4! = 4 \times 3 \times 2 \times 1$)
+ Big-O notation is used to describe the time-wise efficiency of algorithms
+ Searching algorithms include the binary search, $O(\log n)$ (logarithmic time), and the linear search, $O(n)$ (linear time)
+ Sorting algorithms include the merge sort, $O(n \log n)$, and the bubble sort, $O(n^2)$ (polynomial time)
+ Other algorithms use constant time, $O(1)$, exponential time, $O(k^n)$ and factorial time, $O(n!)$
+ Tractable problems can be solved in a reasonable (polynomial or less) time
+ Intractable problems can be solved, but not in a reasonable time (because of hardware limits, for example)
+ Heuristic methods such as reducing complexity or accepting a close-enough solution are used to solve intractable problems
+ Some problems, such as the Halting problem, cannot be solved algorithmically
+ The halting problem states that a program that can check whether or not another program will loop forever, given a specific input, cannot exist
+ The halting problem means that some problems cannot be solved by a computer
+ A Turing machine is a theoretical computing device that can carry out one fixed program
+ A Turing machine has a finite set of states, a finite alphabet, an infinite strip of tape and a read-write head
+ Any algorithm that can be computed can be described using a Turing machine, and vice-versa
+ A Turing machine can be described using a finite state machine, state transition diagrams, state transition tables and transition functions
+ A universal Turing machine can read in the description for any Turing machine and its tape in order to simulate it
+ A universal Turing machine is a theoretical machine, more powerful than any real computer because it has infinite memory / an infinite tape, and provides the theoretical basis for modern computers

Exam practice

1 A 7-bit code, 010 1011 is processed by the finite state machine, as shown.

The code is processed from the most significant bit, so the first value processed will be 0.

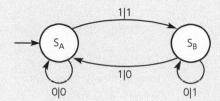

a) State the output when the 7-bit code 010 1011 is processed. [1]

b) The last value that is output from the finite state machine is added to the 7-bit code before it is transmitted. State the purpose of the final bit. [2]

c) The finite state machine could also be represented using a state transition table. Copy and complete the state transition table below. [3]

Starting state	Input	Output	Next state
S_A	0	0	S_A
S_A	1		
S_B			
S_B			

d) A Turing machine to achieve the same outcome is shown, along with its tape, below. The current position is labelled with an asterisk (*).

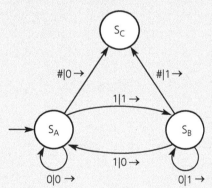

| ... | 1* | 1 | 0 | 0 | 1 | 0 | 1 | # | # | ... | | S_A |

Copy and complete this trace table by hand-tracing the Turing machine. [4]

...	1*	1	0	0	1	0	1	#	#	...		S_A
...										...		
...										...		
...										...		
...										...		
...										...		
...										...		
...										...		
...										...		
...										...		

e) As well as a finite set of states and a tape, identify **two** other features required by a Turing machine. [2]

Check your understanding and progress at **www.hoddereducation.co.uk/myrevisionnotesdownloads**

2 The subroutine `Fold` takes an array of integers as an argument.

The subroutine `Copy` takes two arguments – an array of integers and the index of the first element to be copied. This subroutine will return a copy of the array, starting from the position indicated by the index argument. For example: Calling `Copy([9,8,7,6,5],1)` would return `[8,7,6,5]`.

```
FUNCTION Fold (List)

    IF Len(List) > 1 THEN

        Head = List[0]

        Tail = Copy(List,1)

        return Head * Fold(Tail)

    ELSE

        return List[0]

    ENDIF

ENDFUNCTION
```

a) Copy an complete this trace table by hand-tracing the subroutine call `Fold([3,5,8,2])`. [4]

Call Number	List	Head	Tail	Return
1	[3,5,8,2]			
2				
3				
4				
3				
2				
1				

b) Explain why recursive algorithms are often considered to be space-wise inefficient. [2]

c) State the time-wise complexity for each of the following algorithms. [4]

Algorithm	Time-wise complexity
Linear search	
Merge sort	
Binary sort	
Insertion sort	

d) Explain why the time-wise complexity for a bubble sort is $O(n^2)$. [2]

e) State what is meant by an *intractable problem*. [2]

f) Suggest **two** possible approaches to solving an intractable problem. [2]

g) Explain the significance of the halting problem. [1]

3 Abstraction and automation are essential techniques in computer programming.

a) Explain what is meant by *abstraction*. [2]

b) Copy and complete this table by entering the appropriate letter in each case. [6]

    A Abstraction by generalisation

    B Data abstraction

    C Information hiding

    D Composition

    E Functional abstraction

    F Problem abstraction

Description	Abstraction
Combining individual functions to create compound functions	
Removing unnecessary details until the problem can be recognised as one that has already been solved	
Grouping features of the problem until it can be identified as a particular type of problem	
Hiding the details of how a task should be performed inside a subroutine that returns a value	
Creating structures such as stacks and queues using arrays and pointers	
Hiding the attributes that are stored within an object	

c) List the **four** steps involved in automation. [4]

4 A language is partly described using the finite state machine shown.

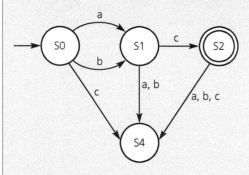

a) State which state is the accepting state. [1]

b) Write the regular expression described by this finite state machine. [1]

c) Explain why the language described by the finite state machine is a regular language. [1]

d) Below is an attempt at describing the language using the following BNF production rules.
State which BNF production rule cannot be represented as a regular expression and explain why not. [2]

```
<code>  ::= <digit><digit><word> | <digit><word>

<word> ::= <letter> | <word><letter>

<letter> ::= a | b | c

<digit> ::= 1 | 2 | 3
```

e) Copy and complete this table by placing a Y or N next to each input that would be accepted by the BNF rules above (regardless of whether the input would be accepted by the finite state machine). [3]

Input	Accepted?
12ab	
ab12	
3ab1	
2abc	
321cba	
21caabc	

5 Fundamentals of data representation

Number systems

Numbers can be grouped into different sets.

Many standard sets of numbers can be indicated using specialised set notations such as ℕ, ℤ, ℚ, and ℝ.

Natural numbers REVISED

The set of natural numbers, ℕ, is the set of positive integers. A handy way to remember this is that, when humans first started counting, these were the numbers that were obvious. 0 people, one person, two people, three people, and so on.

$$\mathbb{N} = \{0, 1, 2, 3, 4, \dots\}$$

The set of natural numbers is infinitely large, so we use the notation '...' to show that the set carries on forever.

> **Natural numbers** Positive integers, including 0. Numbers used to count things.

Integer numbers REVISED

The set of integer numbers, ℤ, is the set of all integers, both positive and negative.

$$\mathbb{Z} = \{\dots, -3, -2, -1, 0, 1, 2, 3, \dots\}$$

> **Integer numbers** Whole numbers, including both positive and negative values.

Rational numbers REVISED

The set of rational numbers, ℚ, is the set of all numbers that can be represented as fractions. This includes integers, since all integers can be written as a fraction of 1 (for example, 3 = 3/1).

ℚ includes $\{\dots, -2, -4/3, 0, 1/100, \dots\}$

> **Rational numbers** Any number that can be represented as a fraction, including an integer.

Irrational numbers REVISED

The set of irrational numbers is the set of all real numbers which are not rational numbers (in other words, numbers that cannot be represented as fractions). It does not use a specialised set notation, though it can be considered as the set of all real numbers, minus all rational numbers (ℝ \ ℚ).

The set of irrational numbers includes $\{\dots, \pi, \sqrt{2}, e, \dots\}$

> **Irrational numbers** Any number that cannot be represented as a fraction, including π and square roots of non-square numbers.

Real numbers REVISED

The set of real numbers, ℝ, contains all rational and irrational numbers. It does not include imaginary numbers, such as i or $\sqrt{-2}$.

It is important to recognise the relationships between the sets. For example, the set of natural numbers is a subset of the set of integer numbers; the set of integer numbers is a subset of the set of rational numbers; the set of rational numbers and the set of irrational numbers are both subsets of the set of real numbers.

> **Real numbers** The collection of all rational and irrational numbers.

103

Ordinal numbers

REVISED

Ordinal numbers are used to describe the order in which numbers appear. For example, in the ordered set {apple, banana, clementine}, ordinal numbers can be used to indicate that 'clementine' is the third item in the set.

Counting and measurement

REVISED

Natural numbers are used for counting. This is because the numbers are discrete and relate to physically countable objects.

Real numbers are used for measurement. This is because the numbers are continuous and can be expressed in more flexible terms (for example, calculating a hypotenuse using a square root, or a measurement of a circle using π)

> **Ordinal numbers** Numbers used to count the order that something appears; for example, 1st, 2nd, 3rd, and so on.
>
> **Discrete** Can only take certain, countable values, such as shoe sizes or ordinal numbers.
>
> **Continuous** Can take any value, such as the length of an object.

Now test yourself

TESTED

1 State the specialised set notation **and** describe the numbers contained in each set.
   a Integers
   b Rational numbers
   c Real numbers
   d Natural numbers

2 Explain why an integer can also be described as a rational number.

3 Place at least one cross (×) in each row to show which sets each value belongs to. A value can belong to more than one set.

Number	$\mathbb{N}$	$\mathbb{Z}$	$\mathbb{Q}$	Irrational	$\mathbb{R}$
7					
4.3					
−2					
$\sqrt{5}$					
0					

4 Which set of numbers is used as ordinal numbers?

Answers available online

Number bases

Numbers are traditionally represented in powers of 10, because humans typically have 10 fingers and thumbs on which to count. This is referred to as base 10, denary, or decimal.

Decimal numbers can be written with the number 10 as a subscript; for example, 43_{10}.

In computer systems, which are based on on/off circuits, numbers are represented in powers of 2. This is referred to as base 2, or binary.

Binary numbers can be written with the number 2 as a subscript; for example, 00101011_2.

> **Number base** The number of digits available in that number system.
>
> **Decimal** Numbers with base 10.
>
> **Denary** An alternative less ambiguous term for base 10 numbers.
>
> **Binary** Numbers with base 2.

Check your understanding and progress at **www.hoddereducation.co.uk/myrevisionnotesdownloads**

A different number system is used as a shorthand for binary that uses one digit to represent each group of four binary numbers. Each set of four binary numbers can have one of 16 values, from 0 to 15. This number system is referred to as base 16, or hexadecimal.

Hexadecimal numbers use the digits 0 to 9 just as in denary, followed by the letters A–F. Hexadecimal numbers can be written with the number 16 as a subscript; for example, $2B_{16}$.

When displaying binary numbers it is easy for humans to make typing errors, or to misread the numbers due to the limited number of characters and the length of the numbers. Binary numbers are also difficult to remember. So, hexadecimal is used as a shorthand for binary numbers.

Each block of four binary numbers can be represented using a single hexadecimal digit, meaning that there is no wasted space.

For instance, the hexadecimal number $3399CC_{16}$ is much easier to recall and recognise than the binary equivalent $0011\ 0011\ 1001\ 1001\ 1100\ 1100_2$.

Converting between binary and decimal

To fully understand how to convert between number bases you must be familiar with the concept of place value. We can write a decimal number such as 503 more formally like this:

Place value	100 ($=10^2$)	10 ($=10^1$)	1 ($=10^0$)
Decimal number	5	0	3

To obtain the decimal number we multiply each decimal digit by its place value: $(5 \times 100) + (0 \times 10) + (3 \times 1) = 503$.

To convert a binary number to its decimal equivalent, we follow exactly the same process. However the place values in binary are different because they are powers of 2 rather than powers of 10.

Starting at the right-hand side, the place value of the least significant bit (LSB), has a value of 1. Each subsequent place value, moving left, is worth double the previous value.

Place value	128 ($=2^7$)	64 ($=2^6$)	32 ($=2^5$)	16 ($=2^4$)	8 ($=2^3$)	4 ($=2^2$)	2 ($=2^1$)	1 ($=2^0$)
Binary number	0	1	1	0	1	0	1	0

The decimal value of the binary number is found by multiplying each binary digit by its place value and adding them all together. In this example the binary number 01101010 is expressed in decimal as:

$(128 \times 0) + (64 \times 1) + (32 \times 1) + (16 \times 0) + (8 \times 1) + (4 \times 0) + (2 \times 1) + (1 \times 0)$

$= 64 + 32 + 8 + 2$

$= 106_{10}$

To convert a decimal number to its binary equivalent there are two main methods. The more intuitive method is to remove the largest possible power of 2, working from the most significant bit (MSB), and removing values one at a time.

Hexadecimal Numbers with base 16.

Exam tip

Be careful not to refer to numbers with a fractional part (such as 12.3) as 'decimal numbers'. This term should only be used to create a distinction between different number bases. To avoid confusion, it is acceptable to use the term denary to refer to numbers represented in base 10, and fractional numbers to refer to numbers with a fractional part.

Note

It is important to remember that computer systems always store and process data in a binary format. These representations may be used for input or output, but computers are only capable of storing values as 0s and 1s.

Least significant bit (LSB) The right-most bit in a binary number. The bit with the smallest place value.

Most significant bit (MSB) The left-most bit in a binary number. The bit with the largest place value.

Convert 123_{10} to binary.

$123_{10} = 64 + 59$

Place value	128	64	32	16	8	4	2	1
Binary number	0	1						

$59_{10} = 32 + 27$

Place value	128	64	32	16	8	4	2	1
Binary number	0	1	1					

This is repeated until the binary value is completed.

$123_{10} = 64 + 32 + 16 + 8 + 2 + 1$

Place value	128	64	32	16	8	4	2	1
Binary number	0	1	1	1	1	0	1	1

The next method is more easily written as an algorithm that can be programmed.

In this method the decimal number is halved, and the remainder is written in, starting with the LSB.

Convert 123_{10} to binary.

$123_{10} \div 2 = 61$ remainder 1.

Place value	128	64	32	16	8	4	2	1
Binary number								1

$61_{10} \div 2 = 30$ remainder 1.

Place value	128	64	32	16	8	4	2	1
Binary number							1	1

$30_{10} \div 2 = 15$ remainder 0.

Place value	128	64	32	16	8	4	2	1
Binary number						0	1	1

This is repeated until the remaining decimal value reaches 0.

$15_{10} \div 2 = 7$ remainder 1

$7_{10} \div 2 = 3$ remainder 1

$3_{10} \div 2 = 1$ remainder 1

$1_{10} \div 2 = 0$ remainder 1

$0_{10} \div 2 = 0$ remainder 0

Place value	128	64	32	16	8	4	2	1
Binary number	0	1	1	1	1	0	1	1

Exam tip

Be very careful when converting to binary to check how many binary digits should be used. If the question states that the answer should be in 8-bit binary, then the decimal number 3 should be written as 0000 0011 and **not** as 11.

> ## Now test yourself
> TESTED ⬤
>
> 8 Convert each of the following decimal values to 8-bit binary.
>   a 17
>   b 84
>   c 133
> 9 Convert each of the following binary values to decimal.
>   a 0110
>   b 1001 1101
>   c 0111 1011
>
> **Answers available online**

Converting to and from hexadecimal

When converting between binary and hexadecimal, each block of 4 binary digits is converted to a single hexadecimal digit.

For binary values under 10, the conversion works exactly as it would with decimal numbers.

$$1001_2 = 9_{16}$$

For binary values of 10 or more, the letters A-F are substituted:

Binary	Decimal	Hexadecimal
0000	0	0
0001	1	1
0010	2	2
0011	3	3
0100	4	4
0101	5	5
0110	6	6
0111	7	7

Binary	Decimal	Hexadecimal
1000	8	8
1001	9	9
1010	10	A
1011	11	B
1100	12	C
1101	13	D
1110	14	E
1111	15	F

Because each binary number is split into blocks of 4 binary digits, even large numbers are quick and simple to convert:

$$1001\ 1101_2 = 9D_{16}$$

The reverse process involves expanding each hexadecimal digit back into its binary equivalent.

$$F3_{16} = 1111\ 0011_2$$

To convert from decimal to hexadecimal it is possible to convert to binary first:

$$173_{10} = 1010\ 1101_2 = AD_{16}$$

Alternatively, the hexadecimal value can be found directly by dividing the decimal number by 16 and representing the division and remainder in hexadecimal.

> ## Worked example
>
> **Convert 173_{10} to hexadecimal.**
>
> $173_{10} \div 16$
>
> = 10 remainder 13
>
> = AD_{16}
>
> As $10_{10} = A_{16}$ and $13_{10} = D_{16}$

When converting via binary, the reverse method can be used:

$$3A_{16} = 0011\ 1010_2 = 58_{10}$$

When converting directly from hexadecimal to decimal we use the concept of place value.

Convert $3A_{16}$ to decimal.

The number $3A_{16}$ is written as:

Place value	16 (=16^1)	1 (=16^0)
Hexadecimal number	3	A

$3A_{16} = (16 \times 3) + (1 \times 10) = 58_{10}$

10 Convert each of the following binary values to hexadecimal.
   a   1011 0101   b   1101 1011   c   0111 1110
11 Convert each of the following hexadecimal values to binary.
   a   F3   b   EA   c   C7
12 Convert each of the following decimal values to hexadecimal.
   a   161   b   67   c   213
13 Convert each of the following hexadecimal values to decimal.
   a   20   b   83   c   79

Answers available online

Units of information

Bits and bytes

A single binary digit is referred to as a bit (a shortening of the words **Binary digit**).

Each bit can take the value of a 0 or a 1.

In order to improve the ease of reading binary data, bits are usually written in blocks of four digits, referred to as a nibble.

For most purposes, eight binary digits are grouped together as a byte.

The number of unique combinations of values within a binary value is always a power of 2.

If there are 2 bits then there are 2^2 possible combinations. $2^2 = 4$.

00, 01, 10, 11

If there are 3 bits then there are 2^3 possible combinations. $2^3 = 8$.

000, 001, 010, 011, 100, 101, 110, 111

If there are 8 bits then there are 2^8 combinations. $2^8 = 256$.

In general, if there are n bits then there are 2^n combinations.

Units

In modern computing a large amount of binary data is stored, transferred or used, and so larger units are required.

As is the case with all metric measurements (grams, metres, and so on), a decimal prefix is used for multiples of 1000 (10^3).

1000 bytes = 10^3 bytes = 1 kilobyte, or 1kB

Exam tip

It is important to be able to convert between number bases for Component 2, and it is also important to understand the algorithms used, as Component 1 can sometimes include programming tasks, trace tables and finite state machines based around number base conversion.

Exam tip

If you are asked to complete a list of all unique combinations (for example, for a trace table) then write out the binary numbers in numerical order. That is, in order of the decimal values 0, 1, 2, 3, and so on.

Decimal prefix A shorthand used for multiples of 1000 (10^3) bytes; for example, kilobyte, megabyte, gigabyte.

$1000\,kB = 10^6$ bytes = 1 megabyte, or 1 MB

$1000\,MB = 10^9$ bytes = 1 gigabyte, or 1 GB

$1000\,GB = 10^{12}$ bytes = 1 terabyte, or 1 TB

The convention is to use an uppercase B for bytes and a lowercase b for bits.

Since 1 byte = 8 bits, a conversion between bytes and bits can be carried out by multiplying or dividing by 8.

$100\,kB = (100 \times 8)\,kb = 800\,kb$

$1600\,Mb = (1600 \div 8)\,MB = 200\,MB$

As the 1000 multiplier is based on powers of ten, an alternative approach for the binary number base is to use a binary prefix which is based on powers of 2 and uses multiples of 1024 (2^{10}).

1024 bytes = 2^{10} bytes = 1 kibibtye, or 1 KiB

$1024\,KiB = 2^{20}$ bytes = 1 mebibyte, or 1 MiB

$1024\,MiB = 2^{30}$ bytes = 1 gibibyte, or 1 GiB

$1024\,GiB = 2^{40}$ bytes = 1 tebibyte, or 1 TiB

> **Note**
>
> Since the number of bits is larger than the number of bytes, it is common for internet service providers to advertise connection speeds in bits. 200 Mbps (megabits per second) sounds more impressive than 25 MBps (megabytes per second).

> **Binary prefix** A shorthand used for multiples of 1024 (2^{10}) bytes; for example kibibyte, mebibyte, gibibyte.

> **Exam tip**
>
> Remember that a letter 'i' in the name always refers to the binary prefix (for example, KiB, MiB, GiB). Always read the question carefully to check whether you are being asked about the metric prefix or the binary prefix.

Binary number system

Unsigned binary

REVISED ○

In unsigned binary, all values are positive.

For a 7-bit binary number the ranges are as follows.

	Minimum value	Maximum value
Binary	000 0000	111 1111
Decimal	0	127

> **Unsigned binary** A system that is only capable of representing positive numbers (0 or larger).

The minimum value for any unsigned binary number is 0.

The maximum number for an unsigned binary number is $2^n - 1$, where n is the number of bits.

A quick way to remember this is to understand that adding 1 to the maximum would require an extra bit – for instance, adding 1 to a 7-bit number adding would give 1000 0000, or 128, which requires 8 bits.

> **Exam tip**
>
> Remember that each additional binary digit always doubles the possible range of values – for example, a 7 bit number has 128 possible values and an 8 bit number has 256 possible values. This fact is critical and questions relying on this knowledge can crop up anywhere in Component 2, or Component 1.

Unsigned binary arithmetic

Addition

To add two unsigned binary numbers, write the numbers out one above the other and add in columns, starting with the least significant bit.

To do this we need to remember sum and carry rules and note the following when adding binary digits:

$0 + 0 = 0$

$0 + 1 = 1$

$1 + 0 = 1$

$1 + 1 = 0$ carry 1

$1 + 1 + 1 = 1$ carry 1

Binary digits can only be 0 or 1, so remember to carry if the answer would be 2 or more in decimal. Always write the numbers in binary.

```
  0   0   1   1   0   0   1   0   +
  1   0   1   1   0   1   0   1
-----------------------------------
  1   1   1   0   0   1   1   1        ← sum
      1   1                            ← carry
```

> **Exam tip**
>
> Marks are given for the method as well as the answer. Always show your working for binary arithmetic questions – never just write the answer.

Multiplication

To multiply two binary numbers the method involves:
+ splitting the small number into a sum of powers of 2
+ multiplying the larger number by each of these powers of 2
+ adding together the results.

> **Worked example**
>
> **Calculate $(11 \times 5)_{10}$ in binary.**
>
> Split the smaller number into powers of 2; in this case, $5 = 2^2 + 2^1 = 4 + 1$
>
> $11 \times 5 = 11 \times (1 + 4)$
>
> $= (11 \times 1) + (11 \times 4)$
>
> Multiplying by powers of 2 can be done by performing left shifts. For each power of 2, perform the appropriate left shifts and then add the resulting values.
>
> $1011 \times 1 = 1011 = 11_{10}$
>
> $1011 \times 2 = 1\,0110 = 22_{10}$
>
> $1011 \times 4 = 10\,1100 = 44_{10}$
>
> Therefore, $11_{10} \times 5_{10} = 1011_2 + 10\,1100_2$
>
> Write this out by putting the smaller number across the top and the larger number across the bottom.
>
> ```
>           1   0   1   1   +
>   1   0   1   1   0   0
> -----------------------------
>   1   1   0   1   1   1
>       1
> ```
>
> Finally, convert the result back to decimal:
>
> $11\,0111_2 = 55_{10}$
>
> We can check that this is correct by noting in decimal that 11×5 is indeed 55.

> **Note**
>
> It is not necessary to perform binary division. Binary subtraction is explained in the next section, on two's complement binary.

Check your understanding and progress at **www.hoddereducation.co.uk/myrevisionnotesdownloads**

Now test yourself

TESTED

18 Add the following binary numbers.
   a   0011 + 0101
   b   0010 1011 + 0110 0101
   c   0101 1101 + 0011 0111
19 Multiply the following binary numbers.
   a   0110 × 10
   b   0001 0110 × 11
   c   0011 0001 × 101

Answers available online

Exam tip

You must show your working in binary in order to demonstrate that you can carry out binary arithmetic accurately, but once you have completed your answer carry out the arithmetic on the decimal values and convert the result to binary in order to check your final answer.

Revision activity

✚ Use a random number generator to choose numbers and practise converting them to binary and adding them. Convert the result back to decimal to check your accuracy.
✚ Use a random number generator to choose one large number (up to 256) and one small number (up to 10), then practise converting them to binary and multiplying them. Convert the result back to decimal to check your accuracy.

Signed binary using two's complement

REVISED

In order to represent negative binary numbers, a method known as two's complement is used. This method involves re-thinking the value of the most significant bit.

A normal 4-bit binary number is written using the following place values:

8	4	2	1
1	1	1	0

Two's complement A representation of binary numbers that includes both positive and negative values.

In this case the number $1110_2 = 14_{10}$

In a two's complement binary number, the left-most bit is negative but otherwise the same rules for converting to decimal apply:

−8	4	2	1
1	1	1	0

In two's complement, $1110_2 = -2_{10}$

As the value 0 is considered to be a positive number, the possible range of values for an 8-bit binary number is between -128_{10} ($1000\ 0000_2$) and $+127_{10}$ ($0111\ 1111_2$). There are 128 possible positive values (including zero) and 128 possible negative values.

Notice that in two's complement, all negative numbers begin with 1 and all positive numbers plus zero begin with 0.

Exam tip

If you are asked to find the decimal representation of a two's complement binary number, or if you want to check your working, remembering to count the most significant bit as a negative number is the quickest and simplest method.

Note

Remember that −1 is larger than −128. This can seem counter-intuitive but consider that having −£1 (owing £1) is better than having −£100 (owing £100).

There are two methods for converting between a positive binary number and its negative equivalent in two's complement.

Worked example

Method 1: flip the bits and add one

One common method for taking a positive number and making it negative is to flip (or invert) the bits and add one.

Original number:	0011 0100
Flip the bits:	1100 1011
Add one:	1100 1100

To check:

−128	64	32	16	8	4	2	1
0	0	1	1	0	1	0	0

$0011\ 0100_2 = 32 + 16 + 4 = 52_{10}$

−128	64	32	16	8	4	2	1
1	1	0	0	1	1	0	0

$11001100_2 = -128 + 64 + 8 + 4 = -52_{10}$

To change a negative number into a positive number, reverse the process. Subtract one and then flip the bits.

Original number:	1001 1101
Subtract one:	1001 1100
Flip the bits:	0110 0011

$1001\ 1101_2 = -99_{10}$

$0110\ 0011_2 = 99_{10}$

Worked example

Method 2: flip from the right

Subtracting binary numbers can sometimes be complicated, and it is possible to carry out the operations in the wrong order. Some people prefer a different method.

Regardless of the conversion (positive to negative, or negative to positive), copy the binary sequence, starting with the right-most bit.

Copy the pattern up to *and including* the first 1 digit, and then flip all of the remaining bits.

Original number:	0011 0100
Copy up to *and including* the first 1:	____ _100
Flip the remaining bits:	1100 1100

We can see that this gives the same result as the first example in method 1.

This method is symmetrical, in that it works the same whether the original number is positive or negative, and is also simpler to program.

Making links

This method of conversion is commonly described using a finite state machine or Turing machine using the techniques described in Chapter 4.

Exam tip

Read the question carefully. The question will always indicate which representation is being used and the answers will be quite different if the question uses unsigned, rather than two's complement, representation.

Exam tip

Both methods are perfectly valid, so use whichever one you are most comfortable with.

Check your understanding and progress at **www.hoddereducation.co.uk/myrevisionnotesdownloads**

20 How can you tell instantly whether a two's complement number is positive or negative?

21 Convert each of the following positive binary numbers into its negative equivalent in two's complement.
   a 0110 1010
   b 0010 1101
   c 0000 0000

22 Convert each of the following negative binary two's complement numbers into its positive equivalent.
   a 1000 0001
   b 1111 1111
   c 1001 0101
   d 1101 1000

Answers available online

Subtraction

Using two's complement binary it is possible to subtract two numbers.

For instance, 73 – 14 can be solved by adding +73 to –14.

Worked example

$73_{10} = 0100\ 1001_2$

$14_{10} = 0000\ 1110_2$

To convert 14_{10} to -14_{10} in binary, we flip the bits and add 1:

$-14_{10} = 1111\ 0010_2$

Now we perform the calculation: 73 +(–14):

```
0   1   0   0   1   0   0   1   +
1   1   1   1   0   0   1   0
0   0   1   1   1   0   1   1
1   1
```

Any remaining carry bits are discarded as an overflow.

The final result can be converted to a decimal number for checking. In this case, $0011\ 1011_2 = 59_{10}$, which is the correct answer.

To calculate the possible range of a two's complement binary value containing n binary digits, remember that the first digit is used to indicate the sign.

An 8-bit number two's complement number can have the same maximum value as a 7-bit unsigned binary number.

The possible range of negative values always seems to be one more than the range of positive values. This is because 0 is considered to be a positive number.

Number of bits	Possible range
4	–8 to +7
6	–32 to +31
8	–128 to +127

In general, for an n bit number, the possible range is -2^{n-1} to $(2^{n-1}) - 1$

23 What is the possible range of values in a 7-bit two's complement number?

24 Use binary arithmetic to add a positive and a negative number.

   a 0011 1011 + 1101 1010

   b 0001 0110 + 1001 0101

   c 0000 0001 + 1111 1111

25 Use two's complement to solve these subtraction problems.

   a 0010 0110 – 0001 1101

   b 0110 1100 – 0000 1001

   c 0001 1011 – 0110 1100

Answers available online

Numbers with a fractional part

REVISED

There are two main methods for dealing with number that have a fractional part. In both cases the numbers have a binary point, which performs exactly the same role as a decimal point for decimal numbers.

Fixed point binary

In fixed point binary the position of the binary point is fixed.

Any value to the left of the binary point increases in powers of two, exactly as happens with the integer representation.

$0100.0000_2 = 8.0_{10}$

The digits to the left of the binary point are assigned the value $\frac{1}{2}^n$ where $n = 1$, 2, 3, and so on.

These can be written as fractional values:

–8	4	2	1	.	$\frac{1}{2}$	$\frac{1}{4}$	$\frac{1}{8}$	$\frac{1}{16}$
0	1	1	0	.	1	0	1	0

Alternatively, they can be written using decimal fractions:

–8	4	2	1	.	0.5	0.25	0.125	0.0625
0	1	1	0	.	1	0	1	0

We can see that:

$0110.1010_2 = 4 + 2 + 0.5 + 0.125 = 6.625_{10}$

Fixed point binary has the advantage of simplicity, though it does introduce significant rounding errors as values such as 10.1 are very difficult to represent accurately.

To find the binary representation of a decimal fraction, remove each fractional power of two.

Converting the decimal fraction 7.5625 into its fixed point binary representation.

Calculate the whole number part, in this case 7:

–8	4	2	1	.				
0	1	1	1	.				

Note that 7.5625 – 7 = 0.5625, which is the value left to find

Check your understanding and progress at **www.hoddereducation.co.uk/myrevisionnotesdownloads**

The first value after the binary point is worth $\frac{1}{2} = 0.5$

-8	4	2	1	.	0.5			
0	1	1	1	.	1			

$0.5625 - 0.5 = 0.0625$ left to find

Second value after the binary point is worth $\frac{1}{4} = 0.25$

0.25 can't be taken from 0.0625

-8	4	2	1	.	0.5	0.25		
0	1	1	1	.	1	0		

Third value after the binary point is worth $\frac{1}{8} = 0.125$

0.125 can't be taken from 0.0625

-8	4	2	1	.	0.5	0.25	0.125	
0	1	1	1	.	1	0	0	

Fourth value after the binary point is worth $\frac{1}{16} = 0.0.625$

$0.0625 - 0.0625 = 0$

-8	4	2	1	.	0.5	0.25	0.125	0.0625
0	1	1	1	.	1	0	0	1

Therefore, $7.5625_{10} = 0111.1001_2$

Now test yourself   TESTED ◯

26 Convert the following two's complement, fixed point numbers to decimal.
  a   011.10100
  b   10110.110
  c   011011.01

27 Convert the following decimal numbers into their two's complement, fixed point binary equivalent.
  a   12.5
  b   −3.75
  c   9.875

Answers available online

Floating point binary

Particularly large or small fractional numbers represented using fixed point binary can be very wasteful of memory, as they will need lots of 0s. Floating point binary provides a more efficient, but more complex, representation of fractional numbers.

The number is represented with a mantissa and an exponent, in a similar way to standard form in mathematics. For example, in decimal. $4\,130 = 4.13 \times 10^3$ where 4.13 is the mantissa and 3 is the exponent.

The mantissa provides the value of the number, while the exponent says how far to move the decimal point

In floating point binary the mantissa is a binary fraction stored in two's complement format, where the MSB is −1 and remaining bits are fractions after a binary point. For example, for an 8 bit mantissa:

-1	.	$\frac{1}{2}$	$\frac{1}{4}$	$\frac{1}{8}$	$\frac{1}{16}$	$\frac{1}{32}$	$\frac{1}{64}$	$\frac{1}{128}$
0	.	1	1	0	0	1	0	0

Floating point binary A method for representing fractional numbers where the position of the decimal point is moved according to the value of the exponent.

Mantissa The part of a floating point binary number which provides the value of that number.

Exponent The part of a floating point binary number which states how far to move the decimal point.

The exponent is also stored in two's complement format. For example, for a 4 bit exponent:

−8	4	2	1
0	0	1	1

Note

Exam questions using the floating point representation will usually use two's complement for both the mantissa and the exponent.

Worked example

Calculate the decimal value of the floating point binary number 01100100 0011.

To calculate the decimal value of the following floating point binary number:

0	1	1	0	0	1	0	0		0	0	1	1
			Mantissa								Exponent	

The first step is to calculate the value of the exponent. In this case, +3.

−8	4	2	1
0	0	1	1

The second step is to move the binary point by that number of positions …

−1	.	$\frac{1}{2}$	$\frac{1}{4}$	$\frac{1}{8}$	$\frac{1}{16}$	$\frac{1}{32}$	$\frac{1}{64}$	$\frac{1}{128}$
0	.	1	1	0	0	1	0	0

… becomes …

−8	4	2	1	.	$\frac{1}{2}$	$\frac{1}{4}$	$\frac{1}{8}$	$\frac{1}{16}$
0	1	1	0	.	0	1	0	0

The third step is to convert this value in the same way as with fixed point binary:

$4 + 2 + \frac{1}{4} = 6.25$

The same method is used for negative numbers. Remember that both the mantissa and exponent are in two's complement, which means if the first bit is 1 then the number is negative.

Worked example

Calculate the decimal value of the floating point binary number 10110000 1111.

1	0	1	1	0	0	0	0		1	1	1	1
			Mantissa								Exponent	

The first step is to calculate the value of the exponent. In this case, −1.

−8	4	2	1
1	1	1	1

The second step is to move the binary point by that number of positions. However, for a negative exponent, rather than moving the binary point to the left instead shift the bits to the right, which achieves the same effect. This is because we do not want the left-most bit to move, as it is used to indicate the sign …

−1	.	$\frac{1}{2}$	$\frac{1}{4}$	$\frac{1}{8}$	$\frac{1}{16}$	$\frac{1}{32}$	$\frac{1}{64}$	$\frac{1}{128}$
1	.	0	1	1	0	0	0	0

… becomes …

Check your understanding and progress at **www.hoddereducation.co.uk/myrevisionnotesdownloads**

−1	.	$\frac{1}{2}$	$\frac{1}{4}$	$\frac{1}{8}$	$\frac{1}{16}$	$\frac{1}{32}$	$\frac{1}{64}$	$\frac{1}{128}$
1	.	0	0	1	1	0	0	0

The third step is to convert the value in the same way as with fixed point binary:

$$-1 + \frac{1}{8} + \frac{1}{16} = -1 + 0.125 + 0.0625 = -0.8125$$

It is also important to know how to convert a decimal number to its floating point equivalent.

+ First, start by writing the number in a fixed point format. Use the minimum number of digits needed, remembering to use two's complement format. This means the left-most bit will indicate the sign.
+ Second, move the binary point so that it comes straight after the first value in order to find the mantissa
+ Thirdly, count the number of positions that the binary point has been moved by in order to find the exponent. Use however many digits are needed, remembering to include the right-most bit to indicate the sign.
+ Finally, write the full binary number down using the number of digits specified in the question, adding leading or trailing digits as necessary

Making links

At the second step it is important that the two digits either side of the binary point should be different. For example:

−1	.	$\frac{1}{2}$	$\frac{1}{4}$	$\frac{1}{8}$	$\frac{1}{16}$	$\frac{1}{32}$	$\frac{1}{64}$	$\frac{1}{128}$
0	.	1						

Or …

−1	.	$\frac{1}{2}$	$\frac{1}{4}$	$\frac{1}{8}$	$\frac{1}{16}$	$\frac{1}{32}$	$\frac{1}{64}$	$\frac{1}{128}$
1	.	0						

This is referred to as normalised floating point binary and is discussed in more detail laer in this chapter.

Worked example

Write the decimal number 11.2510 as a floating point number with an 8 bit mantissa and a 4 bit component.

1 Write the number in fixed point two's complement.

$11.25_{10} = 01011.01_2$

2 Move the binary point so that it comes after the first value.

Mantissa = 0.101101

3 Count the number of positions that the binary point has been moved by and express this value in two's complement. In this case the binary point moved four positions:

Exponent = $4_{10} = 0100_2$

4 Finally, write the full binary number down using the number of digits specified in the question. We were asked for an 8 bit mantissa, so we need to add another bit, of value 0, to the right of the mantissa.

0	1	0	1	1	0	1	0		0	1	0	0
			Mantissa								Exponent	

Exam tip

Floating binary is a topic that often trips students up. Remember that both mantissa and exponent will be written using two's complement binary and ensure you get lots of practical practice converting between decimal and binary numbers, both large (positive exponents) and small (negative exponents).

When using floating point binary it is possible to represent very large and very small numbers. Exam questions will usually specify the number of bits to use for the mantissa and the exponent, with a mantissa of 8 bits and an exponent of 4 bits being typical. Be prepared to work with exponents of up to 6 binary digits.

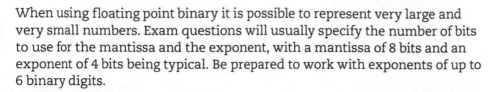

Now test yourself   TESTED

28 Which part of a floating point number is used to describe how far to move the decimal point?

29 Convert each of the following two's complement, floating point binary numbers into their decimal equivalent.

	Mantissa	Exponent
a	0.11010	001001
b	1.0110000	0010
c	0.11000	11110

30 Convert each of the following decimal numbers into their two's complement, floating point binary equivalent. Use a 6-bit mantissa and a 4-bit exponent in each case.
  a 12.5
  b −7.25
  c 0.125
  d −0.9375

Answers available online

Rounding errors

REVISED

Due to the nature of fractional numbers which are written as fractions of powers of 2, it is not possible to store some values with complete accuracy.

Representing 0.5_{10} as a binary fraction is trivial, using 0.1_2.

Representing 0.1_{10} accurately as a binary fraction is impossible, even using an extremely large number of binary digits. It can only be represented approximately as the binary value is rounded up or down.

Absolute and relative errors

REVISED

The absolute error is the difference between the intended value and the actual value that is stored.

The absolute error is always written as a positive number.

For example, the value 9.8_{10} is represented using fixed point binary as 1001.1101_2

Converting this number back to decimal gives a value of 9.8125_{10}

This gives an absolute error of 0.0125.

The relative error is expressed as a percentage of the original value.

The relative error can be calculated by dividing the absolute error by the original value and multiplying by 100. In our example above, the relative error is calculated as:

$(0.0125 \div 9.8) \times 100 = 0.13\%$

Smaller values will typically lead to a larger relative error.

Absolute error The difference between the intended value and the actual value.

Relative error The percentage difference between the intended value and the actual value.

Calculate the relative error when storing the decimal value 0.13_{10} in binary.

0.13_{10} is represented using 4 bits in binary as 0.001_2.

Converting this binary value back to decimal gives 0.125_{10}.

The absolute error is $0.13 - 0.125 = 0.005$.

The relative error is $0.005 \div 0.13 \times 100 = 3.85\%$

Notice that this relative error is much larger than the previous example, even though the absolute error was smaller.

TESTED

31 Will a large number be likely to have a larger or smaller relative error?

32 Calculate the absolute and relative errors for each of these values.
  a   12.26 represented in binary as 1100.01
  b   0.98 represented in binary as 0001.00
  c   7.7 represented in binary as 0111.11

Answers available online

Range and precision

REVISED

There are several considerations when making decisions over which format to use for fractional numbers.

+ Range: The difference between the largest and smallest values.
+ Precision: The reduction of rounding errors.
+ Speed of calculation: The time a processor will take to convert the representation in order to carry out calculations or display the value.

	Advantages	Disadvantages
Fixed point binary	Simpler to convert and allows for quicker processing.	A more limited range, particularly if large magnitude numbers and small magnitude numbers need to be stored using the same system.
	All values can be stored with the same level of absolute precision.	Limited precision.
	Values are processed in a very similar manner to binary integers, meaning that hardware can be re-purposed without needing to be re-designed.	
Floating point binary	A wider range of values are possible by using a large exponent.	The precision of two different values can be very different due to the different exponents.
	More precise as a small exponent can be used.	Processing takes longer.

Normalisation of floating point form

REVISED

Floating point numbers should be normalised. This means that the first and second values in the mantissa should always be opposite.

This means that no space is wasted with leading zeroes in a positive number, or leading ones in a negative number.

In two's complement binary the number 0000 0100 has the same value as the number 0100 – the leading zeroes are not providing any useful information and therefore we want to get rid of them. Similarly, the negative number 1111 1110 has the same value as 10 - the leading ones are not providing any useful information and therefore we want to get rid of them. We can do this by choosing an exponent that ensures the first and second values in the mantissa are opposite.

> **Normalised** The standard way of writing floating point binary, in which the first two bits are opposite to each other.

It is important to be able to recognise whether a floating point binary number is normalised by checking that the first two values are opposite. For example:

−1	.	$\frac{1}{2}$	$\frac{1}{4}$	$\frac{1}{8}$	$\frac{1}{16}$	$\frac{1}{32}$	$\frac{1}{64}$	$\frac{1}{128}$
0	.	1						

Or …

−1	.	$\frac{1}{2}$	$\frac{1}{4}$	$\frac{1}{8}$	$\frac{1}{16}$	$\frac{1}{32}$	$\frac{1}{64}$	$\frac{1}{128}$
1	.	0						

It is also important when converting numbers into floating point binary form to ensure that they are normalised.

Exam tip

Questions about whether a floating point number is normalised are very common. Remember that the first two digits should always be opposite to each other if the number is normalised.

Underflow and overflow

REVISED

When adding or subtracting numbers it is possible that the result will not be stored correctly.

An overflow can occur when adding or multiplying values.

For example, adding the unsigned binary values 1101 and 0110:

```
    1  1  0  1  +
    0  1  1  0
 1  0  0  1  1
 1  1
```

Overflow Where the result of a calculation is too large to be stored in the available digits.

Assuming the answer should be stored using 4 bits, as with the two original values, the extra 1 from the calculation cannot fit in the available space.

Depending on the configuration of the system:
+ this may cause the leading 1 to be dropped, resulting in an incorrect result (in this case suggesting that 13 + 6 = 3)
+ the large result may spill over into the next block of memory.

On some occasions overflow errors are not a problem, for example when adding a positive and negative number using two's complement.

For example, calculating 7 − 4 using two's complement binary:

```
    0  1  1  1  +
    1  1  0  0
 1  0  0  1  1
 1  1
```

Check your understanding and progress at **www.hoddereducation.co.uk/myrevisionnotesdownloads**

The overflow digit can be safely dropped, as the solution is correct. This is because the first digit is used to represent the sign, and so the overflow simply allows for the leading bit to be flipped.

An underflow can occur when a subtraction takes place and the value will not fit in the space available.

For example, adding the two's complement values 1101 and 1000:

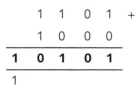

Dropping the leading 1, this gives the erroneous result –3 – 8 = 5. This happens because the correct result is –1110, which cannot be stored as a 4-bit binary number.

> **Note**
>
> In the original version of the computer game Civilisation the character of Gandhi was a peaceful character and was assigned an aggression score of 1. At a particular point in the game each leader's aggression score would reduce by 2 points. As the values were stored as unsigned binary integers, this caused an underflow error and Gandhi immediately became the most aggressive character in the game. In subsequent versions of the game the bug was fixed, however the character of Gandhi has always been given a large aggression score as a reference to this famous mistake.

> **Underflow** Where the result of a calculation is too small to be stored in the available digits.

> **Now test yourself**
>
> 37 Explain what is meant by an *underflow error*.
>
> 38 In a computer game, a player's score goes up by 1 each time they collect a coin. A player has 255 coins and when they collect the next coin their score suddenly jumps from 255 to 0. Explain the most likely cause of this error.
>
> **Answers available online**
>
> TESTED ◯

Information coding systems

Character form of a decimal digit REVISED ◯

The previous topics have all been focused on how to represent a number value in binary so that it can be processed as a number.

Sometimes a number value can be stored as a character value. Think of it as the letter '3' rather than the number 3.

This is useful in situations where the value is intended to be processed as text rather than as a number. For example:

+ telephone numbers have a leading zero and are not generally used in any arithmetic
+ postcodes include numbers and letters.

It is important to make sure you know whether you are dealing with the pure binary representation (for example, unsigned integer, two's complement, fixed point or floating point) or the character code representation (for example, the letter '9').

ASCII and Unicode REVISED ◯

In order to store or transmit text, each character is assigned a numeric value.

This is referred to as a character set.

A character set lists of all the characters which can be understood by a given computer system and their character codes.

> **Character set** The set of all characters that can be understood by a computer system, and their associated character codes.

121

There are two main character sets in use – ASCII and Unicode.

ASCII

ASCII stands for the American Standard Code for Information Interchange.

ASCII is generally agreed to use 7 bits per character, though sometimes an 8th bit is used as a parity bit.

Using 7 bits means that there are 128 possible unique values.

The first 33 codes in the character set are reserved for special characters.

The other 95 values are used for letters and symbols, including:
+ upper case letters
+ lower case letters
+ digits 0-9
+ punctuation
+ mathematical operators.

This is a section of the ASCII character set:

Character	Decimal Code	Binary Code
X	88	0101 1000
Y	89	0101 1001
Z	90	0101 1010
[	91	0101 1011
\	92	0101 1100
]	93	0101 1101

The character codes for upper case letters in ASCII are separated by 32_{10} from lower case letters. This means that only one bit (the sixth bit) needs to be changed to change cases:

Character	Decimal Code	Binary Code
A	65	0100 0001
a	97	0110 0001
B	66	0100 0010
b	98	0110 0010
C	67	0100 0011
c	99	0110 0011

Also note that the last 5 binary digits can be used to identify the letter:

A = 0100 **0001** = 64 + **1**

B = 0100 **0010** = 64 + **2**

Z = 0101 **1010** = 64 + **26**

When a key on a keyboard is pressed, the binary code is transmitted to the computer.

Text files are saved by storing the binary code for each character in the file.

Some codes refer to special characters which are not normally visible when a file is displayed on a screen, such as STX (start of text), BS (backspace), LF (line feed, or new line), and so on.

Unicode

ASCII does not leave enough possible values to represent letters with accents, characters from other alphabets or emojis.

Unicode is an expanded character set which uses a varied character length of between 8 and 32 bits per character. This allows for all 1 million+ valid characters to be uniquely represented.

In situations where these are not needed, ASCII can be preferable as it uses less storage space.

Check your understanding and progress at **www.hoddereducation.co.uk/myrevisionnotesdownloads**

ASCII A 7-bit character set that can represent up to 128 unique characters.

Unicode A variable size character set in which each character code can be 8, 16 or 32 bits in length.

Exam tip

You are not expected to remember individual character codes, but it is useful to know that the last five digits can be used to identify the letter.

Note

There are various specific versions of Unicode including UTF-8, UTF-16 and UTF-32. It is not necessary to be aware of the differences and for the sake of this qualification all forms of Unicode are referred to under that single term.

It is important to note that the first 128 Unicode characters and codes are the same as ASCII, so the two systems are compatible.

Now test yourself   TESTED ◯

39 Describe **two** differences between ASCII and Unicode.

40 Explain why mobile phone text messages, also known as SMS messages, are typically transmitted using ASCII rather than Unicode.

41 If the character A is represented using the character code 0100 0001, write out the character codes needed to spell the word 'BAD'.

Answers available online

Error checking and correction   REVISED ◯

When data is transmitted or stored, there is a possibility that it contains an error.

It is very easy for a bit to misread, or for interference to cause an error in a bit pattern.

There are many ways to try and identify errors, some of which include ways to automatically correct them.

Parity bits

A simple solution is to count the number of 1s in a sequence of binary values and add a parity bit.

In odd parity, there should be an odd number of 1s.

The number of 1s is counted in the data and if there is already an odd number then a 0 is added as the parity bit.

001 1010 – Original data

0001 1010 – Data to be transmitted

If there is an even number of 1s then an extra 1 is added as the parity bit, so that the total number of 1s is now odd.

001 1011 – Original data

1001 1011 – Data to be transmitted

When the message is received, the number of 1s is counted again.

If the number of 1s is still odd then it is assumed that the data is correct.

If the number of 1s is even, then there has been an error, and the data is re-requested.

1001 1011 – Message appears to be correct

1001 0011 – Message contains an error

The parity bit is then discarded and the original value can be processed.

With even parity, the process is identical except that the parity bit is chosen so that the number of 1s is even.

The receiver needs to know whether if the data has been sent using even or odd parity.

Advantages	Disadvantages
Relatively small **overhead** in terms of adding extra data.	Cannot help correct the error.
	If two bits are incorrect, then the error will not be identified.

Note

A technique known as 2D parity can help identify multiple errors and can also correct some errors. This is an interesting technique but is not covered in the AQA A-level specification.

Note

The Unicode Consortium is responsible for defining the code for each character and each year they decide which new emojis to add, and what their character codes should be.

Parity bit A single binary digit added to some data in order to help with error checking.

Odd parity A method of using parity in which each block of data should have an odd number of 1s.

Exam tip

The parity bit can be added to the start or end of the message. Always read the question carefully to check whether the question refers to even parity or odd parity and to check which is the parity bit.

Even parity A method of using parity in which each block of data should have an even number of 1s.

Overhead Additional data added to the original values.

Majority voting

Majority voting involves sending each bit repeatedly.

Each bit must be sent an odd number of times and, within that transmission, whichever digit is seen most commonly is considered to be the correct one.

For example the bit pattern 1010 is being sent using majority voting, and each bit is sent 3 times.

The transmission should be 111 000 111 000.

Due to a timing error, the message received reads 110 000 011 000.

In each block of bits, the majority is considered to be correct and so the data stored is 1010.

An odd number of bits must be used in order to avoid a tie when deciding which is the most common value. Repetitions of 3, 5 and 7 bits are all acceptable.

Advantages	Disadvantages
Makes it more likely that an error can be fixed. Less chance that the data will have to be re-sent.	The extra overhead in data transmission is very high.

> **Majority voting** Transmitting each bit an odd number of times in order to identify and correct any transmission errors.

Checksums

A checksum is a value that can be found by applying an arithmetic algorithm to the original data.

A very simple algorithm might be to add up all of the decimal digits in a large number and store the total.

For an original value of 374 268, the digits added together would total 30.

When the transmission is received the same process is repeated and the total is compared to the checksum.

If the value 375 268 has been received then the sum of the individual digits will be 31. Since this does not match then an error has been identified and the data should be re-requested.

A more complex algorithm might be to add the square of the digits in the even positions to the cube of the digits in the odd positions.

$$8^3 + 6^2 + 2^3 + 4^2 + 7^3 + 3^2 = 512 + 36 + 8 + 16 + 343 + 9 = 924$$

Checksums are effective at identifying errors because two or more errors are very unlikely to cancel each other out.

Simple checksums are not able to locate or correct the exact error.

Advantages	Disadvantages
The transmission overhead is smaller than using majority voting.	The transmission overhead is larger than using parity bits.
Effective at identifying errors because two or more errors are very unlikely to cancel each other out.	Simple checksums are not able to locate or correct the exact error.

> **Checksum** A value derived by following an algorithm, used to check for errors.

> **Making links**
>
> Hashing algorithms can be used to generate checksums. While checksums appear in the specification for Component 2, hashing algorithms are explored as part of the data structures topic in Component 1 (see *Hash tables* in Chapter 2).

> **Note**
>
> One common checksum algorithm is the MD5 algorithm, and large downloads will sometimes have an MD5 checksum file that can be downloaded for checking once the download is complete.

Check digits

A check digit works in almost exactly the same way as a checksum, except the value must be a single digit. This is generally achieved by using a modulo operation, often modulo 10, which provides one of 10 possible outcomes.

One of the more famous uses of a check digit occurs in the ISBN-13 code which is used to uniquely identify books.

> **Check digit** A single digit derived by following an algorithm, used to check for errors.
>
> **Modulo** Finding the remainder when one number is divided by another.

Check your understanding and progress at **www.hoddereducation.co.uk/myrevisionnotesdownloads**

Each book is given a unique 12-digit decimal number.

Starting with the right-most digit, the first value is multiplied by 3, the next by 1, the next by 3 and so on.

The results are added and divided by 10, noting the remainder.

If the remainder is not 0 then a value is added, in the same manner as a parity bit, so that the result of dividing by 10 is 0.

ISBN-13	9	7	8	1	4	7	1	8	6	5	8	2
Weight	1	3	1	3	1	3	1	3	1	3	1	3
Partial sum	9	21	8	3	4	21	1	24	6	15	8	6

Total = 126

Total % 10 = 6

Value to add = 4

The final 13-digit code is therefore 978-1-4718-6582-4 (the spacing is added to aid readability).

When the code is entered, the same calculation is performed on the full code.

ISBN-13	9	7	8	1	4	7	1	8	6	5	8	2	4
Weight	1	3	1	3	1	3	1	3	1	3	1	3	1
Partial sum	9	21	8	3	4	21	1	24	6	15	8	6	4

Total = 130

Total % 10 = 0

As the modulo result is 0, it can be assumed that the values have been recorded or transmitted correctly.

> **Note**
>
> In some cases, such as ISBN-10, there are 11 possible values for the check digit. Using modulo 11 the final value could be a digit (0-9) or an X.

Advantages	Disadvantages
Lower overhead than a checksum, meaning that data can be transmitted more quickly.	With only 10 or 11 possible values for the check digit, it is possible that an erroneous transmission will be identified as correct.

Now test yourself   TESTED ⬤

42 Explain how a parity bit can be used to check a binary value for an error.

43 Describe **one** situation where an incorrect binary value could pass a parity check.

44 Explain the difference between odd and even parity.

45 What rule is used to decide how many times to transmit each bit using majority voting?

46 Describe the difference between a checksum and a check digit.

47 Of the four methods described in this Chapter, only majority voting is capable of correcting errors. Explain why this isn't the most commonly used method.

Answers available online

> **Revision activity**
>
> Carry out your own check digit calculations, using the ISBN numbers on the back of any textbooks and revision guides you have with you.

Representing images, sound and other data

Bit patterns, images, sound and other data

REVISED ⬤

All data in a computer system must be represented using binary numbers.

In addition to numbers and text, techniques have been devised to represent images and sounds using binary numbers as well.

Analogue and digital

Data in the real world is typically analogue. This includes visible light, sound, and physical movement.

Analogue signals are continuous as there are an infinite number of values between each measurement. They are usually represented as a wave with smooth curves.

> **Analogue** A continuous signal, usually represented as a curved wave.

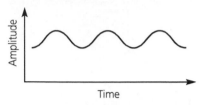

Figure 5.1 An analogue signal

Data in computer systems is usually digital. This is because computer systems generally store and transmit data using systems with two states – on and off, represented in binary.

> **Digital** A discrete signal, often represented using a stepped wave.

Digital signals have a finite set of values and use discrete measurements with no intermediate values. They are usually represented as a stepping, or square, signal.

ON
OFF

Figure 5.2 A digital signal

Analogue/digital conversion

In order for computers to read in analogue data, an analogue to digital converter (ADC) must be used.

An ADC will use an analogue sensor to read in an analogue signal and produce a digital output.

Microphones and digital cameras are examples of devices that use an ADC.

Each digital value will be a close approximation to the analogue signal at any particular moment.

A digital to analogue converter (DAC) is used to convert a digital signal into an analogue signal.

This is used, for example, to convert a digital audio file into an analogue signal which can be used to recreate the sound through a speaker.

> **Data** Values or information.
>
> **Analogue to digital converter (ADC)** Converts an analogue signal into a digital signal.
>
> **Signal** The electric or electromagnetic impulses that are used to transmit data.
>
> **Digital to analogue converter (DAC)** Converts a digital signal to an analogue signal.

Exam tip

Questions about ADCs and DACs are usually written in the context of either digital images or digital sound. Make sure you are able to apply your understanding of ADCs and DACs to the topics on the following pages.

Now test yourself

48 What is the main difference between an analogue signal and a digital signal?

49 Explain why it is not possible to store an analogue signal in a computer system.

50 What device is used to convert a digital signal so that it can be transmitted over an analogue medium?

51 Other than a microphone, name **one** device which contains an ADC.

Answers available online

Bitmapped graphics

A bitmap (or raster) graphic is an image made up of individual blocks of colour called pixels.

Each pixel is a single colour, and the colour of each pixel is recorded using a binary code.

In black and white images each pixel can be represented using a single bit, such as 1 for white and 0 for black.

Data stored in memory

0	1	0	0	1	0	0	1

1	1	1	0	1	1	0	0

Pixels displayed in screen

Figure 5.3 Each pixel in this black and white image is represented by one bit of data

Colour depth

Increasing the number of bits per pixel increases the possible number of colours that each pixel can represent. This is known as the colour depth.

Bits per pixel (colour depth)	Possible colours
2	$2^2 = 4$
4	$2^4 = 16$
8	$2^8 = 256$
16	$2^{16} = 65\,536$

Most high-quality images use a colour depth of 24 bits per pixel – 8 bits each for the amount of red, green and blue (RGB).

Increasing the colour depth allows for a more accurate representation of the image, however it also increases the size of the image file.

Size and resolution

The size of an image is a measure of its pixel dimensions.

size in pixels = width in pixels × height in pixels

Increasing the number of pixels allows the image to be more accurate, however it also increases the size of the image file.

The resolution of the image is the number of pixels per unit of length such as cm or inches. This is also known as the pixel density of an image.

Print and display resolutions are often measured using pixels per inch (PPI) or dots per inch (DPI) (where dots and pixels mean the same thing). An image with a width of 1024 pixels and a display resolution of 72 PPI would be 1024 ÷ 72 = 14.2 inches wide.

The overall file size for an image can be found by multiplying the number of pixels by the number of bits per pixel.

Bitmap An image format that uses a grid of pixels.

Pixel The smallest addressable element of an image.

Colour depth The number of bits used to store the colour of each pixel.

Size The pixel dimensions measured as the width x height of an image in pixels.

Resolution The number of pixels per unit of length, also known as pixel density, often measured in PPI or DPI.

> **Note**
>
> Digital screens, including mobile phones, are usually described according to both their pixel dimensions and their display resolutions.

5 Fundamentals of data representation

127

file size = size in pixels × colour depth

This can also be expressed as:

file size = width (px) × height (px) × bits per pixel

(Note that 'pixel' is often abbreviated to 'px'.)

For example, for an image which is 2000px wide, 2000px tall and has a colour depth of 24 bits per pixel:

size = 2000px × 2000px = 4000000px

file size = 4000000px × 24 bits per px = 96000000 bits

There are 8 bits in a byte, so to convert this to bytes:

96000000 bits ÷ 8 = 12000000 bytes

= 12MB

The major advantage of bitmap images is that they are an effective way to store a photo-realistic image due to the possible complexity of the different shades within each pixel.

> **Exam tip**
>
> Remember that 1 byte = 8 bits. Always read the question carefully and make sure that your answer is presented in the right units.

Metadata

Metadata means data about the data.

While an image file contains the binary data that makes up the colour of each individual pixel, additional data is also needed.

This includes the width, height and colour depth of an image which is necessary to convert the raw binary data back into a usable image.

Other metadata might include the time and date the image was created or saved, the camera settings used (for a photograph), the name of the software used to edit it and GPS data.

> **Metadata** Data about data. Additional data stored in a file.

> **Now test yourself** TESTED ◯
>
> 52 What is meant by a *pixel*?
> 53 Explain **two** effects of increasing the colour depth of an image.
> 54 Explain the impact of increasing the colour depth of an image by 1 bit per pixel.
> 55 What term refers to the number of pixels in an image?
> 56 Suggest **four** pieces of metadata that could be added to a digital photograph.
> 57 Calculate the colour depth for an image with up to 16 colours.
> 58 Calculate the file size in bytes for an image that is 600 pixels wide, 400 pixels tall and with a colour depth of 16 bits per pixel.
>
> **Answers available online**

Vector graphics

REVISED ◯

Vector graphics use geometry to describe the objects that make up an image.

Each object is a shape (also known as a vector primitive), such as a line, polygon, circle, curve or text.

Properties are used to describe each object in the image so that it can be drawn as needed. These properties include co-ordinates, line colour, line thickness and fill colour. Vector graphic files store the details of these properties.

A vector graphic is made up of various vector primitives and the image can be drawn to any scale.

> **Vector graphic** An image made of lines and shapes.
>
> **Vector primitive** Simple objects which can be combined to create a vector graphic.
>
> **Polygon** A shape made of straight lines, for example, rectangle, hexagon, and so on.

Check your understanding and progress at **www.hoddereducation.co.uk/myrevisionnotesdownloads**

• Start coordinate

Figure 5.4 Scaled vector graphics

Vector graphics versus bitmapped graphics

The file size of bitmap images is large as the colour for each pixel must be stored.

With a vector graphic the data that must be stored for each object is much smaller in size.

When a bitmap image is scaled up the pixels are enlarged, making them more noticeable, and the image becomes blocky. The resolution decreases as there are fewer pixels per inch.

With a vector graphic, the scale can be adjusted with no loss of quality as the image is redrawn each time.

Vector graphics are:
✚ not able to store a photo-realistic image as the vector primitives require each image to be made of relatively simple shapes and colours
✚ ideal for use in logos, fonts, and clipart as they can be scaled with no loss in quality and can be edited or split into separate objects.

> **Clipart** A cartoon style image.

Bitmap Images	Vector Images
Large file size.	Small file size.
Loss in quality when scaled.	No loss in quality when scaled.
Suitable for photo-realistic images.	Unsuitable for photo-realistic images.
Less commonly used for logos, fonts, and clipart.	Ideal for logos, fonts, and clipart.

Now test yourself

59 Give **three** properties of vector objects.

60 Explain why scaling a vector graphic does not reduce the quality of the final image.

61 State **one** advantage and **one** disadvantage for storing an image as a bitmap graphic.

62 Suggest **two** cases where a vector graphic would be preferable to a bitmap.

63 Suggest **one** reason why digital photographs are generally stored as a bitmap rather than a vector.

Answers available online

Digital representation of sound

When analogue sounds are recorded digitally, the amplitude of the sound wave is measured at fixed intervals of time.

The value of each sampling point is stored as a binary number.

> **Amplitude** A measure of how large a vibration or oscillation is.

129

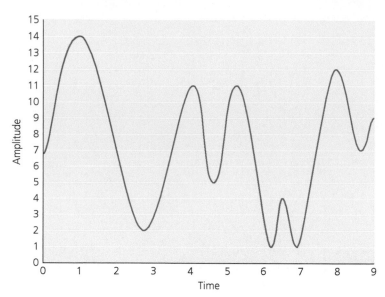

Figure 5.5 Sampling an analogue wave

The fixed interval of time is known as the sample rate and is measured in Hz, where 1 Hz is one sample per second.

A sample rate of 48 kHz means that there will be 48 000 samples per second.

Using a higher sample rate means that more samples will be captured:
+ increasing the accuracy of the recording
+ while also increasing the file size.

The sampling resolution refers to the number of bits per sample to measure the amplitude. (This concept is similar to the colour depth of an image). In Figure 5.5 each measurement of amplitude can take the integer values 0-15. This represents a 4 bit sample resolution (as $2^4 = 16$). For a 3 bit sample resolution the horizontal axis of Figure 5.5 would only have eight values (as $2^3 = 8$).

Using a larger sampling resolution means that the amplitude measurement of each sample will be captured more accurately, again increasing the accuracy of the recording and the file size.

The file size required for an audio recording can be found by multiplying the length of the recording (in seconds) by the sample rate and the sampling resolution.

file size = length of recording (seconds) × sample rate (Hz) × sampling resolution (bits per sample)

For example, for a 2 minute recording at 48 kHz and 16 bits per sample, the file size is:

file size = 120 seconds × 48 000 Hz × 16 bps

= 92 160 000 bits

= 11 520 000 bytes

= 11.52 MB

> **Sample rate** The rate at which samples are taken, typically measured in kHz.
>
> **Sampling resolution** The number of bits per sample.

> **Note**
>
> If audio is recorded in stereo then there will be two recordings – a left channel and a right channel, doubling the overall file size requirements; in this example, the stereo file size would be 23.04 MB

Nyquist's theorem

If the sample rate of a sound wave is too low then it is possible that the recording will miss some peaks or troughs.

In order to ensure that the recorded sound does not miss this data, Nyquist's theorem states that the sample rate should be at least double the maximum hearing range.

Since humans can hear sounds up to around 20 kHz, a minimum sample rate of 40 kHz should be used.

> **Nyquist's theorem** The rule that the sample rate should be at least double the maximum frequency that can be heard.

Check your understanding and progress at **www.hoddereducation.co.uk/myrevisionnotesdownloads**

Sounds recorded at a lower sample rate may still be recognisable, but will not be as accurate.

Telephone calls typically use a lower sample rate, and while this is suitable for speech, music played over a telephone line sounds tinny and lacks definition.

Musical Instrument Digital Interface (MIDI)

Musical Instrument Digital Interface (MIDI), is a protocol and file format that is used to capture certain information about musical notes. This information includes:
+ Pitch (how high or low the note is)
+ Note length
+ Note volume
+ Instrument

MIDI files can be created directly using a computer program or captured as someone plays a MIDI-enabled instrument such as a keyboard.

Rather than capturing the analogue sound wave generated at the time, a MIDI file records information such as which notes should be played, at what volume and for what length of time.

This means you cannot listen directly to a MIDI file – you need some kind of computer hardware and software to interpret it and generate sounds.

A MIDI file can be modified, and each individual note can be edited to change any of its properties. For instance, if a musician played the wrong note this can easily be corrected in the MIDI file.

Once captured, a MIDI file can then be used to generate sounds from any MIDI instrument. For instance, a MIDI file captured from a piano performance could be used to generate the same performance but on a completely different instrument such as a synthesiser.

MIDI produces much smaller files than audio files and are much more easily edited and corrected. Most modern music recordings make at least some use of MIDI.

> **Musical Instrument Digital Interface (MIDI)**
> A type of file that uses the instructions for how to create each note rather than capturing the analogue sound wave.

Now test yourself   TESTED

64 What value is being measured when sound is recorded?

65 Identify **two** effects of decreasing the sample rate of a sound recording?

66 What are the effects of increasing the sampling resolution?

67 Which rule predicts that sound quality will noticeably degrade when the sample rate drops below 40 KHz?

68 Calculate the file size in MB for a 5 minute recording at 40 KHz and a sampling resolution of 8 bits per sample.

69 Give **two** advantages for using MIDI files.

Answers available online

Data compression

Data compression means reducing the size taken up by data. This is useful as it means that less storage space is used on storage devices, and less time is taken to transmit data.

Sound files and image files are often compressed as these files typically use large amounts of data.

Other files, including text files, data files and program files can also be compressed.

> **Compression** Reducing the size of a file.

> **Note**
>
> Video files are made up of image data and audio data. Video files are not explicitly covered in the specification, but it can be assumed that similar techniques apply.

Lossy compression

In lossy compression some data is removed from the file. Once removed this data cannot be replaced.

In image files this can involve reducing the pixel dimensions or reducing the colour depth.

Reducing the resolution means that fewer pixels are needed. While this reduces the image quality, it is often possible to reduce the number of pixels quite significantly without making the image unusable, especially if the image is to be viewed on screen.

Figure 5.6 A high resolution image on the left and a low resolution image on the right

Reducing the colour depth means that each pixel is stored using fewer bits. The cost of this is that fewer colours are available which can lower the overall accuracy of the image.

The advantage of using lossy compression is that the file size can be significantly reduced, often with minimal noticeable effects. The major downside is that the lost data cannot be recovered.

Text files, program code and raw data cannot be compressed with lossy compression as the data would lose its meaning - for example removing every third letter from a piece of computer code would stop the code from working.

Lossless compression

Lossless compression, as the name suggests, does not involve losing or removing any data.

One technique to achieve this is run length encoding (RLE).

A run is a sequence of identical values, and the data can be shortened by recording the data in pairs of values indicating the run length and then the value.

The text data AAAAAAAAABBBBBBBBBAAAAAA could be shortened to 9A 8B 6A.

Another method of lossless compression is to use a dictionary method.

Each unique value in the data is recorded as a key-value pair.

For example the phrase:

"how much wood could a woodchuck chuck if a woodchuck could chuck wood"

could be rewritten using the following dictionary.

Key	Value
1	how
2	much
3	wood
4	could
5	a
6	woodchuck
7	chuck
8	if

Lossy compression
Reducing the size of a file by permanently removing some data.

Lossless compression
Reducing the size of a file without removing any data.

Run length encoding (RLE) A lossless compression technique of recording the length and value of each run in the data.

Run A series of identical values in a file or dataset.

Dictionary A data structure made of key:value pairs.

Check your understanding and progress at **www.hoddereducation.co.uk/myrevisionnotesdownloads**

The phrase could then be stored using just the keys: "1 2 3 4 5 6 7 8 5 6 4 7 3".

Making links

Dictionaries are a type of data structure commonly used in programming, and are included in the specification for Component 1. You can find out more about dictionaries and how they are used in programming in *Dictionaries* in Chapter 2.

The major advantage of lossless compression is that no data is lost and, when decompressed, the original file is recreated exactly as it was. Any file can potentially be compressed using lossless compression.

The major disadvantage of lossless compression is that file size reductions are usually much more limited than with lossy compression. Depending on the number of runs, or the number of unique values in the file, it is even possible that the compressed version will not be any smaller than the original.

Now test yourself   TESTED ⬤

70 Explain the purpose of compressing data.

71 Identify **two** methods of reducing the file size of an image using lossy compression.

72 Why can program code not be compressed using lossy compression?

73 Other than the answer above, give **one** disadvantage for using lossless compression.

74 A digital image is made of repeating patterns. Explain how a dictionary could be used to compress the image file.

Answers available online

Note

Other compression techniques exist, and data compression is a highly important area of research with far-reaching implications. Only those techniques described here are included in the specification.

Revision activity

Find examples of simple 8-bit graphics using an image search and practise representing them using run length encoding

Encryption   REVISED ⬤

Encryption is a method of scrambling data so that it cannot be understood.

Encryption is carried out by starting with a plaintext message and applying a cipher and a key in order to generate a ciphertext message.

Once received, the ciphertext message is then decrypted back into the original plaintext message.

Caesar cipher

One of the most basic ciphers is the Caesar cipher, an example of a substitution cipher.

In this cipher each letter is shifted by a fixed amount, or a key. For example, with a key of 2, each plaintext letter is moved two places further up the alphabet.

Plaintext letter	A	B	C	D	E	...	X	Y	Z
Ciphertext letter	C	D	E	F	G	...	Z	A	B

Making links

Writing a computer program to carry out a Caesar cipher is good practice, and the kind of task that can appear in Component 1, Section B. In order to wrap the alphabet back to the start, the modulo operator can be used. Make sure you are comfortable with the programming techniques in Chapter 1 and try writing your own programmed version of the Caesar cipher.

Encryption A method of hiding the meaning of a message.

Plaintext The original, unencrypted message.

Cipher An algorithm for encrypting data.

Key A value used to encrypt or decrypt data.

Ciphertext The encrypted form of the message.

Decryption A method of converting an encrypted message back to its original form.

Caesar cipher A substitution cipher in which each letter is shifted according to the key.

Substitution cipher A cipher in which each plaintext letter is replaced with a ciphertext letter.

The plaintext message DAZE would be encrypted as FCBG.

Once the message is received, along with the key, the process is reversed, and the ciphertext message FCA would be decrypted as DAY.

133

The Caesar cipher is easily cracked as there are a maximum of 25 possible keys (a key of 26 would mean that the plaintext and ciphertext messages would be identical). Trying every possible key is known as a brute force attack.

In order to speed up the cracking of a message encrypted using the Caesar cipher, frequency analysis can be used. This means that the most commonly used letters (typically E and T in the English language) are likely to occur most often.

Testing the keys where the most frequent letters align with E or T can further reduce the time taken to crack this encryption method, though with only 25 possible keys it is trivially quick to break this code with a computer.

Exam tip

Although not listed directly in the specification, you may be asked a question based on a substitution cipher of a similar complexity to the Caesar cipher (for example, with the letters of the alphabet written backwards, or using space as a 27th character). Practise with both of these examples to ensure that you are comfortable with the principles of substitution ciphers.

Vernam cipher

The Vernam cipher is also known as a one-time pad.

The cipher starts with choosing a random sequence of characters or binary digits as the key. This key is the one-time pad as it must only be used once.

The next task is to write down the binary codes for each character in the plaintext message and in the key.

Plaintext message	n	o	w
Key	g	p	w
Plaintext (binary)	0110 1110	0110 1111	0111 0111
Key (binary)	0110 0111	0111 0000	0111 0111

The individual bits in the plaintext and key characters are passed through an XOR gate in order to generate the cipher text.

Making links

In an **XOR** (or exclusive-OR) gate, the output is 1 if either input is a 1, but not both. If both inputs are 0 or both inputs are 1, then the output is 0. Logic gates are explored in more detail in Chapter 6.

Plaintext (binary)	0110 1110	0110 1111	0111 0111
Key (binary)	0110 0111	0111 0000	0111 0111
Ciphertext (binary)	0000 1001	0001 0000	0000 0000

The decryption process is identical. The ciphertext is passed through an XOR gate with the key, and the plaintext is produced.

Ciphertext (binary)	0000 1001	0001 0000	0000 0000
Key (binary)	0110 0111	0111 0000	0111 0111
Plaintext (binary)	0110 1110	0110 1111	0111 0111
Plaintext	n	o	w

The rules regarding the key state that it should:
+ be truly random
+ be at least as long as the ciphertext
+ not be repeated
+ not be re-used.

Check your understanding and progress at **www.hoddereducation.co.uk/myrevisionnotesdownloads**

If these rules are followed then it is mathematically impossible to reproduce the plaintext message without the key, because each character uses a different, unrelated key to its neighbours and every possible decrypted value is equally likely.

The biggest flaw in the Vernam cipher is that both the sender and receiver must know which key is being used. This means that either the key must be transmitted in a separate message (which could be intercepted) or that both parties must have a copy of the keys in advance, in which case it may be possible to physically retrieve the key.

The Vernam cipher is the only cipher in existence to have been mathematically proven to be completely unbreakable, even given infinite time and infinite ciphertext.

All other ciphers are based on computational security – that is, using algorithms which are so complex that they would take far longer than is useful to break. Theoretically all ciphers other than the Vernam cipher are breakable given enough time and data.

Symmetric The same key is used in encryption and decryption.

Asymmetric Different keys are used for encryption and decryption.

Making links

Both ciphers described in this chapter are **symmetric**, which means they use the same key for encryption and decryption. The importance of **asymmetric** encryption and the use of public/private key encryption is discussed in Chapter 9 (internet security). Note that both topics are often assessed in the same question.

Now test yourself

TESTED ○

75 What is meant by the terms *plaintext* and *ciphertext*?
76 Decrypt the message 'LTTI QZHP' which has been encrypted using the Caesar cipher and the key 5.
77 Describe **two** methods that could have been used to decrypt the message if you did not know the key.
78 State **three** rules for choosing a key to be used in the Vernam cipher.
79 Name **one** cipher which is mathematically impossible to break.
80 Explain why that cipher is not routinely used.

Answers available online

Revision activity

+ Practise encrypting and decrypting messages using the Caesar cipher, using online tools to check your accuracy.
+ Practise encrypting and decrypting messages using the Vernam cipher, using online tools to check your accuracy.

Summary

Number systems

+ Numbers are classified in sets, including $\mathbb{N}$ (natural), $\mathbb{Z}$ (integers), $\mathbb{Q}$ (rational), $\mathbb{R}$ (real) and irrational numbers
+ Ordinal numbers are used to identify the position of a value in a set
+ Natural numbers ($\mathbb{N}$ - positive integers, including 0) are used for counting
+ Real numbers ($\mathbb{R}$) are used for measurement

Number bases

+ Numbers can be represented using any base
+ You are expected to be familiar with numbers in base 2 (binary), base 10 (decimal) and base 16 (hexadecimal)
+ You are expected to be able to convert between numbers in different bases
+ Hexadecimal is used as a shorthand for binary because each hexadecimal digit maps exactly to one binary nibble

Bits and bytes

+ A single binary digit is called a bit
+ Bits are usually grouped into blocks of 8, called a byte

+ Binary values are usually written with a space after each block of 4, called a nibble
+ A block of n binary bits can represent 2^n possible values
+ Multiples of 10^3 (1000) bytes are referred to as 1 kB, 1 MB, 1 GB, 1 TB, and so on
+ Multiples of 2^{10} (1024) bytes are referred to as 1 KiB, 1 MiB, 1 GiB, 1 TiB, and so on

Binary number system

+ Unsigned binary is used to represent natural numbers, with a maximum range between 0 and $2^n - 1$ (where n is the number of bits)
+ It is important to be confident adding and multiplying binary numbers manually
+ Two's complement is used to represent signed (negative) binary numbers
+ In two's complement the MSB a negative number (for example, in a 4 bit number: −8, +4, +2, +1)
+ Subtracting binary numbers can be done by adding the negative version of the second number

→

135

+ The range of a two's complement number is from -2^{n-1} to $2^{n-1} - 1$, because 0 is included as a positive number
+ Fractional numbers can be represented using fixed point or floating point binary
+ In fixed point binary, the decimal place position is fixed and values after this are weighted as $\frac{1}{2}, \frac{1}{4}, \frac{1}{8}$, and so on
+ In floating point binary the value is written using a mantissa and an exponent
+ The binary point in the mantissa is moved by the number of places indicated in the exponent
+ Both exponent and mantissa are usually written using two's complement binary in exam questions
+ You are expected to be able to convert fractions between decimal and binary.
+ Binary fractions cannot represent all decimal fractions with complete accuracy as they use inverse powers of 2 ($\frac{1}{2}, \frac{1}{4}$, and so on)
+ The absolute error is the difference between the original value in decimal to be stored and the binary value that is actually stored
+ The absolute error is always written as a positive value
+ The relative error is found by dividing the absolute error by the original value, multiplied by 100 and written as a percentage (%)
+ Fixed point binary is quicker to process, but less precise and more wasteful of storage
+ Floating point binary takes longer to process, but is more precise and more efficient in terms of storage
+ In fully normalised floating point only one digit is placed before the binary place and this will be the opposite of the first digit after the binary place, in order to avoid wasting space with leading digits
+ Overflow occurs when the result of adding binary values is too large
+ Underflow occurs when the result of subtracting binary values is too small

Information coding systems

+ Numbers can be represented as a pure binary value, or as a character code
+ ASCII and Unicode are coding systems in which each character has a unique binary code
+ ASCII uses 7 bits per character, for a maximum of 128 characters
+ Unicode uses either 8, 16 or 32 bits per character, which is needed to represent other alphabets and symbols including emojis
+ Error checking can be carried out using parity bits, majority voting, checksums, or check digits
+ Parity bits use odd or even parity and append either a 0 or a 1 to a binary message to ensure that is has an odd or even number of 1s
+ In majority voting each bit is transmitted a fixed, odd number of times, and if all bits received are not the same, the majority value is assumed to be correct
+ A checksum uses an algorithm to generate a value based on the data in the original message which can be recalculated once the message has been received to check that the message is identical

+ A check digit is similar to a checksum, but is only represented by a single digit, often making use of the modulo operator

Representing images, sound and other data

+ Analogue measurements are continuous rather than discrete and are often represented with a curved wave
+ Digital measurements are discrete and are often represented with a stepped wave
+ Data can be converted between analogue and digital using an analogue to digital converter (ADC) or digital to analogue converter (DAC)
+ The most common use for a DAC is to convert a digital audio signal to an analogue signal
+ Images can be represented using bitmap images or vector images
+ The size of an image typically refers to its width × height, in pixels (px)
+ Resolution refers to pixel density, measured in dots per inch (DPI)
+ The colour depth of an image refers to how many bits are used to store the colour of each pixel
+ For a bitmap image file: file size = width (px) × height (px) × colour depth
+ Metadata is additional data stored in a file, and for an image file this can include the pixel dimensions, colour depth, data edited and GPS data
+ Bitmap graphics are suitable for photo-realistic images due to the large range of colours and their ability to represent images that are not made of simple shapes
+ Vector graphics are made by combining one or more vector primitive objects, which describe the properties of each object, including its co-ordinates, line colour and fill colour
+ Vector graphics are suitable for logos and clipart due to their ability to scale without quality loss and their small file size
+ Analogue sound is captured by measuring the amplitude of the sound wave at fixed intervals
+ The sample rate is measured in kHz and increasing the sample rate increases the accuracy of the recording
+ Nyquist's Theorem states that the minimum sample rate should be at least double the maximum frequency you wish to sample – for sound waves this maximum frequency is hearing range (up to 20 kHz in humans)
+ The sample resolution is the number of bits per sample
+ For a sound file: file size = length of recording (seconds) × sample rate (Hz) × sampling resolution (bits per sample)
+ MIDI stands for Musical Instrument Digital Interface and is used to represent information about each individual note or sound in a piece of audio
+ Each MIDI note can be individually edited in order to change features such as its pitch or length without affecting the rest of the sound
+ File compression is used to reduce the size of files in order to improve storage capacity and/or transmission times
+ Image and sound files are most frequently compressed, though text files and program files can also be compressed

Check your understanding and progress at **www.hoddereducation.co.uk/myrevisionnotesdownloads**

- Lossy compression refers to compression techniques in which some data is removed (for example, pixels and/or colour depth in an image, samples and/or sample resolution in a sound file
- Any data removed from a file during lossy compression cannot be recovered, but significant savings in file size can be made for a relatively low loss of quality
- Text and program files cannot be compressed with lossy compression as they would become meaningless
- Lossless compression refers to compression techniques in which no data is removed and the decompressed file is identical to the original
- Run length encoding (RLE) is a lossless compression technique in which each run of identical values is recorded as a pair of run:length values
- Dictionary-based methods use a table of key:value pairs in order to represent the data using its keys rather than the full values in each case
- Encryption is a method of scrambling data so that it cannot be understood by anyone but the intended recipient
- The original message is referred to as plaintext and the encrypted message is referred to as ciphertext

- The encryption algorithm is known as a cipher and the value used to encrypt and decrypt the data is known as the key
- The Caesar cipher is a substitution cipher in which each letter is shifted along the alphabet by a fixed amount dictated by the key
- The Caesar cipher is trivially easy to break as there are only 25 possible keys to try
- The Vernam cipher is the only mathematically secure cipher
- Each character to be encrypted is passed through an XOR gate along with a randomly selected key
- Because the key is completely random and each character is encrypted with a different key, the ciphertext is distributed uniformly and each possible decryption value is equally likely
- The Vernam cipher is only effective if the key is completely random and only ever used once
- The major problem with the Vernam cipher is that both sender and recipient must know the exact key
- All other ciphers are based on computational complexity and are therefore potentially breakable given enough time and ciphertext

Exam practice

1 Four numbers are listed below.
   a) For each number, tick one or more boxes to show which sets it belongs to. Some numbers belong to more than one set. [4]

	Natural	Integer	Rational	Irrational	Real
17.4					
√2					
7					
−12					

   b) State which value from the table above is an ordinal number and explain the purpose of an ordinal number. [2]

2. a) Represent the number 113 as an 8-bit unsigned integer. [1]
   b) Represent the number -47 as an 8-bit two's complement integer. [1]
   c) Use binary addition to find the value of 113 – 47. [2]
   d) Using only binary values, calculate the value of 23 × 9. [3]
   e) Name the problem that would occur if finding the value of 27 × 11 using 8-bit unsigned binary. [1]
   f) Represent the number 113 as a hexadecimal number. [2]
   g) Explain why it may sometimes be preferable to represent a value using hexadecimal rather than binary. [2]
   h) Calculate the decimal value of the two's complement fixed-point binary number 1101.0110. [2]

   i) The number 7.8 is represented as 0111.1100. Calculate the absolute and relative error. [3]
   j) Calculate the decimal value of the floating-point binary number with a mantissa of 0.110 1000 and an exponent of 0110. You must show your working. [2]
   k) Write the normalised floating point representation of −426 using a 10 digit mantissa and a five digit exponent. [3]

3 The letter H is represented in ASCII using the binary code 100 1000.
   a) State the binary codes for the letters I and K. [2]
   b) Explain why someone writing in using a different alphabet might not be able to use ASCII encoding and suggest an alternative system. [2]
   c) The letter H is transmitted using odd parity, with the parity bit appended before the most significant bit. State the binary code which is transmitted. [2]
   d) The binary code 1011 0101 is received, still using odd parity. State whether this transmission would be accepted. [1]
   e) Identify **two** flaws with using a parity check. [2]
   f) Another transmission is sent using majority voting in which each bit is transmitted three times. The data received is 111 000 110 011 101. State the original data. [1]
   g) Explain why it would not have been suitable to transmit each bit four times. [1]
   h) Some text has been encrypted using the Vernam cipher. Explain what is meant by *encryption*. [1]
   i) Describe why the message was not encrypted using the Caesar cipher. [1]

137

j) The received message is as follows, and the key is MOFK. The ASCII code for the letter H is 100 1000. Decrypt the message and show the plaintext message. You must show your working. [4]

000 0101

000 1010

000 1010

001 1011

4 A digital photograph is 4000 pixels wide, 3000 pixels tall and has a colour depth of 8 bits.

a) Calculate the size of the file in MB. [2]

b) State the maximum number of colours in the image. [1]

c) Identify **two** effects of increasing the colour depth of an image to 9 bits. [2]

d) Describe **two** advantages for saving the file as a vector graphic, rather than a bitmap. [2]

e) Identify **two** methods of lossy compression that could be applied to a bitmapped image. [2]

f) Explain why run length encoding is unlikely to have a significant impact on the file size of a bitmap image. [1]

g) Explain why lossy compression could not be applied to a program file containing source code. [2]

Check your understanding and progress at **www.hoddereducation.co.uk/myrevisionnotesdownloads**

6 Fundamentals of computer systems

Hardware and software

Relationship between hardware and software

The term hardware relates to the physical components of a computer system. This includes the:
+ internal components (including RAM and the CPU)
+ peripheral components (including secondary storage devices, printers, monitors, keyboards and mice).

The term software relates to the program that run on computer systems. This includes the:
+ operating system
+ utility programs
+ application programs.

Software requires hardware to carry out the instructions, and hardware requires software in order to be given instructions to carry out.

> **Hardware** The physical components of a computer system.
>
> **Peripheral** External hardware devices, on the periphery of the computer system.
>
> **Software** The programs that run on a computer system.

> **Now test yourself** TESTED ⚪
>
> 1 Identify **three** pieces of hardware commonly found as part of a laptop computer.
> 2 Identify **three** pieces of software commonly found installed on a laptop computer.
>
> **Answers available online**

Classification of software

There are two broad classes of software: system software and application software.

System software is intended to allow the computer system to run. This includes:
+ operating systems
+ utility programs
+ libraries
+ translators.

Systems software is there to support the running of the computer system, rather than to achieve a specific outcome for the user.

Application software is intended to allow the computer to serve a useful purpose. This includes:
+ word processing software
+ spreadsheet software
+ web browsers.

General-purpose application software can be used to achieve multiple tasks, for example word processing software can be used to write a letter, make notes or create a display.

Special purpose application software is written with a more specific purpose in mind and cannot easily be used for a different purpose. Examples include audio editing software, flight simulator training software and computer games.

> **System software** Software intended to allow the computer system to run.
>
> **Application software** Software intended to allow the end-user to achieve a task.

139

System software

REVISED

Operating systems:
+ provide an interface between the user and the hardware
+ run application programs
+ manage resources and hardware.

Utility programs are individual programs which help configure, maintain or optimise the computer system. Examples of utility programs include:
+ virus scanning
+ file manager
+ system monitor
+ disk cleanup
+ backup software
+ disk defragmenter.

Library programs are collections of resources or code that can be used by other programs. They include pre-written subroutines which can be called by other programs on the system.

Translators are used to translate high-level source code into low-level machine code. Examples include:
+ assemblers
+ compilers
+ interpreters.

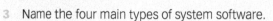

Now test yourself

TESTED

3 Name the four main types of system software.
4 State whether a word processor is an example of application software or system software.
5 Name **three** different examples of utility programs.
6 Describe the purpose of a library.

Answers available online

Role of an operating system (OS)

REVISED

An operating system (OS) serves three main purposes, all of which are related. An OS:
+ hides the complexities of the hardware
+ provides an interface for the user
+ manages and allocates system resources.

User interface

The user interface can be graphical (GUI), command line (CLI), menu driven or voice controlled.

A GUI is commonly used on desktop and mobile devices, and is typically made up of windows, icons, menus and pointers. This is often shortened to the acronym WIMP.

A CLI is often used for remote computers or servers. The lack of graphical cues makes a CLI less user-friendly, but those confident using text-based commands can make changes quickly and efficiently.

A CLI is also ideal for remote connections as no graphical data needs to be transmitted.

A menu-driven interface is often used on devices with few inputs, such as a (non-touchscreen) watch or digital set top box.

Voice controlled interfaces can be used in situations where using a manual input method are not practical. This includes phone-based systems and digital home assistants.

User interface The tools that are provided for a user to interact with a computer system.

Graphical user interface (GUI) An image-based interface that uses windows, icons, menus and pointers.

Command line interface (CLI) A text-only interface which is less user-friendly but often more powerful for knowledgeable users.

Check your understanding and progress at **www.hoddereducation.co.uk/myrevisionnotesdownloads**

Hardware resources

Running the computer hardware includes significant complexities, which are hidden from the user because the operating system handles them in the background.

Tasks include:

+ **Memory management:** Programs are loaded into RAM when run; the most frequently used instructions are loaded into the cache for faster access and the least frequently used instructions are moved into virtual memory.
+ **CPU allocation:** Individual instructions are passed to the CPU with differing levels of priority. Multi-core processors require complex solutions in order to make the most efficient use of the CPU, with minimal delays while dependent tasks are still running.
+ **Peripheral management:** Input/output devices need to be managed, and each data stream needs to be processed in competition with the programs already running.

Making links

In order to fully appreciate the hardware complexities which are hidden by the operating system it is important to understand system architecture, including the role of the CPU and RAM. This topic is discussed in Chapter 7 (*Internal hardware components*).

Now test yourself

TESTED

7 State the main purpose of an operating system.

8 Identify **three** aspects of hardware management which are run by the operating system.

9 Describe **two** features of a graphical user interface.

10 Name **two** types of user interface other than a GUI.

Answers available online

Classification of programming languages

Computer programming has evolved over the lifetime of computers and there are several different classifications for programming languages.

Low-level languages

REVISED

There are two types of low-level language.

Machine code refers to the binary code which is directly acted upon by the processor.

Each type of processor has its own machine code instruction set with individual commands for tasks such as fetching data from memory, saving data to memory, adding values, etc.

The only language that a computer understands is machine code.

Assembly language is a text-based equivalent to machine code. Remembering and correctly entering the exact binary codes is difficult, so assembly language allows each binary instruction to instead be represented by a short code, which is closer to the English language. This makes it easier to program.

> **Low-level language** A programming language which describes exactly how to interact with the computer's hardware.
>
> **Machine code** Each instruction is represented as a binary code.
>
> **Assembly language** Each instruction is represented as a text-based command.

141

For instance, the assembly language instructions:

```
ADD R3, R1, R2
```

would add the value in register 2 to the value in register 1 and store the result in register 3.

Each assembly instruction maps to one machine code instruction, and each type of processor has its own assembly language.

Making links

AQA has developed its own assembly language instruction set and it is normal to include a question in which students are expected to read or write programs using assembly language. The specific details are discussed in Chapter 7 (*The processor instruction set*).

Now test yourself TESTED

11 Name the **two** different examples of low-level programming languages.

12 Explain why **one** of those languages is more commonly used by programmers.

Answers available online

High-level language

REVISED

High-level languages use structured statements (for example, IF statements, WHILE loops, and so on) in order to simplify the task of describing an algorithm.

Keywords and constructs are written in an English-like form which makes them more recognisable.

High-level languages also include features such as local variables, parameters, named constants and indentation – features which are not found in assembly language code.

One line of code from a high-level language might require multiple machine code instructions.

High-level languages include those you will have studied for Component 1, such as:

+ C#
+ Delphi/Pascal
+ Java
+ Python
+ Visual Basic.net

Imperative high-level languages are languages in which the commands are carried out in a programmer-defined order. The term imperative refers to types of programming language where the programmer is describing how the computer should achieve the desired result. All of the examples above are imperative high-level languages.

The alternative to imperative high-level languages is declarative high-level languages, in which the programmer writes a program that describes what the program should achieve, but not how.

For example, the command for searching through a table of data does not contain an explicit loop.

Examples of declarative programming languages include:

+ SQL
+ Haskell
+ LISP
+ Prolog

> **High-level language** A programming language which uses keywords and constructs written in an English-like form.

> **Imperative** A language in which commands are used to say how the computer should complete the task.
>
> **Declarative** A language in which the programmer codes what they want to happen, but not how.

> ### Exam tip
>
> Remember that imperative refers to the specifics of how to solve the problem, whereas declarative refers to what the program should achieve.

Low-level versus high-level

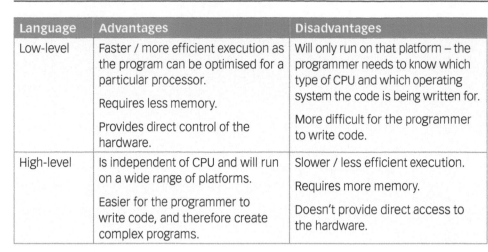

Language	Advantages	Disadvantages
Low-level	Faster / more efficient execution as the program can be optimised for a particular processor. Requires less memory. Provides direct control of the hardware.	Will only run on that platform – the programmer needs to know which type of CPU and which operating system the code is being written for. More difficult for the programmer to write code.
High-level	Is independent of CPU and will run on a wide range of platforms. Easier for the programmer to write code, and therefore create complex programs.	Slower / less efficient execution. Requires more memory. Doesn't provide direct access to the hardware.

> **Note**
>
> While all CPUs of the same type use the same basic instruction set, the choice of operating system also has an impact. This means that a program compiled for an Intel CPU running Windows will not run on the same CPU running Linux.

> **Now test yourself** TESTED
>
> 13 Describe **one** reason why high-level languages are more commonly used than low-level languages.
>
> 14 Explain the meaning of imperative in relation to high-level languages.
>
> 15 Suggest **one** situation where a programmer may prefer to use a low-level programming language.
>
> **Answers available online**

Types of program translator

Programs written in any language other than machine code must be translated. In order for a program to run it must be translated from the original source code into object code.

There are three main types of translator.

> **Note**
>
> Machine code refers to the code directly acted on by the CPU. Object code is a portion of machine code which is not yet fully linked to a complete program. The difference is subtle and it is beyond the scope of A-level. Either term is likely to be accepted.

Source code Code written by a programmer.

Object code Low-level code, translated from the source code.

Translator Systems software for converting one form of code into object code.

Assemblers, compilers and interpreters

Assembler

An assembler is used to translate assembly language instructions into object code instructions.

Because assembly language and machine code map one-to-one, each assembly language instruction is translated directly into its binary equivalent.

Compiler

A compiler is used to translate high-level code into object code. This is a more complex process than with an assembler as one line of high-level code may involve several machine code operations.

A compiler will process all of the code in a program in one batch, and will produce an executable binary file (often with a .exe file extension, though not always).

Assembler Translates assembly language code into object code.

Compiler Translates high-level code into object code as a batch.

143

Once compiled, the executable file can be run multiple times without the need to translate the source code again.

Advantages	Disadvantages	Uses
The executable file is much quicker to run than the source code. Once compiled, the executable file can be run without the need to translate the source code again. The programmer can share the executable file with others, but the program cannot be easily edited or algorithms in the source code copied as only the machine code is present in the file. If the compiler detects any errors then it will try to inform the user of all errors that have been found.	The executable file will be compiled specifically for one set of machine code instructions and the executable file will only run on that platform. The whole program must be fully compiled before it can be run and this can slow down the process of debugging. If there is an error in the program then the program will not compile, meaning that a partially working program cannot be tested.	Producing a program that will be run many times without frequent changes to the source code. Producing a program where the programmer wishes to keep the details of the algorithms secret.

Interpreter

An interpreter achieves the same basic goal as a compiler – translating high-level code into machine code. The main difference is that an interpreter translates and then executes one line of code at a time.

An interpreter doesn't produce an executable file, but must be re-translated each time it is run.

> **Interpreter** Translates and then runs high-level code one section at a time.

Advantages	Disadvantages	Uses
The program can be run on any platform that has an interpreter for that language, making it easier to run the program on different systems. Debugging can be quicker as the whole program doesn't need to be translated in order to test one part. If there is an error in the program then the interpreter will not detect this until it reaches that part of the program, and so a partially completed program will still run, up to a point.	The program must be translated each time it is run, meaning that the program will run more slowly than compiled code. The source code must be made available to anyone running the program, as the user must translate the source code at runtime. The program will stop at the first error it encounters, and so multiple errors will not be identified at once.	Producing a program that may need to run on a variety of different platforms. Debugging a large program that would take a long time to compile.

Bytecode

In order to help compiled programs run on a wider range of devices, some programming languages are compiled to bytecode, rather than object code.

The source code is translated using a compiler, to an intermediate language, called bytecode. When the program is executed the bytecode is executed in a virtual machine. This means that the physical computer system creates a virtual computer system that has a common instruction set, no matter what platform the physical computer system is running.

When the bytecode is executed it is translated by the virtual machine, into object code that can be understood by the physical computer system.

This means that any platform that can support the virtual machine can also run the program.

This allows the compiled program to be run on a much wider range of devices without needing to be recompiled and also allows for optimisation by the virtual machine for that platform.

> **Bytecode** An intermediate code between high-level and object code which can run in a virtual machine.
>
> **Virtual machine** Software that emulates or simulates a computer system.

Now test yourself   TESTED

16 What is the common purpose of all translators?

17 Which translator would be used with code written in assembly language?

18 Describe the main difference between a compiler and an interpreter.

19 Identify **one** advantage and **one** disadvantage for using an interpreter over a compiler.

20 Explain the purpose of bytecode.

Answers available online

Logic gates

Logic gates are physical devices which take one or more inputs and produce an output according to certain logical rules.

There are six basic logic gates which students are expected to recognise and be able to draw.

The function of each logic gate can be described using a truth table, which shows the possible inputs and the equivalent outputs.

Each logic gate can also be represented using a Boolean expression.

> **Logic gate** Device which takes one or more binary outputs and produces a single binary output.
>
> **Truth table** A table showing the possible inputs and their corresponding outputs.
>
> **Boolean expression** A mathematical notation for logic gates and circuits.

Types of logic gate

Symbol	Truth table	
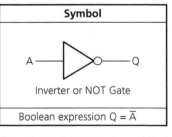 Inverter or NOT Gate	A	Q
	0	1
	1	0
Boolean expression $Q = \overline{A}$	Q = NOT A	

Figure 6.1 A NOT gate and its truth table

> **NOT gate**
> The NOT gate is also referred to as an inverter, as it inverts (or flips) the input value.
>
> Note that this is the only gate which only uses one input.

Symbol	Truth table		
	A	B	Q
	0	0	0
A ─┐ ... B ─┘ Q	0	1	0
2-input AND Gate	1	0	0
	1	1	1
Boolean expression Q = A.B	Q = A AND B		

Figure 6.2 An AND gate and its truth table

AND gate
The AND gate produces an output only if input A AND input B are on.

Note that this gate looks like a letter D, which is the last letter in AND.

Symbol	Truth table		
	A	B	Q
	0	0	0
A ─┐ ... B ─┘ Q	0	1	1
2-input OR Gate	1	0	1
	1	1	1
Boolean expression Q = A+B	Q = A OR B		

Figure 6.3 An OR gate and its truth table

OR gate
The OR gate produces an output if either input A OR input B are on OR both.

Note that each line on the drawing for this gate is curved, as are the letters in OR.

Symbol	Truth table		
	A	B	Q
	0	0	0
A ─┐ ... B ─┘ Q	0	1	1
2-input Ex-OR Gate	1	0	1
	1	1	0
Boolean expression Q = A⊕B	Q = A XOR B		

Figure 6.4 An XOR gate and its truth table

XOR gate
The XOR (or exclusive OR) gate produces an output if either input A OR input B are on but not both.

Note that this gate looks very similar to an OR gate, with an extra curved bar on the input.

Symbol	Truth table		
	A	B	Q
	0	0	1
A ─┐ ... B ─┘ Q	0	1	1
2-input NAND Gate	1	0	1
	1	1	0
Boolean expression Q = $\overline{A.B}$	Q = NOT (A AND B)		

Figure 6.5 A NAND gate and its truth table

NAND gate
The NAND gate is equivalent to an AND gate followed by a NOT gate.
Note the round 'nose' on the front to indicate that the result should be inverted.

Check your understanding and progress at **www.hoddereducation.co.uk/myrevisionnotesdownloads**

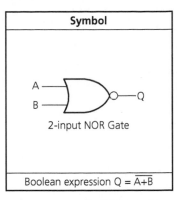

Symbol	Truth table

A	B	Q
0	0	1
0	1	0
1	0	0
1	1	0

Boolean expression $Q = \overline{A+B}$ Q = NOT (A OR B)

Figure 6.6 A NOR gate and its truth table

Now test yourself TESTED

21 State the name of the gate which produces an output of 'on' (or 1) when one input is on, but not both.

22 State the difference in the symbols for an AND gate and a NAND gate.

23 State another name for an inverter.

Answers available online

Logic circuits REVISED

Logic circuits which contain two or more gates can be devised to solve practical problems.

For example, the windscreen wipers (O) on a car may activate if the engine (E) is switched on and either the wiper switch is activated (W) or the rain sensor is activated (S).

The logic circuit for this scenario is shown below, along with the relevant truth table.

Logic circuit A solution to a problem that uses one or more logic gates.

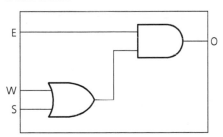

Figure 6.7 Logic circuit diagram for a car's windscreen wiper

E	W	S	O
0	0	0	0
0	0	1	0
0	1	0	0
0	1	1	0
1	0	0	0
1	0	1	1
1	1	0	1
1	1	1	1

The circuit can also be represented using its Boolean expression: O = E.(W+S)

You may be asked a question which involves translating between any two of:
+ a written description of a problem
+ a logic circuit diagram
+ a logical expression.

Draw a logic circuit to represent the Boolean equation A.B̄ + A.C.

The circuit can be created by combining the output of A.B̄ with the output of A.C, using an OR gate.

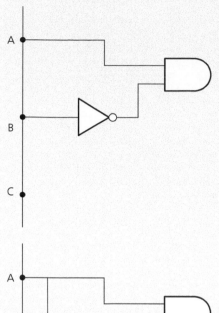

First, draw the part of the circuit that represents. A.B̄.

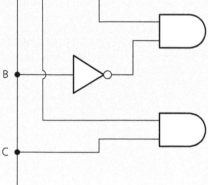

Second, draw the part of the circuit that represents. A.C.

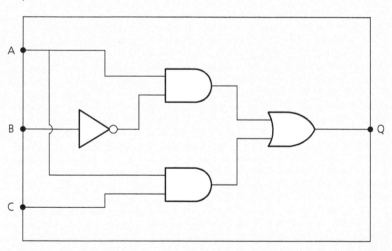

Finally, connect the two using an OR gate.

Figure 6.8

Check your understanding and progress at **www.hoddereducation.co.uk/myrevisionnotesdownloads**

When completing truth tables for complex circuits it can be helpful to include intermediate points.

Complete the truth table for the following logic circuit and write the Boolean expression.

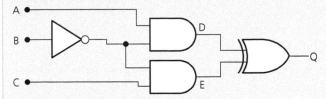

Figure 6.9 A more complex logic circuit

To complete the truth table we would consider the intermediate points labelled D and E on the diagram, and given by the expressions:

D = A.B

E = B.C

Inputs			Intermediate points		Output
A	B	C	D	E	Q
0	0	0	0	0	
0	0	1	0	1	
0	1	0	0	0	
0	1	1	0	0	
1	0	0	1	0	
1	0	1	1	1	
1	1	0	0	0	
1	1	1	0	0	

We would then complete the table by noting that:

Q = D⊕E

Inputs			Intermediate points		Output
A	B	C	D	E	Q
0	0	0	0	0	0
0	0	1	0	1	1
0	1	0	0	0	0
0	1	1	0	0	0
1	0	0	1	0	1
1	0	1	1	1	0
1	1	0	0	0	0
1	1	1	0	0	0

Using the expression **Q = D⊕E** and substituting for D and E we can construct the full Boolean expression:

$Q = A.\bar{B} \oplus \bar{B}.C$

24 a Draw a logic circuit to represent the Boolean equation $Q = \overline{A}.B + \overline{A}.\overline{B}$.

    b Complete a truth table for the Boolean equation.

25 Complete a truth table for the logic circuit in Figure 6.10.

Figure 6.10

Answers available online

Adders

Two of the most important logic circuits are the half adder and the full adder.

The half adder is used to add two binary numbers so that:

$0 + 0 = 0$ carry 0

$0 + 1 = 1$ carry 0

$1 + 0 = 1$ carry 0

$1 + 1 = 0$ carry 1

When written out as part of a larger binary addition it is common to use the following layout.

```
  0          1              1
  1 +        0 +            1 +
  1          1           1 0
```

The outputs are labelled as S (sum) and C (carry).

> **Half adder** A logic circuit to add two binary digits.
>
> **Full adder** A logic circuit to add three binary digits.

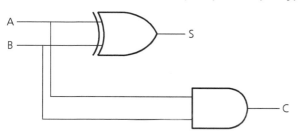

Figure 6.11 A half adder logic circuit

The Sum is calculated using an XOR gate and the Carry is calculated using an AND gate.

> **Exam tip**
>
> You may be asked to construct the circuit for a half adder. If so, start with the truth table and the two gates required can be worked out from there.

INPUT		OUTPUT	
A	B	C	S
0	0	0	0
0	1	0	1
1	0	0	1
1	1	1	0

When adding two digit (or larger) numbers, it is necessary to add 3 inputs – the two numbers being added and the carry from the previous digit. These are labelled A, B and C_{in} (Carry in).

When adding three binary numbers there is an additional possible case:

$1 + 1 + 1 = 1$ carry 1

To do this we need a circuit called a full adder. This is made from two half adders joined with an OR gate to generate the Sum and $Carry_{out}$.

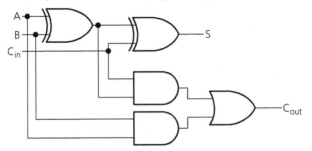

Figure 6.12 A full adder logic circuit

The truth table gives some clues as to the overall purpose of the logic circuit.

INPUT			OUTPUT	
A	B	C_{in}	C_{out}	S
0	0	0	0	0
0	0	1	0	1
0	1	0	0	1
0	1	1	1	0
1	0	0	0	1
1	0	1	1	0
1	1	0	1	0
1	1	1	1	1

> **Exam tip**
>
> You will not be asked to construct a full adder, but you may be shown one and asked to explain its function, or to complete a truth table.

> **Now test yourself**   TESTED ◯
>
> 26 State the two gates used in a half adder.
>
> 27 Describe the difference in purpose between a half adder and a full adder.
>
> 28 Explain why a full adder would be needed to add 4-bit binary numbers.
>
> **Answers available online**

D-type flip-flop   REVISED ◯

The edge triggered D-type flip-flop is a logic circuit which can be used to store a state. This concept is the basis of computer memory.

+ The circuit takes two inputs, a data input, and a clock input signal which changes from 0 to 1 and back again at regular intervals.
+ When the clock input signal changes from 0 to 1 (called the rising edge), the output changes to match the current data input signal.
+ In between the rising edges, at any other point in the clock signal, any changes in the input data has no effect on the output – the old output will still appear, regardless of the current data input.
+ This can be used to check if a value has changed since the last timing signal (by comparing the current output of the signal to its input), or to store data to be used later.

It should be noted that this circuit still requires power and is therefore a type of volatile memory.

> **Edge triggered D-type flip-flop** A logic circuit used to store the state of an input.
>
> **Rising edge** The point at which the clock signal changes from 0 to 1.
>
> **Volatile memory** Memory which can only store a value when supplied with power.

Now test yourself   TESTED ○

29 State the two inputs required for a D-type flip-flop.
30 Explain the purpose of a D-type flip-flop.

Answers available online

Boolean algebra

Using Boolean algebra   REVISED ○

Each logic gate and each logic circuit can be written as a Boolean expression.

More complex logic circuits can often be replaced with a simpler design, and so Boolean expressions are checked to see if they can be simplified.

There are three main steps involved in simplifying a Boolean expression.

Boolean identities

A Boolean identity refers to an expression where there is only one input, and therefore the circuit can be simplified.

> **Boolean identity** A relation that is always true.

For example the Boolean expression **A.1** would produce the following truth table.

A	1	A.1
0	1	0
1	1	1

As the second input is always on (represented as '1'), the output is always the same as the value of A.

Another Boolean expression that can be simplified is $A.\bar{A}$.

A	$\bar{A}$	$A.\bar{A}$
0	1	0
1	0	0

As A and NOT A are opposite, the output from the AND gate must always be 0.

There are eight main Boolean identities to remember:

$A + 0 = A$ $A.A = A$

$A.0 = 0$ $A + A = A$

$A + 1 = 1$ $A.\bar{A} = 0$

$A.1 = A$ $A + \bar{A} = 1$

In the Boolean expressions above, whilst A is a single input it could represent a more complex expression.

Take the expression Q = A + 0 which can be represented by the logic diagram:

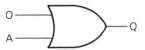

Figure 6.13 Q = A + 0

Now consider the following diagram:

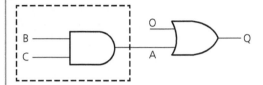

Figure 6.14

Now we can see that A is in fact the output of B.C and, therefore, the expression above can be written as:

Q = B.C + 0, where A = B.C

and, since A + 0 = A,

B.C + 0 = B.C

In fact, it doesn't matter what expression is contained within dotted box – if the box has one output then you can think of it as: 'box + 0 = box'. And the same goes for any of the Boolean identities above.

Now test yourself   TESTED ○

31 Simplify each of these Boolean expressions using a Boolean identity.
  a B + 1
  b D + D
  c C.$\overline{C}$
  d (A.B).1

Answers available online

Rearranging Boolean expressions

The rules for rearranging Boolean expressions work in exactly the way you would expect based on traditional algebra taught in maths.

Boolean expressions are commutative.

This means that:
+ A.B can be rewritten as B.A (just as 3 × 5 = 5 × 3).
+ A + B can be written as B + A (just as 3 + 5 = 5 + 3)

Boolean expressions are associative.

This means that brackets can be rearranged as long as the operations are equal. For example:

A + (B + C) = (A + B) + C, and

(A.B).C = A. (B.C)

BIDMAS *applies.*

This means that in the Boolean expression A + $\overline{A}$.(A + B) the AND operator takes precedence over the OR operator between A and $\overline{A}$.

The first two terms cannot be removed as a Boolean expression because the A.- must be multiplied first.

Expanding and factorising brackets

As with traditional algebra, brackets can be expanded, and factorising can reduce common factors.

Expanding brackets involves multiplying each term in the brackets by the value outside:

➤ A.(B + C) = A.B + A.C

Factorising is the reverse process, identifying common factors and removing them:

➤ A.B + B.C = B.(A + C)

Note that a single input can be factorised by itself:

➤ A + A.B = A.(1 + B)

This then leads to the use of Boolean identities to further simplify:

➤ A.(1 + B) = A.1 = A

Expanding two sets of brackets together can be completed remembering the acronym **FOIL**:

➤ (A + B). (A + $\bar{B}$) =

First (the first term in each bracket): A.A +

Outer (the two outer most terms):   A.$\bar{B}$ +

Inner (the two inner most terms):   B.A +

Last (the last term in each bracket): B.$\bar{B}$

➤ = A.A + A.$\bar{B}$ + B.A + B.$\bar{B}$

We can then apply Boolean identities (since B.$\bar{B}$ = 0):

➤ = A + A.$\bar{B}$ + B.A + 0

And again (since X + 0 = X):

➤ = A + A.$\bar{B}$ + B.A

We can now factorise as A is a common factor:

➤ = A. (1 + $\bar{B}$ + B)

And again apply Boolean identities:

➤ = A.1

➤ = A

Now test yourself

TESTED ⬤

32 Simplify each of the following Boolean expressions
  a   A.B + B
  b   C.(D + $\bar{D}$)
  c   (A + B). ($\bar{A}$ + $\bar{B}$)
  d   C.D.(C + D)

Answers available online

De Morgan's laws

Given a Boolean expression with a bar over two or more inputs, the bar can be split:

➤ $\overline{A + B}$ = $\bar{A}.\bar{B}$

The reverse is also true, and the bar can be joined:

➤ $\bar{A} + \bar{B}$ = $\overline{A.B}$

De Morgan's laws can be simplified to a simple phrase: 'Break the line, change the sign'.

Note

AND operations should be considered to have the same level of precedence as a multiply operation.

OR operations should be considered to have the same level of precedence as an addition operation.

Expanding brackets The process of removing brackets by multiplying.

Factorising The process of removing a common factor.

Common factor A term which appears in 2 or more parts of an expression.

De Morgan's laws Break the line, change the sign (and vice versa).

Check your understanding and progress at **www.hoddereducation.co.uk/myrevisionnotesdownloads**

Using this technique it is common to find you have a double bar. Applying the first De Morgan law:

➤ $\overline{\overline{A} + \overline{B}} = \overline{\overline{A}} . \overline{\overline{B}}$

Alternatively applying the second De Morgan law gives:

➤ $\overline{\overline{A} + \overline{B}} = \overline{\overline{A} . \overline{B}}$

Since passing a value through two NOT gates returns the same result, a double bar cancels itself out in both cases; that is:

➤ $\overline{\overline{A} + \overline{B}} = A.B$

A good strategy for simplifying Boolean expressions is to look for opportunities to apply, in this order:

+ Boolean identities
+ De Morgan's laws
+ Expanding or factorising

After each step, start the list of strategies again, and if you hit a dead end then step backwards and look for an alternative route.

Summary

+ The term hardware describes the physical components of a computer system
+ The term software refers to the programs that run on that system
+ Software can be classified as systems software or application software
+ Systems software is concerned with allowing the computer system to run and includes the operating system, utility programs, libraries, and translators
+ Application software is not associated with the operation of a computer but instead allows it to serve a useful purpose by performing tasks
+ The operating system is a piece of systems software which hides the complexity of the hardware and provides a user interface
+ The operating system also performs resource allocation, specifically memory management, controlling CPU access and peripheral management
+ Utilities are programs which deal with one aspect of running the computer system
+ Examples of utility programs include disk defragmenters, back-up software, virus scanners and disk cleanup
+ Libraries are collections of subroutines which can be accessed by other programs
+ Translators are programs that convert source code into object code – assemblers, compilers and interpreters
+ The low-level languages are machine code and assembly language
+ Machine code is a set of instructions for a particular CPU made up of individual binary codes

+ Assembly language code is written in a form closer to English
+ Each machine code and assembly language is specific to one platform
+ Each assembly language instruction is equivalent to one machine code instruction
+ High-level languages use structured statements and English-like keywords and constructs
+ High-level languages support the use of local variables, parameters, named constants and indentation
+ Imperative high-level languages describe how a problem should be solved, step by step
+ Declarative high-level languages describe what should happen, but not how
+ High-level languages make it easier for programmers to write code and can be run on different platforms
+ Low-level languages use less memory and can be optimised for the platform on which it runs
+ An assembler is used to translate assembly language code into object code
+ A compiler or an interpreter can be used to translate high-level code into object code
+ A compiler translates all of the code at once and produces an executable file which can be run without further translation
+ An interpreter translates and then executes one line of code at a time, and does not produce an executable file
+ A compiler will attempt to identify all errors when compiling and ensures that the source code can be kept secret, as only the executable file is distributed
+ A compiled program will only run on the system it has been compiled for

- ✚ An interpreter will re-translate the program each time it is run, so that the same source code can be run on more platforms without needing to provide a different executable file
- ✚ An interpreter can allow for faster debugging as a partially complete program will still run
- ✚ When sharing an interpreted program, the source code must be shared, and the program must be re-translated each time it can run
- ✚ Bytecode is used in some languages as an intermediate step as this bytecode can then be executed in a virtual machine, allowing compiled programs to run on a wide range of platforms
- ✚ Logic gates take one or more binary inputs and produce a single binary output
- ✚ The six main logic gates are the NOT, AND, OR, XOR, NAND and NOR gates
- ✚ Each logic gate has its own truth table, which describes the range of possible inputs and the corresponding outputs
- ✚ Logic gates can be combined to create a logic circuit, which can be used to solve a larger range of problems
- ✚ A half adder is used to add two binary numbers
- ✚ A full adder is used to add three binary numbers

- ✚ A D-type flip-flop stores the state of the input and can therefore be used as a unit of memory
- ✚ A D-type flip-flop has two inputs – a data signal and a clock signal
- ✚ Boolean expressions use the '+' symbol to mean OR and the '.' operator (meaning multiply) to mean AND
- ✚ BIDMAS rules apply, and so AND operations should be applied before OR operations
- ✚ Boolean identities can be used to simplify Boolean expressions, for example, A.1 = A
- ✚ Boolean expressions can be factorised, and brackets expanded, just as in normal algebra
- ✚ A bar over any part of a Boolean expression refers to a NOT operator
- ✚ De Morgan's Law means that if you break a line, you change the sign
- ✚ The reverse is true, and two bars can be joined, with the operator where the break was being changed
- ✚ A rule of thumb when simplifying Boolean expressions is to look for opportunities to use De Morgan's Law, followed by looking for Boolean identities and finally looking for opportunities to use brackets (factorising or expansion)

Exam practice

1 A computer has been newly set up, with an operating system, disk defragmenter, hard disk drive and a compiler
   a) State which item from the list above is an item of hardware. [1]
   b) State which category of system software a disk defragmenter belongs to. [1]
   c) Describe two different types of resource management carried out by the operating system. [2]
   d) Identify **one** other feature of the operating system. [1]

2 Dani has written a computer program using an imperative high-level language.
   a) Explain the meaning of the term *imperative high-level language*. [2]
   b) Suggest **two** reasons why Dani may have chosen to use a high-level language rather than a low-level language. [2]
   c) State the name of **one** low-level language. [1]
   d) State the purpose of a compiler. [2]
   e) Describe **two** advantages to Dani for choosing to use a compiler. [4]
   f) Describe **one** disadvantage to the end-user of Dani's program if she had chosen to use an interpreter. [2]
   g) Dani's program is compiled to bytecode instead of object code. Suggest **one** reason why she has chosen this method. [1]
   h) Explain the process of executing the bytecode. [2]

3 a) State the name of this logic gate. [1]

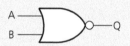

   b) Copy and complete the truth table for this logic gate. [2]

A	B	Q
0		
0		
1		
1		

   c) Draw the circuit diagram for the logical expression. [4]

$$Q = \overline{A.B + \overline{B.C}}$$

   d) Copy and complete the truth table for the logic circuit described in part c). [3]

A	B	C	Q

→

Check your understanding and progress at **www.hoddereducation.co.uk/myrevisionnotesdownloads**

e) Use the truth table to draw a simplified logic circuit. [3]

f) State the name of this logic circuit. [1]

4 Simplify each of these Boolean expressions.

    a) $1 \oplus \bar{B}$ [1]

    b) $A.B + B$ [3]

    c) $(A + B).(\bar{A} + \bar{B})$ [4]

    d) $\overline{A + \overline{B.B.C}}$ [5]

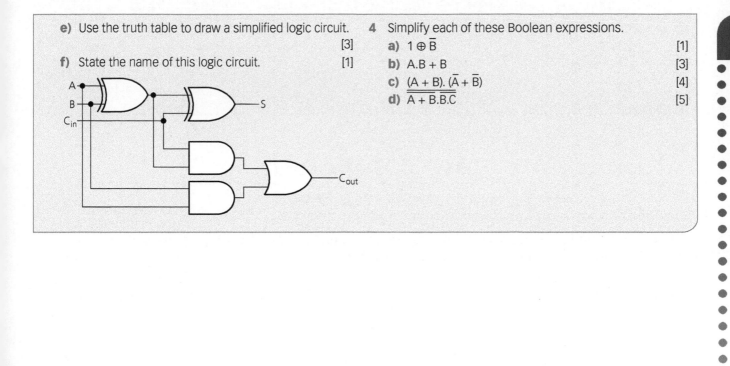

7 Computer organisation and architecture

Internal hardware components

The internal components of a computer system vary slightly between computing platforms, however the basic requirements are the same.

In almost every case the components are connected to a single printed circuit board (PCB) referred to as the motherboard, or logic board.

These components include:
+ processor
+ main memory
+ I/O controllers
+ buses
  + control bus
  + address bus
  + data bus

> **Internal components** The components essential to a computer system.
>
> **Motherboard** The circuit board to which all other components are connected.

The components

REVISED

Processor

The processor, or central processing unit (CPU), is used to process instructions.

Every other aspect of computer hardware is designed around passing instructions and data to the CPU in order to be processed, and then returned.

In some systems it is possible to remove and replace the processor in order to upgrade the system, while in other systems the processor is permanently fixed and cannot be replaced.

The individual components of a processor are discussed later in this chapter.

Main memory

Main memory stores data and instructions that are directly accessed by the CPU. There are two main forms of main memory: RAM and ROM.
+ RAM (random access memory), is volatile storage used to hold the instructions and data for programs that are currently running.
+ ROM (read only memory) non-volatile storage used to hold the startup instructions for the computer

RAM can be easily upgraded in most desktop and laptop computers as each memory module is built onto a small circuit board with standardised connectors.

> **CPU** Electronic device used to process instructions.
>
> **Main memory** Memory that can be directly accessed by the CPU.
>
> **RAM** Short term storage for currently running programs and currently used data.
>
> **ROM** Long term storage for startup instructions.
>
> **Volatile** Data is lost when electrical power is removed.
>
> **Non-volatile** Data is retained even when electrical power is removed.
>
> **Virtual memory** A portion of secondary storage used to store the least frequently-used instructions and data.

> **Note**
>
> When a computer system runs out of main memory a portion of the secondary storage can be allocated as **virtual memory**. The least frequently accessed contents of main memory are placed in virtual memory, which has significantly slower data access times due to the physical limitations (for example, spinning up a magnetic hard drive).

Addressable memory

Inside main memory, each block of memory is given a unique address so that the correct data can be retrieved and passed to the CPU. Without using blocks, the whole of the memory would need to be retrieved each time.

The address is written as a sequence of binary numbers (often represented using hexadecimal).

Instructions and data from different programs are typically grouped together in order to improve efficiency.

I/O controllers

I/O devices (input/output devices) are required to enable computer systems to be used effectively.

Instructions and data must be passed to the memory and processor and the results returned from the system in order for the computer to serve a practical purpose.

External devices include:
+ storage devices (such as HDDs, SSDs, memory cards, optical disc drives)
+ input devices (such as keyboards, mice, webcams, microphones, sensors)
+ output devices (such as monitors, speakers, motors).

I/O controllers provide a hardware interface between the internal computer components and the I/O devices.

> **Note**
>
> In order for an external device to communicate with the computer system it needs a hardware I/O controller and a software device driver.

Each type of I/O controller requires specific hardware for that device; for example:
+ a disk controller (for connecting a HDD or SSD)
+ a keyboard controller (for connecting a keyboard)
+ a video display controller (for connecting a monitor).

These controllers are typically built into the motherboard and use a physical socket for connecting the devices.

> **Now test yourself**   TESTED ◯
>
> 1 Identify **three** pieces of internal hardware.
> 2 Describe the purpose of main memory.
> 3 Give **one** reason why memory should be addressable.
> 4 Identify **three** devices which connect through an I/O controller.
>
> **Answers available online**

Buses

Three buses are used to allow communication between the processor, RAM and the I/O controllers.

Control bus

The control bus is used to send and receive control signals to each device. These signals include commands from the processor and status signals (for example, indicating read or write mode).

The control bus is bi-directional. This means that the messages can be sent both to and from the processor.

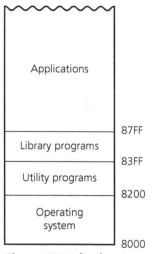

Figure 7.1 A basic memory map

Applications	
Library programs	87FF
Utility programs	83FF
Operating system	8200
	8000

> **I/O devices** Input and output devices such as keyboard, mice, printers and monitors.
>
> **I/O controller** The physical interface between an I/O device and the internal components.

> **Note**
>
> I/O ports are general-purpose controllers that allow a wider array of devices to be connected, for example, USB sockets which allow the use of mice, printers, and even remote-controlled toy rocket launchers.

> **Bus** A communication system for transferring data.
>
> **Control bus** A bus for transmitting control and status signals.
>
> **Bi-directional** Data travels in both directions.

Address bus

The address bus is used to indicate the physical address of the data which is to be accessed (for example, the specific block of memory in RAM).

The address bus is uni-directional. This means that the processor sends out the addresses but does not receive them.

Data bus

The data bus is used to carry the actual data that is required to be transmitted.

The data bus is bi-directional. However in many situations data only travels one way along the data bus (for example, when data is passed to the video display controller, or received from the input controller). Any status messages are passed over the control bus, which is bi-directional.

The three buses work in unison. If some data is required to be fetched from memory then:

+ the control bus carries signals indicating the status of memory (for example, ready to read, ready to write, busy or in error) and indicates that, for example, a read operation is to take place
+ the address bus carries the address of the memory which is to be read (in this example), sent by the processor
+ the data bus carries the data stored in the required memory location to the processor.

It can be helpful to consider a graphical representation of a computer system (Figure 7.2).

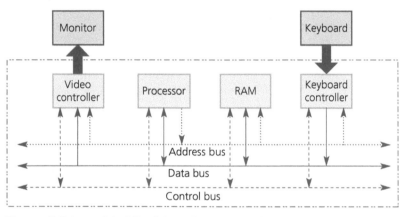

Figure 7.2 A model of the internal components

Note the directionality of each bus.
+ The control bus is bi-directional at all points.
+ The address bus is uni-directional away from the processor.
+ The data bus is sometimes bi-directional, but data only comes in from the keyboard controller and out to the video controller.

> **Address bus** A bus for transmitting memory addresses.
>
> **Uni-directional** Data only travels in one direction.
>
> **Data bus** A bus for transmitting data.

Now test yourself TESTED ⬤

5 Name the **three** buses used in computer architecture.

6 What is transported using the control bus?

7 Which bus is always directed away from the processor?

8 Which bus is often shown on diagrams as being bi-directional at the processor and RAM, but uni-directional at different I/O controllers?

9 On a diagram, how can you identify which bus is the control bus?

Answers available online

Check your understanding and progress at **www.hoddereducation.co.uk/myrevisionnotesdownloads**

von Neumann vs Harvard architecture

Computer architecture refers to the underlying design principles.

In a von Neumann architecture the computer system uses main memory to store both instructions and data.

In a Harvard architecture the computer system uses separate memory for instructions and for data.

> **von Neumann architecture** A computer system design with one shared memory for instructions and data.
>
> **Harvard architecture** A computer system design with separate memory for instructions and data.

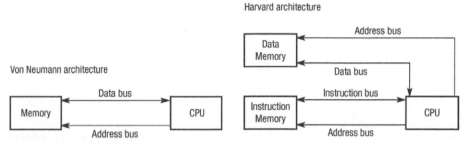

Figure 7.3 von Neumann and Harvard architectures

	von Neumann architecture	Harvard architecture
Advantages	It is flexible because each block of memory can be used for instructions or data as needed. This allows for situations where there are more instructions than data, or more data than instructions.	Can read both instructions and data simultaneously, meaning that it can carry out the instructions more quickly without having to wait for two sequential read operations to be carried out.
Disadvantages	Cannot read instructions and data simultaneously, meaning processing is typically slower.	The ratio of data and instructions stored in memory is fixed, making this system less effective for general-purpose computing
Uses	Used in almost all general-purpose computers due to the increased flexibility.	Used extensively in **digital signal processing (DSP)** hardware. This includes recording and playing back audio, processing images in a digital camera and working with sensors.

10 Which architecture uses two separate areas of memory?

11 For what purpose is Harvard architecture extensively used?

12 Why is von Neumann architecture preferable for general-purpose computer systems?

Answers available online

> **Digital signal processing** Manipulating digitised data relating to analogue signals.

The stored program concept

Whereas early computers required that the program was input as it was run (for example, on punch cards), the stored program concept allows programs to be stored in memory before being run.

✚ In the stored program concept, machine code instructions are stored in memory.
✚ Each instruction is then fetched, decoded, and executed, in order, by a processor.
✚ The processor performs operations on the data – such as arithmetic or logical operations.

> **Machine code** Binary code instructions which can be read and understood by a processor.
>
> **Arithmetic** Mathematical operations such as addition, subtraction and multiplication.
>
> **Logical** Operations using computation logic such as AND, OR and NOT.

Now test yourself TESTED ○

13 How is it possible to execute a computer program without the stored program concept?

14 What **three** steps need to be carried out in order to execute a stored program?

Answers available online

Structure and role of the processor and its components

The processor and its components

REVISED ○

The processor is made up several components, as outlined below.

Arithmetic logic unit

The arithmetic logic unit (ALU) performs arithmetic and logical operations such as addition, subtraction and logical AND operations.

Control unit

The control unit (CU) supervises the fetch-execute cycle, sends and receives control signals and decodes each instruction once it has been fetched from memory.

Clock

The clock generates timing signals which are used to synchronise the tasks within the fetch-execute cycle.

Clock speed is measured in Hz (where 1 Hz = 1 state change per second) and most modern processors operate in the range 1 to 4 GHZ (up to 4 billion state changes per second).

General-purpose registers

General-purpose registers are used to temporarily store data in the processor.

The result of a calculation may be placed in a register if it is known that it will be needed again imminently.

The exact number of general-purpose registers varies, however it is typically in the region of 16-32 for modern desktop processors.

Dedicated registers

Some registers (called dedicated registers) are dedicated to a specific purpose.

The following registers are all used directly as part of the fetch-execute cycle.
✚ Program counter (PC) – stores the address of the next instruction
✚ Current instruction register (CIR) – stores the instruction currently being executed

> **Arithmetic logic unit (ALU)** Carries out arithmetic (mathematical) and logical operations.
>
> **Control unit (CU)** Decodes instructions and sends/receives control signals.
>
> **Fetch-execute cycle** The process by which instructions are fetched from memory, decoded and executed.
>
> **Clock** Generates timing signals.
>
> **General-purpose registers** Registers that can be used to store any data.
>
> **Registers** Small areas of memory inside the processor.
>
> **Dedicated registers** Registers which are dedicated to holding data for a specific, functional purpose.

Check your understanding and progress at **www.hoddereducation.co.uk/myrevisionnotesdownloads**

- Memory address register (MAR) – stores the address of the item in memory currently being addressed. This could refer to an instruction or to data
- Memory buffer register (MBR) – stores the data that is currently being fetched from memory
- Status register (SR) – stores the current state of the processor, such as whether an overflow has been detected

Exam tip

Be familiar with the acronyms for each dedicated register, but make sure you can state each one's full name

Now test yourself   TESTED ○

15 Name the **five** main components in a processor – both the full names and the abbreviations.

16 What two tasks are carried out by the ALU?

17 Which part of the processor is used to decode instructions?

18 What data can be stored in a general-purpose register?

Answers available online

The fetch-execute cycle   REVISED ○

The fetch-execute cycle (sometimes referred to as the fetch-decode-execute cycle, or FDE cycle) describes the steps involved in executing a stored program.

At the start of each cycle the PC (program counter) already stores the address of the next instruction.

Fetch

In this part of the cycle the next instruction is fetched from memory.
1 The contents of the PC are copied to the MAR
2 The contents of the PC are incremented.
3 The address bus transfers the contents of the MAR to main memory.
4 The data at that memory location is transferred to the processor via the data bus.
5 This fetched data is stored in the memory buffer register (MBR).
6 The data (which is an instruction) is transferred to the CIR.

Decode

In this part of the cycle the contents of the CIR are decoded by the processor's control unit.

Execute

The final part varies significantly depending on the exact instruction.

If the instruction involves fetching data from memory then:
- the address of that data is stored in the MAR
- the address bus transfers the contents of the MAR to main memory
- the data at that memory location is transferred to the processor via the data bus
- the fetched data is stored in the memory buffer register (MBR).

If the instruction involves writing data to memory, then the process will be almost identical, except that the data will be transferred from the MBR to main memory via the data bus.

Sometimes the cycle is described in five steps:
1 MAR ← [PC]
2 a PC ← [PC]+1
  b MBR ← [Memory]$_{addressed}$
3 CIR ← [MBR]
4 Decode instruction
5 Execute instruction

163

In this style of question, the square brackets read 'the contents of' and the arrow, ←, reads 'copied to'. For example, Step 1 reads 'The contents of the program counter are copied to the memory address register'.

Note that steps 2a and 2b can occur simultaneously, as both tasks use different registers and do not rely on the result of the other operation.

Now test yourself

TESTED

19 Identify the **three** main stages in the fetch-execute cycle.
20 Describe the first part of the fetch stage.
21 What is the purpose of the program counter?
22 Which register communicates via the address bus?
23 Which register communicates via the data bus?

Answers available online

The processor instruction set

REVISED

Each instruction is made up of an opcode and an operand.

The opcode describes:
+ what operation is to be carried out (for example, add, load, and so on)
+ the addressing mode.

The operand describes:
+ the value(s) which are to be processed.

Each processor has its own processor instruction set.

This instruction set describes the binary machine code for each available operation.

Note that in machine code the addressing mode is included as part of the opcode. In assembly language the addressing mode is typically shown as part of the operand in order to make the assembly language instruction easier to follow, however the addressing mode bit is still stored as part of the opcode.

> **Exam tip**
>
> Questions referring to the fetch-execute cycle are typically longer-answer questions. Make sure you are confident explaining the fetch part of the cycle in particular, including the use of both buses and registers.

> **Opcode** An operation code, describing what operation is to be carried out.
>
> **Operand** The value on which the operation is to be carried out.
>
> **Instruction set** The list of machine code values for each available operation.

opcode							operand(s)							
basic machine operation						addressing mode								
1	0	0	1	1	1	1	1	1	1	0	0	0	1	1

Figure 7.4 An example machine code instruction

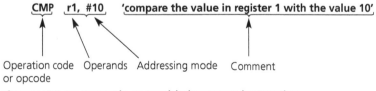

CMP r1, #10 'compare the value in register 1 with the value 10'

Operation code or opcode | Operands | Addressing mode | Comment

Figure 7.5 An example assembly language instruction

Addressing modes

REVISED

The addressing mode describes whether the operand is an immediate value, or the address of a value.

Immediate addressing is when the operand of an instruction contains the number itself. For example:

```
ADD R1, R2, #3
```

This instruction will add the number 3 to the value in register 2 and store the answer in register 1.

Direct addressing is when the operand of an instruction contains an address (either a register number or an address in memory). For example:

```
ADD R1, R2, R3
```

> **Addressing mode** Either immediate or direct.
>
> **Immediate addressing** The operand is the value, which is to be processed.
>
> **Direct addressing** The operand is the address of the value which is to be processed.

Check your understanding and progress at **www.hoddereducation.co.uk/myrevisionnotesdownloads**

This instruction will add the value in register 3 to the value in register 2 and store the answer in register 1.

The exact format of the addressing mode in machine code is specific to that processor's instruction set.

> **Now test yourself** TESTED
>
> 24 What is the purpose of an opcode?
> 25 What is the purpose of an operand?
> 26 Which addressing mode is used for a memory address?
> 27 Why is an addressing mode necessary?
>
> **Answers available online**

Machine code and assembly language operations

REVISED

Each processor has its own instruction set, detailing the specific operations that can be carried out by that processor.

AQA has its own instruction set which is used in Component 2 examinations.

Note

The AQA Assembly Language Instruction Set can be found under 'Other assessment resources' on the AQA website, aqa. org.uk. Search for '7516-7517' and then scroll down to 'Past papers and mark schemes'.

Exam tip

The instruction set is **always** included in the question paper with details of what each operation does and how it should be structured, so you do not need to memorise this content.

Questions may ask you to write your own assembly language code, or to trace an existing algorithm (or both).

This section often causes some confusion for students, so while you don't need to memorise the instruction set, you do need to have practical experience of using it.

Almost all operations include a command and a register address. This is where the result of each operation will be stored. For example:

```
ADD R0, R1, R2
```

The operation is ADD R0, the two operands are R1 and R2.

Thus, the values in register 1 and register 2 will be added and the result stored in register 0.

The operand will either use a # symbol to indicate immediate addressing (such as #25) or Rn to indicate direct addressing, where *n* is the address of a register (such as R4).

Exam tip

Be careful not to mix up your technical vocabulary. The instruction includes both the operation and the operand(s). Referring to the whole instruction as the operation, or vice versa, can cost you marks.

At the start of the following examples the contents of the registers and main memory are as follows.

Registers						Main memory			
R0	R1	R2	R3	R4	R5	100	101	102	103
10	20	5	0			8	12	25	

Load and store

The operation LDR will load, or fetch, data from memory and store it in one of the registers.

The operation STR will store data from a register to an address in memory.

```
LDR R0, 100

STR R2, 103
```

Load Fetch a value from memory into a register in the processor.

Store Copy a value from a register in the processor and save it in memory.

165

The first instruction will fetch the item from memory location 100 and copy it into register 0.

The second instruction will copy the item from register 2 into memory address 103.

Registers						Main memory			
R0	R1	R2	R3	R4	R5	100	101	102	103
8	20	5	0			8	12	25	**5**

Arithmetic

With arithmetic, remember that the first register is the location for storing the result.

```
ADD R4, R0, R1

SUB R5, R1, #2

MOV R3, R5
```

The first instruction adds the value from register 1 to the value in register 0 and stores the answer in register 4.

The second instruction subtracts the decimal value 2 from the value in register 1 and stores the answer in register 5.

The third instruction moves the value FROM register 5 and stores it in register 3.

Registers						Main memory			
R0	R1	R2	R3	R4	R5	100	101	102	103
8	20	5	**18**	**28**	**18**	8	12	25	5

> **Exam tip**
>
> Putting the answer into the wrong register is a very common mistake. For each assembly instruction, fill in the operations as you would a maths problem.
>
> When you see the instruction SUB R5, R1, #2 think (but do not write!) R5 = R1 - #2.

Now test yourself | TESTED ○

28 For the instruction LDR R2, 102, which one of these statements is true?
   A The value 102 will be stored in register 2
   B The value stored in register 2 will be copied into memory
   C The value stored at memory address 102 will be copied into register 2

29 Write the assembly language code for storing the value in register 4 into the memory address 101.

30 What symbol is used to indicate immediate addressing?

31 Explain the effect of executing the instruction MOV R4, R0.

32 If R1 = 10, R2 = 20 and R3 = 30, state the values stored in each register after executing the instruction SUB R2, R1, R3.

Answers available online

Compare and branch

The compare and branch operations allow programmers to create selection and iteration structures in assembly language code.

Remember that you cannot branch on a condition unless you have performed a comparison first.

A selection structure can be created as follows:

```
CMP R3, R5

BEQ same

B diff
```

The first operation will compare the values in register 3 and register 5. The result will be either:
+ EQ (equal to)
+ NE (not equal to)
+ GT (greater than – if R3 > R5)
+ LT (less than – if R3 < R5)

> **Compare** The operation used to check the condition between two values.
>
> **Branch** Jump to a labelled part of the program.
>
> **Selection** A method of choosing whether to execute the following instruction(s).
>
> **Iteration** A method of repeating a section of code.
>
> **Condition** A comparison to see if two values are equal, or whether one is greater/less than the other.

Check your understanding and progress at **www.hoddereducation.co.uk/myrevisionnotesdownloads**

The second operation will branch (or goto) the part of the program with the label 'same' if the result was EQ.

Alternative operations that would also be based on the result of the comparison would be:
+ BNE <label>
+ BGT <label>
+ BLT <label>

The third operation will always branch to the part of the program labelled 'diff'.

In this case the third operation can only be reached if the branch condition in line 2 is not met. This structure works in the same way as a selection statement with an IF and an ELSE component.

An iteration structure can also be created. For example, the code below would create an infinite loop.

```
start:
    ADD R0, R1, R2
    STR R0, 100
    B start
```

And the code below would create a while loop that repeats until the value of register 0 goes beyond 100. After this the section of code labelled 'done' is executed.

```
start:
    ADD R0, R1, R2
    CMP R0, #100
    BGT done
    B start
```

Note that labels for sections of code are written using their name followed by a colon.

All other lines in the program are slightly indented (though always to the same extent).

Bitwise logic

There are four bitwise logic operations and each one involves applying that logical operation to each bit one at a time.

```
AND R0, R1, R2
```

The values of register 1 and register 2 would be processed using a bitwise AND.

Label A named point in the program.

Now test yourself

33 Which operation must immediately appear before a conditional branch?

34 Which opcode would be used to branch if operand 1 was less than operand 2?

35 True or false? Once a branch has been completed, the execution returns to the point at which the branch was made.

Answers available online

TESTED ◯

Bitwise An operation that works on one bit at a time.

Worked example

For the operation AND R0, R1, R2, **calculate the value of register 0 if register 1 has the value 20_{10} and register 2 has the value 5_{10}.**

In binary, register 1 is 0001 0100 and register 2 is 0000 0101.

The AND operation means perform the AND operation on equivalent bits from each register.

Starting with the right most bit (or LSB), we can see that
+ 0 AND 1 = 0   + 1 AND 1 = 1   + and so on.
+ 0 AND 0 = 0   + 0 AND 0 = 0

This gives the result:

```
0001 0100
0000 0101 AND
0000 0100
```

where 0000 0100 is 4_{10} and, therefore, register 0 has the value 4.

Making links

For a more in-depth discussion of logical operations, see *Logic circuits* in Chapter 6.

167

		Registers					Main memory		
R0	R1	R2	R3	R4	R5	100	101	102	103
4	20	5	18	28	18	8	12	25	5

Exam tip

One possible question is to describe the purpose of performing a bitwise AND operation with an operand of 0. This can be used to reset a register to 0 as A.0 is always 0.

Exam tip

To find out if a value is even or odd, perform a bitwise AND operation with an operand of 1_{10}. If the result is 0 then the LSB of the other operand must be 0, meaning that it is an even number. For example:

```
  1110
  0001  AND
  0000
```

The result shows that the value (14) is even.

A similar technique could be used to test the MSB in order to check if a two's complement number is positive or negative. In this case the operand should be a number whose MSB is 1 and all other bits 0. If the result is 0, then the two's complement number is positive, otherwise it is negative.

For example, to show that a) the 4-bit two's complement number –1 is negative, b) the 4-bit two's complement number 4 is positive, using a bitwise AND operation:

```
  1111
  1000  AND
  1000
```

Non-zero result means the two's complement number is negative.

```
  0100
  1000  AND
  0000
```

Zero result means the two's complement number is positive.

The other logical operations all use three characters in the AQA assembly language.

ORR R1, R1, #10

EOR R2, R3, #20

MVN R3, R3

The first instruction will perform a bitwise OR between the value in register 1 and the decimal number 10, storing the result in register 1.

The second instruction will perform a bitwise XOR (exclusive OR) between the value in register 3 and the decimal number 20, storing the result in register 2.

The third instruction will perform a bitwise NOT (move NOT) on the value in register 3 and store the answer in register 3.

```
  0001 0100          0001 0010
  0000 1010  OR      0001 0100  XOR      0001 0010  NOT
  0001 1110          0000 0110          1110 1101
```

Exam tip

To find out if two values are equal, an XOR operation can be used. A XOR 2 (A⊕2) will return 010 if and only if A = 2.

		Registers					Main memory		
R0	R1	R2	R3	R4	R5	100	101	102	103
4	**30**	**6**	**237**	28	18	8	12	25	5

Check your understanding and progress at **www.hoddereducation.co.uk/myrevisionnotesdownloads**

Logical shifts

A logical shift will move all bits to the left or right a given number of places, filling any gaps with zeroes.

```
LSL R0, R0, #1
```

This operation will apply a logical shift left, meaning each of the bits in the value of register 0 will be moved one place to the left. For example:

```
0000 0100 LSL, #1
```

```
0000 1000
```

This has the effect of doubling the value.

+ A left shift multiplies a value by 2^n, where n is the number of shifts.
+ Performing a left shift of magnitude 4 will multiply by $2^4 = 16$
+ This can lead to a loss of accuracy as any overflow is discarded

```
LSR R3, R2, #1
```

This operation will apply a logical shift right, meaning each of the bits in the value of register 2 will be moved one place to the right. The result will be stored in register 3.

```
0000 0110 LSR, #1
```

```
0000 0011
```

This has the effect of halving the value.

+ A right shift divides a value by 2^n, where n is the number of shifts.
+ This can lead to a loss of accuracy as any underflow is discarded.

For example:

```
LSR R4, R2, #2
```

```
0000 0110 LSR, #2
```

```
0000 0001
```

The original number is 6 and the right shift of 2 means 'divide by 4'. The result is calculated as 1 which is not accurate due to underflow.

		Registers						Main memory	
R0	R1	R2	R3	R4	R5	100	101	102	103
4	30	6	**3**	**1**	18	8	12	25	5

HALT

The only operation with more than three letters, the HALT instruction will end the program.

Logical shift An operation involving moving each bit in a given direction.

Logical shift left Moving all of the bits left, doubling the value each time.

Overflow When data is lost because the result is too large.

Logical shift right Moving all of the bits to the right, halving the value each time.

Underflow When data is lost because the result is too small.

Trace tables

A common question is to ask students to hand trace an assembly language program.

Hand trace Manually step through each instruction in an algorithm.

Trace table A table for recording the values stored in each register and memory location.

Worked example

Registers						Main memory			
R0	R1	R2	R3	R4	R5	100	101	102	103
2	10	12	8			3	12	25	

```
    LDR R4, 100
    CMP R4, #1
    BLT labelb
    AND R0, R0, #0
labela:
    ADD R0, R0, R3
    SUB R4, R4, #1
    CMP R4, #0
    BGT labela
    STR R0, 103
labelb:
    HALT
```

Making links

Hand tracing algorithms is an essential skill which is assessed using high-level pseudo-code in Component 1. General advice for hand tracing algorithms is discussed in *Trace tables* in Chapter 4.

- In the first line of the trace table we write down the initial values of the registers and memory locations.
- We work through the code and a new line to the trace table every time a value changes. The first change is to load the value of memory address 100 to R4.
- R4 is not less than 1, so we do not branch, nor add anything to the trace table.
- The next change is `R0 AND 0`. The result is 0, stored in R0.
- Moving on to `labela`, the next change is adding R3 to R0 and storing the result in R0.
- 1 is subtracted from R4.
- These last two lines are repeated until R4 = 0, at which point the value in R0 is stored in memory address 103.

Registers						Main memory			
R0	R1	R2	R3	R4	R5	100	101	102	103
2	10	12	8			3	12	25	
				3					
0									
8				2					
16				1					
24				0					24

This program multiplies the value in register 3 by the value in memory address 100 and stores the result in memory address 103.

Lines 2 and 3 of the program will jump to the **HALT** operation if the value in register 4 is less than 1.

44 Copy and complete the trace table for the following program.

```
MOV R1, R0
ADD R1, R1, R2
SUB R2, R1, R3
EOR R4, R2, R3
LSL R5, R4, #3
```

Registers					
R0	R1	R2	R3	R4	R5
10		15	12		

Answers available online

Interrupts

REVISED

The processor is continually processing instructions, even when a computer seems to be idle.

It is important to be able to get the processor's attention and to alter the sequence of instructions which is about to be processed. This might happen for a number of reasons, such as:
+ timing interrupts; for example, at fixed intervals the screen must be redrawn
+ program error interrupts; for example, if a program has attempted to divide by 0
+ hardware error interrupts; for example, a printer reports a paper jam
+ I/O interrupts; for example, the user has pressed a key.

An interrupt is sent to the processor in order to ensure that it can deal with this event.

In order for the processor to recognise this, the FDE cycle includes a step to check for an interrupt.

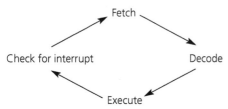

Figure 7.6 A fetch-execute cycle model with a check for any interrupts

Because programs will require a large number of instructions to be processed, when an interrupt is detected then that program's execution must be paused.
+ The current state of the processor and its registers is saved on a stack.
+ The source of the interrupt is identified.
+ The appropriate interrupt service routine is called.
+ The state of the processor is restored from the stack.

An interrupt service routine (ISR) is a software routine which will take an interrupt and examine it in order to determine the best course of action.

This will usually involve adding new instructions to the queue of instructions to be processed.

> **Interrupt** A signal sent to the processor in order to alert it to an event.
>
> **Interrupt service routine (ISR)** A program which will examine an interrupt and handle the event.
>
> **Stack** A data structure in which the most recently added item is returned first.

171

Different ISRs are written for different types of interrupt as the responses to different interrupts will need to deal with that specific event.

TESTED ○

45 Give an example of an event that might trigger an interrupt.

46 When in the fetch-execute cycle is there a check for an interrupt?

47 Explain the purpose of an interrupt service routine.

48 Describe what happens when an interrupt is detected.

Answers available online

Factors affecting processor performance

REVISED ○

There are many factors which can affect the performance of a processor.

Cores

A single-core processor can carry out one instruction at a time.

A dual-core processor can carry out two instructions at a time.

A quad-core processor can carry out four instructions at a time.

… and so on.

However, it is not true that a quad-core processor will be four times faster than a single-core because:
+ some tasks cannot be run in parallel
+ other tasks may cause a delay while waiting for the result of another instruction
+ there is a processing overhead in splitting the task into separate threads.

That said, a quad-core processor will typically complete a set of tasks more quickly than an equivalent single-core processor.

Cache memory

A cache is a small amount of memory located on the processor chip which acts as main memory for the most frequently accessed instructions and data.

The cache can be accessed much more quickly than RAM and, therefore, increasing the size of the cache reduces the average time it takes to fetch frequently-used instructions and data from memory.

Single-core A processor containing a single CPU.

Dual-core A processor containing two CPUs, both working simultaneously.

Quad-core A processor containing four CPUs, both working simultaneously.

Cache A small unit of volatile memory placed on the same circuit board as a processor for fast access.

Clock A component in the processor for generating timing signals.

Note

Most desktop and laptop processors will have three levels of cache: L1, L2 and L3.

L1 is the smallest and offers the quickest access.

L3 is the largest and offers the slowest access – though it is still faster than accessing RAM.

Clock speed

The clock is the processor component that generates timing signals.
+ Most modern processors have a clock speed of at least 1 GHz, which means there are 1 billion state changes per second.
+ Increasing the clock speed means that each instruction is processed more quickly.
+ One significant downside of increasing clock speed is that this generates more heat which will ultimately shorten the lifespan of the processor and make it more prone to errors.

Word length

A binary word is a piece of binary data that can be processed in one unit.

+ Using a 4-bit word length for example, means that only 4 bits can be processed at once. This would mean that adding two 16-bit numbers would be time consuming and would take multiple cycles.
+ Using a larger word length means that larger values can be processed in fewer cycles, improving the overall speed at which a computer will complete its processing.

Most modern desktop computers use a 32- or 64-bit word length.

Address bus width

The address bus is used to transport the address of an item in main memory.

The range of available addresses is limited by the size of the address bus.

If the address bus is:
+ 8 bits wide, then only 256 (= 2^8) addresses can be used
+ 16 bits wide, then 65536 (= 2^{16}) addresses can be used.

Increasing the address bus means that more memory can be addressed.

Data bus width

The data bus is used to transport data from memory to the processor, and vice versa.

Increasing the width of the address bus means that more data can be transferred in one fetch cycle, meaning that less time is lost waiting for data to arrive at the processor.

> **Word** The maximum number of bits that can be processed in one instruction.
>
> **Address bus width** The maximum number of bits that can be used to address a memory location.
>
> **Data bus width** The maximum number of bits that can be transferred at one time.

> **Exam tip**
>
> In the case of word length, address bus width and data bus width, remember that adding 1 bit will **double** the range of possible values. This often catches students out.

> **Now test yourself** TESTED ⬤
>
> 49 Identify **three** aspects of a processor which can affect its performance.
> 50 Explain the difference between increasing the number of cores and the clock speed.
> 51 a What term is used to describe a small, fast block of memory built onto the same circuit board as the processor?
>   b What data is stored in this block of memory?
> 52 What is the significance of the word length?
> 53 What happens to the number of memory addresses that can be accessed if the address bus width is increased by 1 bit?
>
> **Answers available online**

External hardware devices

Input and output devices

REVISED ⬤

There are many input devices and output devices. Four are covered in detail here.

Barcode reader

A barcode reader is an automated input device.

The reader is made of three main components.
+ Light emitter: shines red light at a pattern of black and white vertical bars.
+ Light sensor: reads the pattern of reflected light.
+ Decoder: converts this pattern into digital data.

Barcodes are made of a series of vertical bars, printed in a black and white pattern. They are commonly seen on products such as books as the barcodes themselves are small, cheap and easy to manufacture.

> **Barcode reader** A device for reading barcodes.
>
> **Barcode** A black and white image consisting of vertical bars of different widths to represent data.

The barcode scanner needs direct line of sight in order to function. Obscured, folded or damaged barcodes cannot be read.

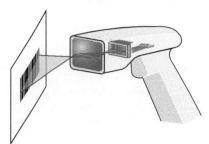

Figure 7.7 A barcode reader and barcode

Digital camera

A digital camera uses a lens to focus light through the camera's body and onto an array of sensors.

+ Each sensor represents one pixel in the image.
+ A colour filter is used to separate the amount of red, green, and blue light being captured.
+ Each sensor reacts to the incoming light and generates an electrical signal.
+ The signals are processed by an ADC and turned into binary data.
+ Each pixel is generated based on the combination or red, green and blue light.

The major advantage of a digital camera as an input device is that it captures a large amount of data compared to a barcode or other simple optical reader.

If the camera is to be used as an automated input device (for example, to identify items passed through a checkout till) this means that a lot of processing is required in order to derive any meaning from the data (as opposed to a barcode scanner).

Digital cameras can be used effectively to recognise objects and to identify faces, though these can be obscured, and identification is not always accurate.

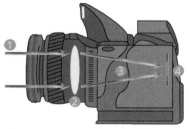

Figure 7.8 A digital camera: light is let in through the shutter (1) and focused by the lens (2); it is directed through RGB filters (3) before being focused onto the sensor array (4)

Radio frequency identification

A radio frequency identification (RFID) tag is used to transmit a small amount of data using a radio frequency over a short distance.

+ Many RFID tags are passive, meaning that they have no internal power source and do not broadcast for most of the time. Instead an RFID scanner broadcasts a radio signal which provides enough power for the RFID tag to respond.
+ Active RFID tags use a battery to allow them to broadcast the signal and have a longer range.
+ RFID scanners are very accurate as it is difficult to distort or obscure the signal accidentally.
+ RFID tags do not require line of sight.
+ However, RFID signals can be shielded using materials which block the radio frequency signal.

> **Note**
>
> Barcodes can be thought of as a one-dimensional data pattern, much like an array of numbers. QR codes are a two-dimensional equivalent, using small squares of black and white to store more data using the same technological principles. QR codes are not covered in the specification, however it may be useful to recognise the similarities.

Digital camera A device for taking photographs stored as digital data.

Pixel The smallest addressable unit of an image.

ADC Analogue to digital converter.

RFID Radio frequency identification.

RFID tag A small device capable of emitting data using radio frequencies.

RFID scanner A device for reading the data from an RFID tag.

Check your understanding and progress at **www.hoddereducation.co.uk/myrevisionnotesdownloads**

- RFID tags are fairly cheap, as well as being small and light. They are slightly more expensive than printing a barcode.
- RFID tags are often used for advertising on public transport, for contactless payment and contactless passports.

Laser printer

A laser printer is a device for creating a physical copy of a document or image on paper.

- When a document is sent to a printer it is converted into a bitmap image.
- Inside the printer a round printer drum is coated in a static electrical charge. A laser is aimed at the drum using a mirror, and the laser beam is modulated (switched off and on) to draw the image.
- Wherever the laser beam touches the drum the charge is removed, and this is where the toner is intended to stick.
- The toner is a powdered form of ink and is given the same static electrical charge as the drum. This means the charged areas of the drum will repel the toner. The drum picks up the toner where the laser has removed the static charge.
- In a colour printer there are four different drums for each coloured toner. The four toner colours are known as CMYK (**c**yan, **m**agenta, **y**ellow, and **k**ey, which is black).
- The paper is rolled over the drum in order to transfer the toner to the paper. Once this is done the toner is fused to the paper using heated rollers.

Laser printers take a short amount of time to warm up, making them slightly slower to print one page. However, they are much faster, much cheaper to run and far less prone to failures than inkjet printers.

Exam tip

Barcode readers, digital cameras and RFID scanners are all methods of data input. As well as understanding their main principles of operation it is common to be asked to compare the suitability of each device for a given scenario.

Laser A device for creating an intense beam of light.

Printer A device for creating a hard copy of a document, usually on paper.

Drum A round device used to attract the toner.

Toner A powdered form of ink with a static charge.

CMYK In a colour printer the colours used are cyan, magenta, yellow and key (black).

Note

The primary colours in printing (CMYK) are different from the primary colours in monitors (red, green and blue (RGB)). This is because monitors use additive colour to add light to an otherwise black display. Printers use subtractive colour to absorb light from an otherwise white piece of paper.

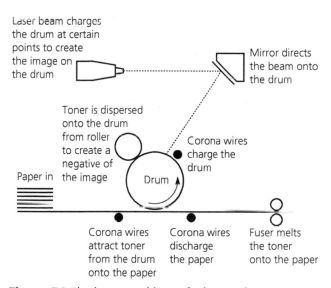

Figure 7.9 The inner workings of a laser printer

Now test yourself

TESTED ◯

54 What are the **three** main components in a barcode scanner?

55 What happens to light when it enters a digital camera?

56 What technology does an RFID scanner use to read data?

57 Give **three** advantages to using RFID as an automated input device rather than a barcode scanner.

58 Name **three** different components in a laser printer.

Answers available online

175

Secondary storage devices

Secondary storage refers to non-volatile storage of programs and data. It is necessary because all volatile data (that is, RAM) will be lost when the system is powered down. Programs and data stored on a secondary storage device can be retrieved at a later date.

> **Exam tip**
>
> Questions on storage devices generally fall into one of two categories:
> 1 Explain the workings of one particular type of storage device in detail.
> 2 Compare the advantages and disadvantages of different storage devices for a given scenario.
>
> For questions of type 1, focus on learning and using the technical vocabulary and you can construct your answer around these key terms.

Mechanical hard disk drive

A mechanical hard disk drive (HDD) uses a metal disk, called a platter, which is coated in a thin film of magnetic material.

+ The film is made up of concentric rings, or tracks, each of which is split up into sectors.
+ Each sector is made up of thousands of magnetic charges, to indicate 0s or 1s that represent data.
+ The platter spins at high speed and a read/write head is moved over the platter, which can both detect and change the magnetic charges in that sector.

Most mechanical hard drives use multiple platters, each with its own read/ write head.

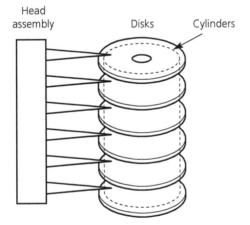

Figure 7.10 HDD platters

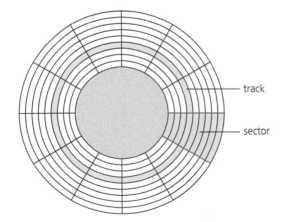

Figure 7.11 HDD tracks and sectors

Secondary storage Persistent, non-volatile storage.

Non-volatile Retains data when powered down.

Volatile Loses data when powered down.

> **Exam tip**
>
> Many students incorrectly assume that secondary storage only refers to backups. In order to avoid this trap, whenever you see the term 'secondary storage', just think 'storage'.

Hard disk drive (HDD) A storage device which saves data using magnetic film.

Platter A metal disk used to store the data in a HDD.

Track A concentric ring on a platter.

Sector A small section of a track.

Read/write head The device used to read and write magnetic data to each to sector.

Solid state disk drive

A solid state disk drive, often referred to as a solid state drive (SSD), has no moving parts.

+ An SSD is made up of NAND flash memory, and a controller.
+ NAND flash memory is non-volatile and is based on floating gate transistors.
+ The storage is split up into blocks, and each block is split up into pages.
+ Pages cannot be over-written – they must be erased first. However the whole block must be erased.
+ The controller is used to manage these complexities.

SSDs have lower latency and faster access speeds than HDDs, due to the lack of moving parts. However they have a limited number of read and write actions before the flash memory degrades.

As well as SSDs there are several types of solid state storage device, including SD cards and USB sticks.

Solid state drives are gradually replacing HDDs in desktop and laptop computer systems.

Figure 7.12 shows the principle of NAND flash memory. When the control gate is turned on, electrons flow from the source to the drain, and some of those electrons are attracted into the floating gate. When the control gate is turned off, the electron flow stops and electrons in the floating gate are trapped there. The presence, or not, of electrons in the floating gate corresponds to a '1' or '0' state.

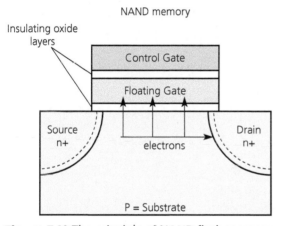

Figure 7.12 The principle of NAND flash memory

Optical disk

Optical disks include the CD (compact disc), DVD (digital versatile disc) and BluRay. Optical refers to light, and the data is read using a laser beam which is a form of light.

+ Data is stored on one spiral track that covers the disk, and this track uses pits (indentations) and lands (bumps).
+ The laser beam is shone at the disk, focused at a point on the track
+ The laser light is reflected back to a sensor while the disk spins at a constant linear velocity.
+ Where a pit or land continues, a certain amount of light is reflected back to the sensor, representing a 0.
+ Where there is a transition between a pit and a land, the light is scattered which means a different amount of light is reflected back to the sense – this represents a 1.

> **Note**
>
> Because the distance around the outside of the disk is much further than the inside of the disk, the disk will spin at different speeds so that the portion of the track being read by the laser moves at a constant velocity relative to the laser.

Solid state disk drive (SSD) A storage device with no moving parts that uses flash memory and a controller.

NAND flash memory Memory which can be electrically erased and reprogrammed.

Controller A component of an SSD which manages the reading and writing.

Floating gate transistor Used as a memory cell in flash memory.

Block A subdivision of the storage on an SSD.

Page A subdivision of a block.

Latency The time taken for the first signal to reach its destination.

> **Note**
>
> The spelling 'disk' is generally used in computing terms, though the terms CD and DVD are standards defined using the spelling 'disc'. You will not be penalised for your choice of spelling.

Optical disk A storage medium which uses light to read the data.

CD Compact disc, typically used for audio and small computer programs.

DVD Digital versatile disc, typically used for medium quality video and medium sized computer programs.

BluRay A high-capacity optical disc typically used for high definition video and large computer programs.

Track A spiral line that covers the CD, containing pits and lands.

Pits Small indentations in the track.

Lands Small bumps in the track.

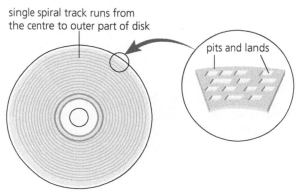

single spiral track runs from
the centre to outer part of disk

pits and lands

Figure 7.13 The workings of an optical disk

Comparing capacity and speed

It is important to be able to make a practical judgement about the suitability for different storage devices in different circumstances.

The technology (and particularly the cost and the capacity) are constantly changing; however the basic principles remain consistent.

The main areas for comparison are capacity and access speed, however cost and robustness are also factors to consider.

	Hard disk drives	Solid state disk drives	Optical disks
Capacity	Typically have a very large storage capacity (frequently measured in TB).	Have a range of capacities, typically measured in GB and increasingly available in the TB range.	Small storage capacity (700 MB for CDs up to 50 GB for BluRay).
Access time	Access time is quite slow.	Access time is extremely fast due to the lack of moving parts.	Access times are extremely poor and is by far the slowest of the three technologies discussed here.
Cost	The overall cost of storage is very low.	The cost is higher than for an equivalent capacity HDD.	The cost to produce one disk is very low, though the overall cost per GB is quite high.
Robustness	Fairly robust, although they can be damaged if dropped and can be affected by very strong magnetic fields.	Very robust and difficult to accidentally damage. However, there are a limited number of read and write actions before the memory degrades.	Robust – they can be dropped without too much damage. However, they are easily scratched and exposure to UV light can degrade the tracks.
Applications	An effective solution for archived storage of large quantities of data.	An effective solution as a storage device in a laptop or desktop due to their fast response time.	Suitable for transporting data in small batches, such as computer programs, films and music.

Capacity The amount of data that can be stored.

Access speed The time taken to read or write data.

Cost This can mean the cost per device, or cost per GB.

Robustness How likely the device is to break or be damaged.

Exam tip

When asked to compare solutions it is vital to refer back to the scenario given in the question, as the effectiveness of each solution will depend heavily on the requirements in that specific case.

Now test yourself

62 Which storage device has the fastest access time?

63 Which storage device typically has the largest capacity?

64 Which storage device would be most suitable for use in a mobile phone? Justify your answer

65 Which storage device would be most suitable for sharing copies of a computer program? Justify your answer

Answers available online

Summary

+ The internal hardware of a computer system includes the processor, main memory, I/O controllers, and buses
+ Main memory is addressable so that each section of memory can be retrieved when needed
+ I/O controllers are hardware interfaces between the internal components and external devices
+ The three buses are the control bus, address bus and data bus
+ The control bus is used to transmit control and status signals
+ The address bus is used to transmit the address where data is to be read or written, from the processor to memory
+ The data bus is used to transmit data to and from different components
+ von Neumann architecture uses one area of memory for both instructions and data, and is used in general-purpose computers
+ Harvard architecture uses two distinct areas of memory, one for instructions only and one for data only, and is used in embedded systems such as digital signal processing systems (DSPs)
+ Programs can be saved in memory so that they can be executed repeatedly without having to input the program each time
+ Machine code instructions are fetched from main memory and executed by the processor
+ The processor is made of five key components – the arithmetic logic unit (ALU), control unit, clock, general-purpose registers and dedicated registers
+ The ALU carries out all arithmetic and logical operations
+ The control unit decodes instructions and sends control signals to other devices
+ The clock generates a timing signal so that each process can be synchronised
+ General-purpose registers are used to store data that is being worked on by the processor
+ Each dedicated register is used for a specific purpose, mostly related to the fetch-execute cycle
+ The dedicated registers are the program counter (PC), memory address register (MAR), memory buffer register (MBR), current instruction register (CIR) and the status register (SR)
+ The fetch-execute cycle is often referred to as the fetch-decode-execute cycle as there are three phases
+ It is important to be familiar with the steps involved in the fetch phase of the F-E cycle
+ Each processor has its own instruction set, describing the machine code for each operation

+ Each instruction is made up of an opcode (including the addressing mode) and an operand
+ When using immediate addressing the operand should be treated as the value (also known as the datum) to be operated on
+ When using direct addressing the operand should be treated as the address of a value in memory or a register
+ In assembly code programming each opcode is represented as a short piece of text
+ AQA examinations use a consistent assembly language instruction set which is provided in the exam paper – it is important to be familiar with using this assembly language instruction set to write simple programs and to hand trace existing programs
+ Basic AQA assembly language operations include: load, add, subtract, store, branching, compare and halt
+ Bitwise logical operations such as **AND**, **OR (ORR)**, **XOR (EOR)** and **NOT (MVN)** are carried out one bit at a time
+ Logical shifts involve shifting the binary values to the left (**LSL**) or right (**LSR**) a given number of times
+ A logical shift left has the effect of doubling the value each time
+ A logical shift right has the effect of halving the value each time, though at the risk of loss of accuracy due to underflow
+ Interrupts are signals which need to get the processor's attention as it carries out the F-E cycle
+ There are four main types of interrupt – timing, program error, hardware error and I/O interrupt
+ When an interrupt is triggered the state of the processor is stored on a stack, the source of the interrupt is identified, the appropriate interrupt service routine (ISR) is called and the state of the processor is restored
+ An ISR is a program designed to decide on the best course of action to follow for a given interrupt
+ Increasing the number of cores in a processor means that more instructions can be carried out simultaneously
+ Increasing the clock speed of a processor means that each instruction takes less time to complete
+ A cache is a small, very fast area of memory used for storing the most frequently accessed instructions and data
+ The word length dictates the number of bits which can be processed in a processor core in any one cycle
+ The address bus width limits the range of available memory addresses
+ The data bus width limits the amount of data which can be fetched from memory in one cycle
+ A barcode reader emits a red light which is aimed at a black and white image made of bars

+ The sensor in the scanner reads the reflected light and the decoder converts this into a digital code
+ Barcodes are cheap, small and light, but require line of sight and can easily be obscured or damaged
+ A digital camera uses a lens to focus the incoming light onto a sensor chip with an array of sensors which produces an electrical signal
+ Each sensor represents one pixel
+ A colour filter is used to separate the amount of red, green, and blue light being captured.
+ Each sensor electrical signal is processed by an ADC
+ Digital cameras collect a large amount of data, which requires a lot of processing in an automated system
+ RFID (radio frequency identification) is able to transmit data over a short distance using radio waves
+ Active RFID tags use a battery to allow them to broadcast the signal and have a longer range.
+ Passive RFID tags take power from the radio frequency energy taken from the signal sent by the RFID scanner
+ RFID tags are cheap, small, and light, and do not require line of sight
+ A laser printer applies electrical static charges to a drum and toner and uses a laser beam, switching on and off, to remove the electric charge on the drum and attract toner to areas that should be black
+ The drum rolls over the paper, transferring the toner which is then fused to the paper
+ A mechanical hard disk drive (HDD) uses platters split into tracks and sectors
+ The platter of a HDD is coated in a magnetic film which can be read and written to using a read/write head
+ A solid state disk drive contains NAND flash memory and a controller
+ The SSD data is stored using floating gate transistors and is split into blocks and pages
+ An optical disk uses a single spiral track filled with pits and lands
+ A laser beam is used to read the data on an optical disk, with a transition between a pit and a land representing a 1
+ HDDs typically have a large capacity and a medium access time
+ SSDs typically have a medium capacity and a fast access time
+ Optical disks typically have a small capacity and a very slow access time

Exam practice

1   A general-purpose computer is being designed.
    a) Name **three** internal components that must be included in the design. [3]
    b) State whether the computer should use von Neumann or Harvard architecture. [1]
    c) Justify your answer to part b). [2]

2   A computer system has a 2 GHz, dual core processor.
    a) Explain why a 1.5 GHz, quad core processor might be able to complete a task more quickly. [2]
    b) A computer has an address bus of 7 bits. Describe the impact of increasing the size of the address bus by 1 bit. [2]
    c) Identify **two** other ways to improve the performance of a processor and explain the impact of each. [4]
    d) Describe the steps involved with fetching and executing an instruction from memory using the full names for any registers involved. [6]

3   a) Look at this assembly language program. Follow the program to copy and complete the trace table. [4]

```
label1:
    AND R4, R1, #1
    CMP R4, #0
    BNE label2
    LSR R1, R1, #1
    LSL R2, R2, #1
    B label1
label2:
    STR R1, 101
    STR R2, 102
    HALT
```

Registers						Main memory			
R0	R1	R2	R3	R4	R5	100	101	102	103
	12	1							

    b) Explain the purpose of the instruction AND R4, R1, #1. [1]
    c) Explain the effect of applying a logical shift left by 4. [2]
    d) Explain the potential problem with applying a logical shift right. [2]

Check your understanding and progress at www.hoddereducation.co.uk/myrevisionnotesdownloads

4 Write an assembly language program to carry out the following high level algorithm.

The mathematical operator // represents an integer division.

Assume that register R1 holds the value of A, R2 holds the value of B, R3 holds the value of C and registers R4-R10 are available if needed. [8]

```
B ← A // 4

B ← B * 4

IF B = A THEN

    C ← 1

ELSE

    C ← 0
```

5 A new footwear shop is considering how to enter customer purchases into its computer system. The options available are using a barcode scanner, digital camera or RFID scanner. Discuss the advantages and disadvantages of each and identify a suitable recommendation. [8]

6 A student is buying a new laptop for college and is unsure whether to purchase a laptop with a mechanical HDD or a solid state disk drive.

a) Identify **two** components that make up a mechanical HDD. [2]

b) Identify **two** components that make up a solid state drive. [2]

c) Describe the advantages and disadvantages for each option and identify a suitable recommendation. [6]

Moral, ethical, legal and cultural issues and opportunities

The increasingly widespread use of technology has brought about many changes, most of which feature a combination of positive and negative consequences.

It is important to be able to discuss both previous examples (case studies) and potential future developments (hypotheticals).

Questions on this topic may be asked in relation to some technical details covered in other chapters (for example, networks in Chapter 9, encryption in Chapter 5, automated input devices in Chapter 7, or robust program design in Chapter 1). However, no new technical knowledge is required specifically for this topic.

> **Hypothetical**
> Consideration of a 'what if...' scenario.

Definitions

`REVISED`

+ Moral and ethical issues relate to what is right or wrong, and how consequences might affect individuals and groups of people. For example, an automated telephone answering system might mean that a company makes more profit by reducing the need for human call handlers, however it might mean that the user experience for the customer is less satisfying and will likely have a negative consequence for the staff who are no longer needed.
+ Legal issues relate to the law. This might refer to those making laws, enforcing laws and those who may break laws.
+ Cultural issues relate to how the culture of a society changes. For example, the widespread availability of computing equipment and fast internet access has allowed many more people to work from home. This has both positive and negative consequences such as reduced travel costs, but also a lack of social interaction that previously happened in the workplace.

Communication and information flow

`REVISED`

Governments, companies, organisations, and even individuals are increasingly able to capture vast quantities of data about people. This includes:
+ location data
+ browsing data
+ shopping habits
+ contact details
+ political opinions.

This data may be collected, stored, analysed and even sold without our knowledge or understanding. With so much data available:
+ behaviour can be monitored – for instance, enabling your mobile phone location and Bluetooth allows third parties to collect an incredible level of detail about where you are every second of the day
+ multiple sources of data can be combined and analysed to build up very detailed pictures about someone – for instance where they shop, how much they spend, who they spend time with, how much they earn, how fit they are
+ This data may be published and distributed outside the user's control – for instance, when material such as photographs are uploaded to social media sites, their terms and conditions normally allow the site to reuse as they wish – even though you might think it is 'your' photograph.

Users' personal data and personal preferences can be used in a variety of ways, with or without their consent, and the consequences of how this data is collected and how it is used has a significant impact on individuals, society, and on the culture of that society.

Software engineers and computer scientists must make decisions about the algorithms they design, the systems they build and the software they write in order to benefit, rather than harm, individuals and societies. They must ensure that appropriate moral and cultural values are embedded within their software. This can mean many things, but examples could include:

+ voice recognition systems that struggle to interpret regional accents
+ facial recognition systems that display racial bias.

In both of these examples, appropriate moral, ethical and cultural values have not been embedded into the software.

> **Personal data** Data that relates to an identifiable person.
>
> **Moral** Relating to the principles of right and wrong.
>
> **Cultural** Relating to the ideas, customs and behaviour of a society.

Negative consequences may also occur because of …	Example
… a deliberate act.	A programmer includes a secret login so that they can access data without detection once the system is running.
… poor anticipation of consequences.	A Google street view car captures and publishes images of someone getting changed in front of a window.
… poor design decisions.	A programmer chooses not to encrypt data before it is transmitted over a network.
… a mistake.	An error in the way the login process is handled means that a user can trick the system into giving them administrator access.

The people who develop systems must think carefully about what data is to be collected, how it can be collected, how it should be stored, what processing will occur and how the results of the processing should be used.

Another point to consider is that software is scalable. This means that:

+ once written and compiled, the internet allows the same software to be easily distributed to almost anywhere in the world
+ one piece of software could be installed on literally millions or even billions of computers.

> **Scalable** Used to describe a product, service or business that can cope with increased demand.

This represents the tremendous impact that software developers and computer scientists can have, and why they must consider all of the ethical, moral, legal and cultural impacts of their code.

> **Now test yourself** TESTED ○
>
> 1 Identify **four** items of personal data that are typically stored in online systems.
> 2 When creating software, suggest **three** ways that inappropriate consequences could be introduced into the program.
>
> **Answers available online**

Legislation

REVISED ○

It is not necessary to have a detailed knowledge of computing-related legislation, though it may be useful to have a basic knowledge of some key examples.

Computer Misuse Act

This legislation is used to prosecute individuals who attempt to gain unauthorised access to a computer system. This includes attempting to gain access, copying data, editing data and deleting data. The emphasis is on discouraging people from committing malicious acts on another system and making hacking illegal.

Data Protection Act

As organisations collect, store and process personal information, steps should be taken to ensure that the data cannot be accessed by unauthorised parties, and that the data cannot be tampered with. This may well involve password protection, data encryption, anti-malware and other protective measures.

The Data Protection Act puts the emphasis on organisations who hold data to make sure that the data is protected. It is important to note that small, community-based organisations who keep a mailing list of email addresses are subject to the Data Protection Act just as much as multi-national corporations.

> **Note**
>
> The Data Protection Act was updated in 2018 to implement the General Data Protection Regulation (GDPR). A detailed understanding of legislation is not required however and either term would be accepted.

> **Making links**
>
> Encryption is an important aspect of ensuring that data cannot be understood. Techniques for encryption are explored in Chapter 5.
>
> Network security concerns, including malware, are discussed in Chapter 9.

Copyright, Designs and Patents Act

Often shortened to simply 'copyright', this legislation sets out what can and cannot be legally reproduced or copied. Any original piece of work (such as an image, script, video, music or software code) is automatically protected by copyright law which means it cannot be copied, used, or re-distributed without permission, with a few small exceptions.

Regulation of Investigatory Power Act (RIPA)

RIPA aims to describe what powers the police and other authorities have to demand access to personal data stored by online services, such as social networking companies, internet service providers and mobile phone manufacturers.

The aim is to strike a balance between protecting individual freedom for users, with the need to allow investigations that are in the interests of national security, convicting criminals and helping to locate missing persons.

Other relevant legislation

Depending on the context of the question, other legal issues may well occur. For example, in a partially automated factory there may be health and safety considerations, driverless cars may be subject to road traffic legislation, and consumer law may be relevant if the consequences affect customers.

Challenges for legislators

It takes a long time for new legislation to be written and for existing legislation to be updated.

As technology continues to change at an increasingly rapid pace it can be very difficult for legislators to keep up with these changes and to make sure that the legislation is effective, unambiguous and relevant.

> **Now test yourself** TESTED
>
> 3 What piece of legislation makes it illegal to distribute films, games and albums without permission?
>
> 4 Other than computing-specific legislation, suggest **two** other legal issues relating to self-driving cars.
>
> 5 Dave keeps a list of email addresses and phone numbers for the players in a small, local football team. What legislation does he need to consider?
>
> **Answers available online**

Check your understanding and progress at **www.hoddereducation.co.uk/myrevisionnotesdownloads**

Case studies

In order to explore the topic of the consequences of computing, it can be useful to look at past examples and to discuss both the technological details and the moral decisions behind a particular event.

Self-driving cars

Some cars currently include a semi-driverless mode, in which sensors are used to keep the car from drifting out of its lane and the car can steer itself as well as controlling throttle and brake application in order to avoid potential hazards. Drivers are instructed that they are still responsible for the vehicle and should remain in control at all times.

Collisions which occur when drivers are using semi-driverless mode tend to be high profile, and in many such cases the drivers have been distracted and not in full control of the car at the time of the collision.

+ Is it safe to force cars to stop if the driver lets go of the steering wheel?
+ Could cameras be used to track drivers' eye movements in order to ensure they are paying attention to the road?

Many sensors are used on automated vehicles in order to identify potential hazards and obstructions, however it is very difficult to create programs that can accurately identify objects under all conditions and contexts.

Despite the higher profile new coverage of collisions involving automated vehicles, the overall rate of accidents per mile is typically far lower than that for manually driven cars.

> **Making links**
>
> Fully autonomous cars will use machine learning to acquire the skills needed to drive. It requires vast amounts of data to learn from – there is more on Big Data in Chapter 11.

Google street view

Google street view allows users to see locations before they visit. Vehicles with roof-mounted cameras drive along roads, capturing images in all directions. These images are then made available on the internet so that the public can view them.

This is helpful for people planning journeys and also to help people look at the surrounding area before deciding to visit or move to that area. These images can also be used in news stories to help provide viewers and readers with a geographical context.

There are several potential ethical issues relating to the use of Google street view.

+ Many people are concerned about an invasion of privacy and are unhappy at the idea of Google storing and sharing images of them without permission.
+ Personal details such as faces and number plates are blurred using image recognition techniques, though it cannot be guaranteed that all personal data has been obscured.
+ There are concerns that there are potential security risks with showing exact routes and features. This includes areas of high risk such as government buildings, but also private homes and businesses.

Malicious programmers

There have been many cases where a programmer has written code that will collect personal data that is not necessarily needed or has created a method by which they can collect data that they should not have access to.

Relevant legislation such as the Computer Misuse Act and the Data Protection Act is appropriate for discussion here, and it is reasonable to ask how the situation could have been prevented.

The sharing and auditing of code within an organisation is important in order to be able to recognise situations where a programmer has, either maliciously or accidentally, introduced inappropriate code. Security vulnerabilities can then be fixed and, if a programmer has made an inappropriate ethical decision, this can be resolved.

> **Exam tip**
>
> It is common for questions of this type to not have a 'right' and 'wrong' answer. Credit is awarded for identifying, discussing and evaluating potential issues.
>
> | |
> |---|
> | Marks are awarded for identifying relevant knowledge; for example, suggesting appropriate input devices for collecting data or identifying the methods by which wireless data transmissions can be intercepted. |
> | To reach the top mark bands it is important to follow a line of reasoning, using your knowledge to write in connected sentences in a way that makes sense and relates to the context of the question. Explaining how each point links to the scenario and adding as much technical detail and vocabulary as you can makes it more likely that you will score well on this type of question. |
> | Always make sure you back up any arguments or suggestions you make with facts, logical arguments and technical details, as unsubstantiated statements don't demonstrate your understanding. |

Now test yourself TESTED

6 What technological solutions could be used to encourage the drivers of semi-driverless cars to maintain focus and control of the vehicle?

7 How can a company reduce the likelihood that a programmer will add inappropriate or malicious code into a product?

8 What could a company such as Google do to help reduce complaints of invading privacy when capturing and sharing street view images?

Answers available online

Hypotheticals

REVISED

Another strategy for preparing for these types of questions is to ask 'what if...?'.

Web-based social networking and cloud storage systems

A system that allows users to upload and share information and resources is a common context for questions on the consequences of computing.

A decision must be made regarding what data is to be collected and stored, including geographical information, user preferences, and how much access the administrators of the service should have to the content uploaded by individual users.

In terms of legislation, it is the responsibility of the administrators to ensure that data is protected. This means that data should be stored securely, communication should be encrypted and password policies should be enforced.

It is also important to consider copyright implications, as the creators of the service could be held liable if the users are distributing material which cannot legally be shared.

Users have the right to be forgotten, that is the right to have all personal data removed from an organisation. It is a legal, but also an ethical consideration as to whether any posts, files or other items uploaded are removed, or simply anonymised.

The Internet of Things (IoT)

The Internet of Things refers to the use of internet enabled, 'smart' devices. This includes:

+ plugs
+ lights
+ televisions
+ fridges
+ coffee machines
+ doorbells
+ thermostats
+ washing machines
+ security cameras
+ digital assistants.

Each device is designed to be accessed by the user over the internet so that they can access information and issue instructions to the device while away from home.

Login systems must be robust so that unauthorised users cannot access the device. A baby monitor, security camera or doorbell camera could give a potential intruder detailed information about the layout and contents of a home as well as information about typical routines and when the home is empty.

Systems that control objects means that a malicious user, or an error in the code, could cause devices to malfunction and potentially cause damage. For example:

+ a smart device for managing the environment in a tropical fish tank could lead to temperatures too high or too low for the fish to survive
+ altering a smart thermostat could lead to an empty house suffering frozen pipes or an increase in heating bills.

> **Internet of Things (IoT)** Physical devices able to share data or to be controlled using a connection to the internet.

> **Making links**
>
> The Internet of Things and the increasing use of smart devices means that a vast amount of data is being captured at high speed and in many different forms. This is referred to as Big Data, and the approaches for storing and processing Big Data are discussed in Chapter 11.

> **Revision activity**
>
> Find or create a list of as many smart devices as you can. For each one, identify potential ways in which a malicious user could take advantage of the device if they had access to it.

8 Consequences of using computers

> **Now test yourself** TESTED
>
> 9 Identify **two** potential legal issues with creating a system in which users can upload and share content.
>
> 10 Suggest **two** security risks associated with the use of smart, IoT devices.
>
> **Answers available online**

Summary

+ Computer systems make it easier and more common for organisations to collect personal data
+ How that personal data is used has significant consequences that affect individuals, groups, and larger societies
+ Moral and ethical consequences are those that affect individuals and groups of people. These consequences can be positive or negative, and are usually elements of both
+ Cultural consequences affect the way that a society works, thinks or behaves
+ Computer scientists and software engineers have a responsibility to ensure that systems are developed with these consequences in mind
+ Design decisions should consider how data is to be collected, stored, processed and used
+ Consideration should be taken of the impact on individuals and on society at large
+ Computer-based legislation includes the Computer Misuse Act, Data Protection Act, Copyright, Regulation of Investigatory Powers Act, and Designs and Patents Act

+ Other legislation is often relevant depending on the circumstances, including health & safety, road safety and consumer rights legislation
+ Legislation often lags behind changes in technology as it takes time to recognise the need for it and then create tightly defined legislation to deal with the consequences of that technology
+ Case studies of current and recent ethical consequences of computing issues are an effective way of preparing for questions on this topic
+ Hypothetical, what if, questions are a useful approach to preparing for this topic
+ Questions on ethics will often include a technical element that relies on knowledge of other topics such as network security, data collection methods and effective program design
+ To reach the top mark bands it is important to follow a line of reasoning and to back up your points with facts, logical arguments and technical details

Exam practice

1 A company wishes to produce an automated garage door opener. The door should automatically open when the homeowner returns.

Discuss a range of technologies that could be used to allow the automated garage door opener to function and consider the moral, ethical, legal and cultural consequences of using this device. [12]

9 Fundamentals of communication and networking

Communication

Communication methods

In serial data transmission each bit is sent one after another. This can be done with a single wire, or a single track on a circuit board.

In parallel data transmission multiple bits are sent simultaneously. To achieve this there must be multiple wires or multiple tracks on which to send the data.

In theory it is quicker to send data over a parallel connection as more data can be transferred at once. However, there are several reasons why most communication is sent serially:

+ Crosstalk occurs when the signal in one wire causes electrical interference with the signals on the neighbouring wires.
+ Data skew can occur, meaning that one or more bits can be read incorrectly by the receiver if the transmission is not correctly synchronised.
+ The hardware for serial communication is simpler (and, therefore, cheaper) to produce.

In synchronous data transmission both sender and receiver must be in sync. This means that a common clock must be used and the timing signal must be sent in addition to the data.

In asynchronous data transmission there is no common clock.

The sender will send a start bit at the beginning of a transmission to indicate that the data is about to be sent. A stop bit will be sent at the end of that transmission. A start bit will be 0 and a stop bit will be 1.

The process then repeats, and the receiver is able to use the start bit to synchronise its clock to that of the sender. This synchronisation is carried out each time a start bit is received.

Additionally, a parity bit might be added before the stop bit in order to allow error checking to occur.

Finally, the transmission is often shown in reverse, indicating which bits will be received first by the receiver. If so, then the MSB would be on the right hand side.

A typical transmission of an ASCII character using odd parity might work as follows:

Character to transmit: M

ASCII value: 77_{10} or $100\ 1101_2$

Parity bit : 1

Data transmitted:

Stop bit	Parity bit	Data							Start bit
1	1	1	0	1	1	0	0	1	0

Notice that the data is represented in reverse order.

Serial data transmission Data is sent down one wire, one bit after another.

Parallel data transmission Data is sent on several wires, simultaneously.

Crosstalk Interference caused when two or more worse are in close proximity.

Data skew When data that was sent at the same time arrives at a slightly different time to each other.

Synchronous data transmission Where data is sent along with a timing signal.

Asynchronous data transmission Where data is sent without a timing signal.

Clock Used to provide a timing signal.

Start bit A bit sent at the start of a message in order to provide timing data.

Stop bit A bit sent to mark the end of a message.

Parity bit A bit used in error detection.

ASCII A 7-bit code used for representing characters as binary numbers.

Exam tip

Parity bits are sometimes included in questions on start and stop bits.

Now test yourself | TESTED ◯

1 Describe the main difference between serial and parallel data transmission.

2 In synchronous data transmission, what is transmitted other than the data itself?

3 In asynchronous data transmission, what is transmitted other than the data itself?

Answers available online

Communication basics

REVISED ◯

When data is transmitted a signal is sent which changes at fixed time intervals to indicate a new value.

Each signal can represent more than one binary digit by using more than one possible value. For example, an electrical current can be sent with a different voltage.

The baud rate is the number of state changes per second and is measured in Hz. For example, at a baud rate of 100 kHz there are 100 000 changes to the signal per second.

The bit rate is the maximum number of bits that can be transferred per second. This can be calculated by multiplying the baud rate by the maximum number of bits per signal.

The bandwidth describes the range of possible signals, and a larger bandwidth means that a larger number of distinct values can potentially be sent in one signal.

The bit rate is directly proportional to the bandwidth; in other words, if the bandwidth doubles, then there are twice as many possible unique symbols that could be sent. This means that the bit rate doubles as well.

The latency describes the time it takes for the first signal to reach its destination. This is not linked to the baud rate, bit rate or bandwidth of a connection. For instance, a high bandwidth connection can have a high or low latency depending on a number of other factors such as physical distance.

A protocol is a set of rules or standards, and a number of transmission protocols exist. These are essential as different systems need to be able to communicate with each other.

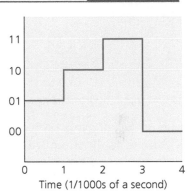

Figure 9.1 Sending multiple bits per value at a baud rate of 1 kHz and a bit rate of 2000 bits per second

Baud rate The number of state changes per second.

Bit rate The number of bits that can be transmitted per second.

Bandwidth The range of possible signals that can be sent in one signal.

Latency The time taken for the first signal to reach its destination.

Protocol A set of rules or standards.

Now test yourself | TESTED ◯

4 What term refers to the range of possible values in one received signal?

5 What term refers to the time it takes for a signal to arrive at its destination?

6 What term refers to the number of signals that can be sent or received per second?

7 How is the total bit rate calculated?

8 What is the definition of a protocol?

Answers available online

Networking

Network topology

The topology of a network describes the physical or logical layout of that network.

Bus topology

In a bus topology a main cable, or bus, is used to transmit all data across the network.

Each device connects to the bus, meaning that no central switch is necessary.

> **Topology** The physical or logical arrangement of connections in a network.
>
> **Bus topology** A network arranged with a main cable, or bus, connecting all devices.

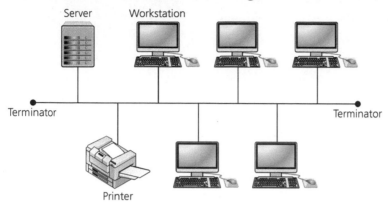

Figure 9.2 A bus network

Advantages of a bus network:
+ Simple cabling requirements.
+ Easier to add new devices as the new cabling doesn't need to go all the way back to a central point.

Disadvantages of a bus network:
+ Affected by high traffic as all traffic must use the main bus.
+ Weaker security as all data is transmitted to all devices.
+ Weaker reliability due to the reliance on the main bus – if that fails, the whole network fails.

Star topology

In a star topology, a central switch is used to connect each device on the network together. All data transmissions are passed through a link to the switch which then forwards the data on to the intended recipient.

Many small networks, and almost all home networks, are based on this topology.

> **Star topology** A network arranged with a switch (or hub) at the centre.
>
> **Switch** A device that receives and forwards data on a network.
>
> **Link** A physical connect between two devices.

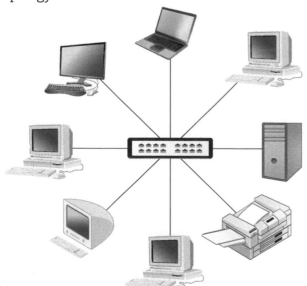

Figure 9.3 A star network

Check your understanding and progress at **www.hoddereducation.co.uk/myrevisionnotesdownloads**

Advantages of using a star network include:
+ copes well with high traffic as only the links between the switch and the relevant devices are used, meaning that data can be transferred between the switch and different devices at the same time
+ improved security – the data is only sent to and from the intended device
+ improved reliability – if one device or link fails then the rest of the network is unaffected.

Disadvantages of using a star network include:
+ cabling requirements can be complex as multiple cables are needed
+ adding new devices means running an extra cable back to the central switch
+ adding devices quite far away from the switch increase the cabling complexities
+ if the central switch fails then the whole network fails.

It is possible to use a hub instead of a switch at the centre of a star topology. A hub will broadcast all signals it receives, creating a logical bus network topology. This means that whilst it has been arranged as a physical star network, it actually operates like a bus network – for instance, all data will be transmitted to all devices. This approach is not advised or common practice any more.

> **Logical bus network topology** A star network that uses a hub as the central device, which causes it to operate like a bus network.

> **Note**
>
> An increasingly common network topology is the mesh network. In a mesh network each device can be connected to two or more other devices, allowing for more possible routes across the network.
>
> The internet is the most significant example of a mesh network, and many larger Wi-Fi networks make use of a mesh topology.
>
> The mesh is not covered in the specification and is unlikely to appear in an exam, however it is an important topology to understand if you wish to study networking in more detail.

Logical versus physical topologies

The physical topology refers to the physical layout or arrangement of the cabling and connections between devices on the network.

The logical topology refers to the way that the data flows around a network.

It is possible for a physical star topology to behave as if it were a bus topology by transmitting all data to all devices.

> **Now test yourself** TESTED ⬤
>
> 9 What device is always used in a star network?
> 10 What does the word 'bus' refer to in a bus network?
> 11 What is the definition of a physical topology?
> 12 How can a network have a different physical topology and logical topology?
>
> 13 Give **two** advantages and **one** disadvantage for using a star network.
>
> **Answers available online**

Types of networking between hosts

Client–server

In a client–server network, a server controls access to a centralised resource; for example:
+ files, in a file server
+ emails, in an email server
+ web pages, in a web server.

The client requests access to the resource and the server then processes the request, decides whether access should be granted and provides the service or response.

> **Client–server network** A network in which clients make requests to servers.
>
> **Client** A device which makes requests.
>
> **Server** A device which controls centralised access to a resource.

191

Client–server networks are used where the central resource must be managed; for example:

+ selling seated tickets to a show
+ assigning seats on an aeroplane
+ managing a centralised backup
+ managing centralised security (anti-virus, firewalls, software updates, and so on)
+ managing a centralised login system.

In client–server networks security is increased as there can be a centralised login or permissions system. However, configuration of the network is more complex and running a separate central server requires additional work.

For small, simple networks a server can be a fairly low powered machine such as a standard workstation. For most situations, however, a server should be a specialised computer with a lot of processing power and memory.

One example of a client–server network is a school network with a centralised file server, print server, and email server.

Peer-to-peer

In a peer-to-peer network all devices have an equal status, and no resource is centrally controlled.

Each resource can be stored on one or multiple devices on the network and can be accessed by any other device on that network.

This effectively shares the storage and processing load across the devices and is useful for situations where no central control is needed, or when a large number of requests might cause delays if relying on a central server.

Peer-to-peer networks are frequently used for accessing or sharing large files, as segments of the file can be stored on and copied from any device on the network with that segment.

Peer-to-peer networks don't require a central server and are typically easier to set-up and maintain. Management of security is more difficult, however, and it is difficult to ensure data consistency across the network.

One example of a peer-to-peer network is a simple home WiFi network in which files can be sent to or from any device on the network.

> **Peer-to-peer network** A network in which all devices are peers.
>
> **Peer** Of equal standing, able to act as a client or a server.

	Advantages	Disadvantages
Client–server	Better security – software and security updates managed centrally, logins and access to files/folders also controlled. Data backups easier to manage as all held in one place.	If the server goes down then all clients are affected. Access times may be slow if the server gets too many requests from different clients at the same time. More expensive because of the costs involved with maintaining the central server. A hacker targeting the server can bring down the network.
Peer-to-peer	Easy to set up. Less expensive to set up – doesn't require specialist hardware. Network unaffected if one device fails.	Less secure – all devices have to have software and security updates run individually, so outdated security is more likely. Multiple versions of files on different devices. Each device needs to be backed up individually.

> **Exam tip**
>
> Questions on client–server or peer-to-peer networks tend to be longer discussion and comparison questions. Make sure that you consider the context of the question and remember that a server is always used in systems where centralised control is important.

Check your understanding and progress at **www.hoddereducation.co.uk/myrevisionnotesdownloads**

Now test yourself TESTED ◯

14 Describe the role of a server.
15 Describe the role of a client.
16 What is meant by a peer-to-peer network?
17 Give **three** advantages and **two** disadvantages for using a client–server network.

Answers available online

Wireless networking

REVISED ◯

Wireless networking uses radio frequencies in order to transmit data over a relatively small area (such as a house or office), called a local area network (LAN).

Wi-Fi is an international communication standard for wireless networking.

No cabling is required in a wireless network, meaning that devices can be moved easily without disrupting communication.

In order to connect to a wireless network, a wireless access point must be used. This is a device which broadcasts and receives the wireless signal to and from the devices on the network.

A wireless access point can be, and frequently is, connected to a wired network in order to allow both wired and wireless connections, as necessary.

Each device connecting to the wireless network requires a wireless network adapter. This can be built into the device (for example, on a computer's motherboard) or added later (for example, through an expansion card or USB wireless adapter).

Each wireless network has a service set identifier (SSID) which appears as the 'name' of the network. Enabling the broadcast of the SSID makes it easier for new users to join a network.

Wireless security

The nature of wireless networking means that any device within range of the wireless signal will be able to intercept and read the data being transmitted, without needing to gain physical access to the network.

There are several methods for dealing with this security risk:
+ Disabling SSID broadcast.

  Broadcasting of the network's SSID can be disabled. Disabling the broadcast means that only users who are aware of the network and know its SSID will be able to connect.
+ Strong encryption

  Data sent over a wireless network should be strongly encrypted. Several encryption methods exist including WEP and WPA. Most wireless networks use WPA2 encryption as this offers significantly stronger encryption than other methods.

  Only users with the encryption key are able to send and receive data over the wireless network, and while other devices can read the data being transmitted, this cannot be understood without the key.
+ MAC address whitelist

  A MAC address (or media access control address) is a unique hardware address assigned to each network interface card (which includes wireless network adapters).

  By enforcing a whitelist, only those MAC addresses on the whitelist will be able to access the network and any other devices will be refused access.

Wireless network A network that allows devices to transmit data using radio frequencies.

Wi-Fi A set of technology standards that allows devices to communicate using radio frequencies.

Wireless access point A hardware device for allowing other devices to connect to an existing wireless network.

Wireless network adapter A hardware device for enabling devices to communicate using Wi-Fi.

SSID Service set identifier- an identifier, or name, for a wireless network.

Note

Wi-Fi is not an acronym and is not a directly shortened form of any longer words.

Wi-Fi is not the only wireless communication method. Bluetooth, 5G, NFC and Zigbee all make use of radio frequencies to allow wireless communication.

Encryption A method of scrambling data so that it cannot be understood.

MAC address A physical address, uniquely assigned to each piece of network hardware.

Whitelist A list of things considered to be acceptable or trustworthy.

193

18 What technology does a wireless network use for communication?

19 What two hardware devices are needed to create a wireless network?

20 What is an SSID?

21 What two pieces of information are usually required for a device to access a wireless network?

22 Identify **three** ways to ensure that wireless data transmissions are secure

Answers available online

Avoiding collisions

If two or more devices attempt to transmit data at the same time, there will be a collision and the data will be unreadable.

To avoid this there are two systems in use, often used together.

CSMA/CA stands for carrier sense multiple access with collision avoidance.

The aim of CSMA/CA is to allow devices to recognise when a duplicate broadcast is occurring and to wait a random period of time before broadcasting again. It works as follows:

+ Sending device checks for traffic.
+ If another device is broadcasting, the sending device waits before repeating the process.
+ If no other device is broadcasting, the data is transmitted.

RTS/CTS stands for request to send / clear to send.

Using RTS/CTS the device wishing to transmit sends an RTS request and waits for a CTS response from the receiver. If the CTS response is not received, the sender wait a random amount of time before sending the RTS again.

The random amount of time is used to ensure that, if two devices attempt to broadcast at the same time, it is unlikely that both will attempt to broadcast at exactly the same time again.

Once a CTS response has been received, the data is transmitted.

Finally, the receiver should respond with an acknowledgement (ACK). If this is not received then the data is resent.

The full process can be written as follows.
+ Sending device checks for traffic.
+ If another device is broadcasting, the sending device waits before repeating the process.
+ If no other device is broadcasting, an RTS signal is sent.
+ The receiving device sends a CTS response if it is ready to receive the transmission.
+ If no CTS response is received, the sending device waits a random period of time before repeating the process.
+ If a CTS response is received, the data is transmitted.
+ The receiving device sends an acknowledgement (ACK) once all data has been received.
+ If the sending device does not receive an ACK then it repeats the process.

Collision Where two items of data are transmitted at the same time, causing both to be lost.

CSMA/CA Carrier sense multiple access/collision avoidance. A method of collision avoidance by checking for existing transmissions.

RTS/CTS Request to send / clear to send. A method of collision avoidance by requesting clearance to transmit.

23 What is the main aim of using CSMA/CA and RTS/CTS?

24 How does CSMA/CA improve wireless transmissions?

25 When a wireless device sends a request to send, what does it aim to receive?

26 When a wireless device has finished sending a message using RTS/CTS, how does it know if the transmission has been received?

Answers available online

Check your understanding and progress at **www.hoddereducation.co.uk/myrevisionnotesdownloads**

The internet

The internet and how it works

The internet is a global collection of networks, all able to communicate with each other.

Packet switching

With so many networks connected together, the internet uses a mesh topology in which each network is potentially connected to many other networks.

This means that data can take many different routes in order to reach its intended destination.

Each time data is sent over the internet it is split into equal sized portions, or packets. These packets contain a portion of the original data as well as a header that provides the packet number and information relating to each layer of the TCP/IP stack (see *TCP/IP Layers* below).

Each packet can take different routes across the internet, meaning that bottlenecks can be avoided and if a packet is lost then only that packet needs to be re-sent rather than the whole of the original data.

This is known as packet switching.

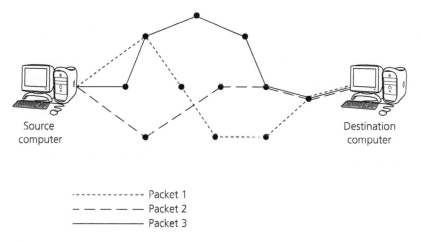

Figure 9.4 An example of packet switching showing the paths of three different packets

While a switch is used inside a network to direct packets to their destinations, a different device is needed to connect a network to other networks and the internet.

Router

+ A router is used to connect different networks together. When a router receives a packet it will read the destination IP address (see *IP address* section below).
+ If the packet is intended for that router's network then the packet will passed into the network. If the packet is intended for another network then it will be forwarded to another router.
+ A router will try to pass the packet to its destination via the fastest route possible. This is done either by using the fewest number of steps or using the route that is least congested at that moment.
+ In order to complete this task a routing table is created which is used to store the routes to particular network destinations.

> **Note**
>
> As described in *Network topology* above, the mesh topology is increasingly common, but is not covered in the AQA specification and so you should not be asked any questions relating to this topic.

> **Mesh topology** A network topology in which each device can be directly linked to several other devices.
>
> **Packet** A small parcel of data, including a header.
>
> **Header** Extra data added to a packet such as the destination address or packet number.
>
> **Bottleneck** A congested path within a network.
>
> **Packet switching** The process of sending individual packets on different routes.
>
> **Router** A network hardware device for connecting different networks together.

Gateway

+ A gateway also connects different networks together. The unique function of a gateway is to connect networks that use different protocols.
+ While a router can check the destination address and then forward a packet, a gateway will strip most of the header data away and create new headers so that the packet can be transmitted through the next network.

> **Gateway** A network hardware device for connecting networks that use different protocols.

Now test yourself TESTED ◯

27 What is the name for a small parcel of data?
28 What hardware device is used to connect networks using different protocols?
29 What hardware device is used to connect networks using the same protocol?
30 Give **two** advantages for using packet switching.

Answers available online

URLs and domain names

A uniform resource locator (URL) is a method for addressing a resource on another network.

The most commonly known example of a URL is a web address, though URLs are also used for other purposes including email and file transfer (FTP).

A URL is made up of several component parts.
+ Protocol: HTTP or HTTPS for webpages, FTP for file transfer, and so on.
+ Domain name: The identifier for the network.
+ Path: The names of any folders and/or the file to be accessed.

> **Making links**
>
> There are several key network protocols covered in this chapter. They are discussed in more detail later in Chapter 9.
>
> A number of protocols use URLs to locate resources. More information on specific protocols can be found in Chapter 9.

$$\underbrace{\text{http://}}_{\text{protocol}}\underbrace{\text{www.awebsite.co.uk}}_{\text{domain name}}/\underbrace{\text{index.html}}_{\text{path}}$$

Figure 9.5 An example URL

Domain names are used to identify the organisation or individual on the internet, and use a string format with each component separated by full stops.

The elements of a domain name are processed from the right hand side, with the top level domain (TLD) typically indicating the nature or location of the domain's subject, such as .co.uk, .gov, .org

The central part of the domain name indicates the organisation or individual that the resource is linked to. For example, www.aqa.org.uk is a website run by and about the AQA exam board.

The left-most part of the domain name is the hostname, which usually refers to a specific computer or server within that domain. It is typical for webservers to use the www hostname (www.awebsite.co.uk), while email servers will often use the mail hostname (mail.awebsite.co.uk), etc.

A fully qualified domain name (FQDN) addresses an exact resource and can only be interpreted in one way. In order to achieve this they must include a hostname.
+ awebsite.com/index.html is not a fully qualified domain name
+ www.awebsite.com/index.html is a fully qualified domain name

However, when packets are sent to a server over the internet the packet is addressed to an IP address rather than to a domain name.

> **Uniform resource locator (URL)** A standard structure for addressing an online resource using alphanumeric strings.
>
> **Protocol** The standard or rule for that type of communication.
>
> **Domain name** The identifier for an individual or organisation's online presence.
>
> **Path** The location of the file or folder on a server that is being addressed.
>
> **Top level domain (TLD)** The right-most term in a domain name, such as .com or .uk
>
> **Hostname** The device within the network that is being addressed.
>
> **Fully qualified domain name (FQDN)** A domain name that addresses an exact resource, including a hostname.

IP address

An IP address is a numeric addressing method that identifies devices on the internet. The current most version uses four 8-bit numbers, each written in decimal between 0 and 255, separated by full stops. An IP address is typically represented in dotted-decimal format; for example, 107.162.140.19.

Examples:

123.456.789.123 – invalid, no number can be greater than 255.

217.83.4 – invalid, there must be four numbers.

4.0.0.1 – valid.

IP addresses are long, difficult to remember and easy to mistype. The IP address for a particular network or server can also change from time to time, and so humans use domain names which are much easier to remember and are much more meaningful.

In order to translate between a domain name and an IP address the domain name system (DNS) is used.

DNS uses a lookup table to find the corresponding IP address for a given domain name, just as a mobile phone contacts list is looked up when a phone call is made.

A computer will send a request to a DNS server in order to find the correct IP address, and will then send packets to the required server with that IP address.

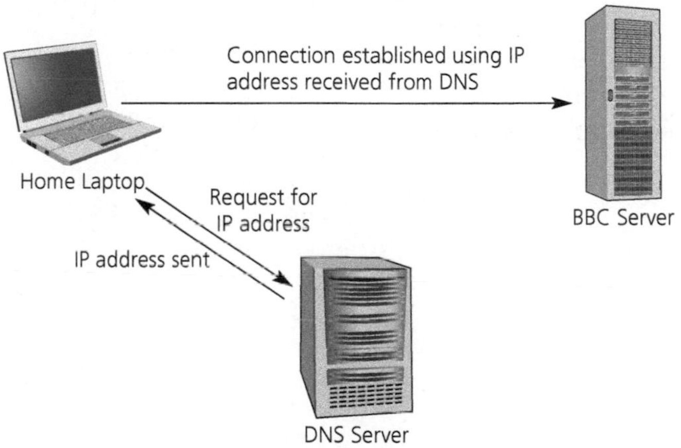

Figure 9.6 Carrying out a DNS lookup before requesting data from a server

Internet registries are organisations responsible for the allocation of IP addresses. There are a very small number of registries, each covering a different geographical area, in order to ensure that address allocation is strictly controlled.

> **IP address** A numerical address for a device on a network.
>
> **Dotted-decimal** A format for writing an IP address with decimal values separated by dots.
>
> **Domain name system (DNS)** A system for looking up domain names to find their corresponding IP address.
>
> **Internet registry** A body responsible for allocating IP addresses.

Now test yourself   TESTED ◯

31 Name the three main parts of a URL.

32 State **three** rules describing the format of an IP address.

33 Explain why domain names are used instead of IP addresses.

34 What system is used to convert a domain name to an IP address?

35 Describe the process of accessing a web page, based on entering a URL

36 How is it possible to avoid two domain names having the same IP address?

Answers available online

Internet security

The nature of the internet means that data is routed across several other networks before it reaches its destination. This means that packets can be intercepted and that any device connected to the internet can also be subject to a potential attack.

Firewalls

A firewall is used to check and potentially stop packets entering or leaving the network. It can be a piece of software on each individual computer or a hardware device that acts as a proxy server.

+ Stateful inspection refers to examining the contents of a packet in order to decide whether the data itself is suspicious. The firewall keeps a record of all current connections in order to identify whether a packet is part of an ongoing communication.
+ A proxy server is a physical device that sits between a private network and a public network. All data to and from the private network goes via the proxy server. It can therefore stop packets that have left a computer before they reach the public network and can prevent packets from the public network entering the private network, before they get to the computer.
+ Packet filtering refers to stopping packets based on their destination or source IP address or their protocol. A firewall can be configured to allow web traffic, but to block FTP packets, or can refuse to send or receive packets addressed to or from a suspicious IP address. This can help prevent data being unknowingly sent from the device and can stop a malicious program downloading other malicious files.

Proxy servers give each device inside a private network a level of anonymity as the public network can only communicate with the proxy server. It also allows for packet filtering to occur for the entire network, at an institutional level, regardless of the configuration of each individual device within a network.

Encryption

Encryption is a method of scrambling data so that, if intercepted, it cannot be understood.

Making links

Encryption is an important principle that is used extensively in network communications, but also in non-networking situations as well. The basic principles of encryption, as well as two examples of symmetric encryption ciphers, are discussed in *Encryption* in Chapter 5.

Symmetric encryption refers to encryption where the same key is used to encrypt and decrypt the data. Symmetric encryption can be secure, however the need for both the sender and the receiver to have access to the same key creates a significant security risk.

In asymmetric encryption a different key is used to encrypt and to decrypt the data. Knowing the key used to encrypt the data does not allow the data to be decrypted. This works as follows:

+ The intended recipient of some data generates a public key and a private key that are mathematically related. The public key is made publicly available, but the private key is not.
+ The sender uses the public key to encrypt the data which cannot be decrypted without the private key. Therefore, only the intended recipient can decrypt the data and they are never required to share the private key.

Figure 9.7 Private/public key encryption

Firewall A software or hardware service that blocks or allows individual packets from entering or leaving.

Stateful inspection Inspecting the data contained in a packet.

Proxy server A device that sits between a private and a public network.

Packet filtering Stopping packets based on their IP address or protocol.

Now test yourself

37 Is a firewall a piece of hardware or a piece of software?

38 One way in which a firewall secures network traffic is packet filtering. Identify **two** others.

39 Explain how packet filtering is used to keep a device secure.

Answers available online

TESTED

Encryption Scrambling data so that it cannot be understood.

Symmetric encryption The same key is used to encrypt and to decrypt a message.

Key A value used to encrypt or decrypt an encrypted message.

Asymmetric encryption Different keys are used to encrypt and to decrypt a message.

Public key A key that is made public. Has a matching private key.

Private key A key that is kept secret. Has a matching public key.

9 Fundamentals of communication and networking

Check your understanding and progress at **www.hoddereducation.co.uk/myrevisionnotesdownloads**

This method of encryption is used in almost all online transactions, including login pages and financial transactions. Removing the need to transmit the private key (as is the case in symmetric encryption) vastly reduces the risk of the data being breached.

Digital certificates

One potential flaw in the use of asymmetric encryption is that an impersonator could share a public key, claiming it is the public key for an intended recipient.

Digital certificates are provided by a certification authority and include a serial number, an expiry data, the name of the organisation, their domain name, and a copy of the public key.

If a website has a public key but no valid certificate this will trigger a warning when trying to communicate with that server as the authenticity of the public key cannot be verified.

Digital signatures

A digital signature uses a checksum to ensure that a message has not been altered during transmission.

The original message is passed through a checksum algorithm to produce a digest. The digest is then encrypted with the sender's private key which means that it can be decrypted by anyone with the sender's public key.

The digest is included at the end of the original message before it is encrypted with the recipient's public key and transmitted.

When the recipient receives the message it is decrypted with the recipient's private key, and the digest can then be additionally decrypted using the sender's public key.

The checksum algorithm can be applied to the decrypted message and compared to the decrypted digest. If the two do not match it is assumed that the message was altered in some way during transmission.

> **Digital certificate** A digital document indicating that a public key is valid.
>
> **Certification authority** A body capable of providing digital certificates.

> **Digital signature** A method of checking that an encrypted message has not been altered.
>
> **Checksum** A value, calculated by an algorithm, based on the contents of the original data.
>
> **Digest** A checksum value used in a digital signature.

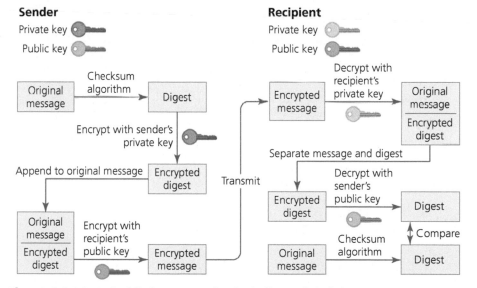

Figure 9.8 Private/public key encryption including a digital signature

Making links

Checksum algorithms are used in a variety of stations to verify that data has not been damaged or altered, not just in networking. The topic of error checking, including a more detailed look at checksum algorithms, is discussed in Chapter 5.

Exam tip

It is very easy to mix up the terms digital certificate and digital signature. Remember that you cannot award yourself a certificate, that must be done by someone else (a certification authority). You can sign a document yourself though, and this method uses the encrypted checksum/digest.

Now test yourself

TESTED

40 Who can issue a digital certificate?

41 What is the purpose of using a digital signature?

42 In a digital signature, why is the digest encrypted using the sender's private key?

43 Identify at least six of the 10 steps involved in using a digital signature.

Answers available online

Malware

There are several types of malware that are used to try to cause damage or intercept data.

Some malware will attempt to delete or destroy data, others will capture data such as usernames and passwords which can be sent back to the malware's creator.

Virus

+ A virus is a small piece of malicious code which attaches itself to an existing program. The virus remains inert until the program it is attached to runs, at which point the malicious code is executed.
+ A virus will typically add a copy of itself to another program and will often attempt to distribute itself to other devices by automatically sending emails with an infected attachment or infecting files in shared workspaces.
+ The key feature of a virus is that the host program must be run in order to execute the malicious code.

Trojans

+ A Trojan is a piece of malware that is disguised as a useful program. When the program is run then the malicious code is executed.
+ Unlike viruses, Trojans do not attempt to replicate themselves into other programs. Trojans are typically spread through user interaction, for example downloading a program or opening an email attachment.

> **Note**
>
> A Trojan gets its name from the story of the Trojan horse. A Greek carpenter built a giant statue of a horse which was then filled with soldiers and left as a gift for the Trojans who were at war with the Greeks. The Trojans brought the horse into their fortified city and the soldiers were able to climb out at night and open the gates, allowing the rest of the army in. This is also why the word Trojan is usually capitalised.

Worms

A worm functions in a manner similar to a virus in that it is self-replicating. However, worms do not need to attach themselves to a file in the way that a virus does, and instead spreads over a network.

Once a worm is active it exploits vulnerabilities in the systems software to replicate and transmit its code to other devices on the network.

Protective measures

There are many ways to protect a system from malware.
+ Firewalls can be used to monitor packets being sent across a network. They can identify unusual or suspicious communication and prevent packets from being sent or received.
+ Anti-virus programs scan files and emails for malicious code. It is vital to keep anti-virus software up to data as new malicious code is always being created.
+ Education for users can help prevent people from running suspicious files or downloading content from suspicious emails.
+ Code quality is key. Bugs, errors, and edge-cases in software programs can all be exploited by malicious programmers.

Malware Malicious software.

Virus Malicious code that attaches to another program and self-replicates when executed.

Trojan A malicious program that pretends to be a useful program, does not self-replicate.

Worm A malicious program that copies itself over a network.

Anti-virus Software that scans programs for malicious code.

Bug A mistake in a computer program that causes unexpected results.

Edge-case A problem that only occurs in an extreme setting.

> **Note**
>
> The detailed nature of specific techniques to avoid security flaws is beyond the scope of this topic, however it is a tremendously important and a growth industry in the field of computer science and software engineering.

Now test yourself   TESTED ⬤

44 What is meant by *malware*?

45 Name **two** types of malware that can copy themselves.

46 Name **one** type of malware that does not copy itself.

47 Which type of malware can copy itself over a network without needing other users to run it?

48 Identify **four** ways of protecting against malware.

Answers available online

Check your understanding and progress at **www.hoddereducation.co.uk/myrevisionnotesdownloads**

The Transmission Control Protocol/Internet Protocol

TCP/IP

REVISED ⬤

There are lots of processes involved in sending a data packet around the internet. To simplify this, different processes are separated into layers and each layer follows a set of rules, or protocols, to complete each process.

TCP/IP is a fundamental protocol used in network communications and is split into four layers.

TCP/IP layers

Each data packet is processed at each layer in order to add the additional data necessary so that the packet can be directed and checked until it arrives safely at its destination.

At the application layer an individual application will format the data so that it can be recognised by that application. This is done using a protocol, many of which are described in the next section. An example is HTTP – the protocol used to transmit websites to web browsers.

This formatted data will then be dealt with at the transport layer, which is responsible for two main jobs:
+ Checking that all packets have arrived and are in the correct order. To achieve this the transport layer adds a packet number to the original data.
+ Identifying which application layer software should deal with the packets. To achieve this the transport layer adds a port number to the packet. The port number indicates which application layer protocol should be used when the packet is received.

The network layer deals with addressing and routing of the data packet, carrying out three main jobs.
+ Adding the sender IP address and recipient IP address.
+ Routing a packet to the next host.
+ Adding error checking bits (when sending data) and checking for errors (when receiving data).

> **Exam tip**
>
> Always try to be as specific as possible. If asked about the function of the network layer, the response 'adding an IP address' is not detailed enough. 'Adding the sender's IP address' is a much more specific answer.

The link layer is responsible for the physical transmission of the packet. This differs between data sent over a wired network and a wireless network, for example.

Once a packet has been sent from one device to another it is processed in reverse order. For this reason it is often referred to as the TCP/IP stack.

> **Making links**
>
> A stack is a LIFO (last in, first out) data structure which is useful in a range of situations. This, and other data structures, are explored in Component 1 and it is expected that you will be familiar with using stacks in a programming context. For more detail please refer to *Stacks* in Chapter 2.

> **Making links**
>
> Ports are discussed and explained in *Sockets and ports* below.

> **Transmission Control Protocol / Internet Protocol (TCP/IP)** One of the main protocols used in network communications.
>
> **Application layer** Formats data according to the application to be used.
>
> **Transport layer** Adds a port number, packet number and error detection data.
>
> **Port number** Extra data added to a packet that identifies what application layer protocol should be used to process the data.
>
> **Network layer** Adds sender and receiver IP addresses.
>
> **Link layer** Deals with the physical medium used for transferring the data.
>
> **TCP/IP stack** The use of the TCP/IP layers to add header data which is then processed in reverse order.

If a packet has been sent to a wireless access point then the receiving device will remove the data relating to the link layer in order to check the destination address, before adding new link layer data required to send the packet over a wired part of the network to a router.

The router might then send the packet over the internet to another router which will, again, strip off the link layer data, check the destination address and add new link layer data to send the packet to the next router.

After arriving at the destination, the link layer data will be stripped off, the IP address verified at the network layer and the transport layer will then check the packet for errors, check the port number and attempt to reorganise the packets in the correct order before passing the data back to the application layer for processing.

Note

There are several models for the TCP/IP stack, including 4-layer, 5-layer and even 7-layer versions. AQA explicitly use the 4-layer model described here.

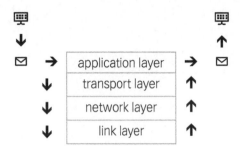

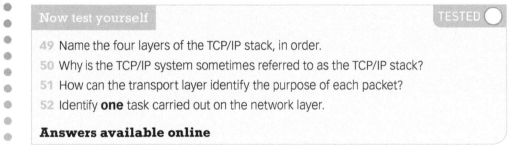

Figure 9.9 The layers in the TCP/IP stack

Exam tip

To help remember the four layers in the TCP/IP stack it can be useful to use a mnemonic. For example, **A**ll **T**eachers **N**eed **L**lamas. If the image of your teacher hanging around on their day off with a pet llama isn't memorable enough you can always create your own.

Now test yourself TESTED ◯

49 Name the four layers of the TCP/IP stack, in order.
50 Why is the TCP/IP system sometimes referred to as the TCP/IP stack?
51 How can the transport layer identify the purpose of each packet?
52 Identify **one** task carried out on the network layer.

Answers available online

Sockets and ports

An IP address is sufficient to identify a device on a network. However, more information is needed to help identify what should happen to a packet once it reaches its destination.

A port number is added to each packet at the transport layer which indicates which protocol, and therefore which type of application, should deal with the data.

Some commonly used ports include:

Port Number(s)	Purpose	Protocol
80	Unencrypted web pages	HTTP
443	Encrypted webpages	HTTPS
25	Receiving mail	POP3
110	Sending email	SMTP
21	File transfer	FTP
22	Remote shell access	SSH

Exam tip

Make sure you can remember the relevant port numbers associated with different protocols.

When the port number and IP address are both known, this is commonly written using a colon as a separator; for example:

107.162.140.19:80

The combination of IP address and port number is described as a socket. The socket provides an end-point for the communication.

Individual sockets can be opened or closed by a firewall, either allowing or blocking traffic addressed to that socket.

MAC addressing

Each network interface card (NIC) has a unique Media Access Control (MAC) address. This is sometimes referred to as the physical address as it is permanently configured at the hardware level and does not change.

The link layer uses MAC addressing to identify exactly which device it is sending the data to within that network in order to ensure that the data is sent to the correct device.

> **Now test yourself** TESTED
>
> 53 What port number is associated with email?
> 54 What service or protocol is associated with port 22?
> 55 What is the difference between a packet sent over port 80, and one sent over port 443?
> 56 What two pieces of information are needed to make up a socket?
> 57 Why does the link layer of the TCP/IP stack use a MAC address rather than an IP address?
>
> **Answers available online**

Standard application layer protocols

REVISED

There are several common application layer protocols, each one relating to a different practical purpose.

It is not necessary to know all of the standards and rules within each protocol, but it is important to be able to identify the purpose for each.

Protocol	Full name	Purpose
FTP	File Transfer Protocol	Transferring files
HTTP	Hypertext Transfer Protocol	Transferring (unencrypted) web pages
HTTPS	Hypertext Transfer Protocol Secure	Transferring encrypted web pages
POP3	Post Office Protocol version 3	Transferring email
SMTP	Simple Mail Transfer Protocol	Transferring email
SSH	Secure Shell	Remote management

FTP

An FTP server manages access to a store of files and a client using FTP client software can request access to those files. Permissions can be granted on a file by file and folder by folder basis, allowing the client to potentially download and/or upload files remotely.

FTP servers can also be configured to require a login, or to provide anonymous access.

> **Exam tip**
>
> It is helpful to have had practical experience using FTP software, although questions will not be asked in reference to specific examples of FTP programs.

HTTP/HTTPS

A web server functions in a similar way, storing the resources and layout information for web pages. A web browser acts as a client, requesting particular information which is generated and returned by the web server.

Once the data has been received the web browser renders the data in the appropriate format on the screen.

Data that does not need to be secure can be sent using HTTP, which is unencrypted. Data that does need to be secure is sent over HTTPS, which is encrypted using private/public key encryption.

SMTP/POP3

An email server receives email messages and stores them securely until the data is accessed. If an email client program is used, then the email messages are downloaded to the client software. If a web browser is used then the emails stay on the server but are transmitted as a web page.

New emails are composed on the client device and sent to the email server which forwards the messages on to the intended recipient's email server.

SMTP is the protocol used for sending emails from a device to an email server. POP3 is a protocol used for receiving emails from the email server.

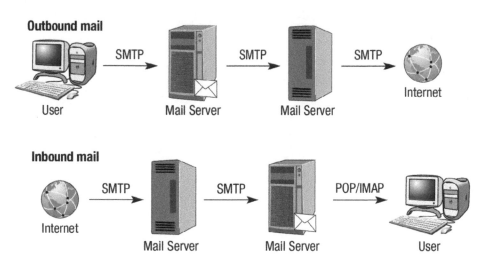

Figure 9.10 SMTP and POP protocols

Note

There are several other protocols in common usage, for example FTPS is the secure equivalent of FTP, however only those listed above are required for the AQA specification.

SSH

SSH is an encrypted method for remotely managing a computer and is often used to provide remote access to a server. The client is provided with a command line interface which can be used to interact with the server.

SSH can be used to access data using other application layer protocols. For instance, an SSH client can connect on port 80 to carry out web requests using commands such as GET, or port 25 to carry out email requests.

Now test yourself

58 What protocol is used to connect to a remotely manage a computer?

59 What service is accessed using POP3 and SMTP?

60 What is FTP used for?

61 How can SSH be used to access data that relies on other protocols?

Answers available online

TESTED ◯

Exam tip

It is helpful to have had practical experience using SSH to connect to a remote computer and it is possible that questions will check your knowledge that SSH can be used to carry out commands using other application layer protocols. However, it is not necessary to be familiar with commands specifically relating to remote server management.

IP address structure

An IP address is a numeric addressing method that uses four 8 bit numbers, each between 0 and 255, separated by full stops. An IP address is typically represented in dotted-decimal format, such as 107.162.140.19.

Each IP address is made up of a network identifier and a host identifier.

A typical IP address for a device on a home network is 192.168.0.3. This network uses a 16-bit network identifier and a 16-bit host identifier. All devices on this network will have the same network identifier; in other words, they will all be in the format 192.168.*.*. A device on the network can then have any IP address between 192.168.0.0 and 192.168.255.255.

For our home network example the network identifier is 192.168.0.0 and the host identifier is 0.0.0.3

Written in binary, the two parts of the IP address can sometimes be easier to spot.

Network identifier	Host identifier
1 1 0 0 0 0 0 0 . 1 0 1 0 1 0 0 0	0 0 0 0 0 0 0 0 . 0 0 0 0 0 0 1 1
1 1 0 0 0 0 0 0 . 1 0 1 0 1 0 0 0	0 0 0 0 0 0 0 0 . 0 0 0 0 0 1 0 1

In order to separate devices on the network this can be further divided into subnets, which restricts the range of IP addresses for that that particular type of device.

A software company's network is going to be split so that there is one subnet for admin purposes and one subnet for development work.
+ Devices on the admin network will have an IP address between 192.168.0.0 and 192.168.191.255.
+ Devices on the development network will have an IP address between 192.168.192.0 and 192.168.255.255.

Therefore, if a device has an IP address of 192.168.192.23, then we know that it is on the development network.

192.168.192.23:

Network identifier	Host identifier
1 1 0 0 0 0 0 0 . 1 0 1 0 1 0 0 0	1 1 0 0 0 0 0 0 . 0 0 0 1 0 1 1 1

Subnet masking

Subnet masking is used to identify the network identifier in an IP address.

This is achieved by applying a logical AND between the IP address of any device on the network and the subnet mask.

For a 192.168.x.x network this can be achieved using the subnet mask 255.255.0.0 on a device on the network, such as one with the address 192.168.0.3

```
11000000.10101000.00000000.00000011          192.168.0.3

11111111.11111111.00000000.00000000  AND     255.255.0.0
AND

11000000.10101000.00000000.00000000          192.168.0.0
```

This has the effect of cancelling out, or zeroing, the host identifier. With this example it is fairly straightforward to see how this works using the decimal representation of the IP address, though it is easier to work directly in the binary format.

In the example above the first 16 bits are used for the network identifier and the last 16 bits are used for the host identifier. This means that there could be 216 (65,536) possible devices on the network.

Network identifier The first part of an IP address, indicating the network.

Host identifier The second part of an IP address, indicating the device on that network.

Subnet A subdivision of a network.

Subnet mask A 32-bit number used to isolate the network identifier in an IP address.

Logical AND The operation of applying an AND function between the individual bits in two binary numbers.

Exam tip

The most likely question on this topic is to be asked to write out a subnet mask given the number of bits allocated to the network identifier and to calculate the maximum number of devices that can be connected to the network at the same time.

In the following example the first 26 bits are used for the network identifier and the last 6 bits are used for the host identifier. This means that there could be 2^6 (64) possible devices on the network. For a device on this network with the IP address 230.117.156.130 then:

Making links

For more on logical AND see Chapter 6.

```
11010110.01110101.10011100.10000010              230.117.156.130

11111111.11111111.11111111.11000000  AND         230.117.156.192
AND

11010110.01110101.10011100.10000000              230.117.156.128
```

Now test yourself

62 Name the two parts of an IP address.

63 If a network uses a 28-bit network identifier, how many devices can exist on that network?

64 State the subnet mask for an IP address with a 24-bit network identifier.

Answers available online

TESTED ○

IP standards

REVISED ○

The examples of IP address so far have all referred to IPv4 (version 4).

IPv4 was the default standard for IP addresses for a large number of years. However the range of possible IP addresses for a 32 bit number is 2^{32} (4.3 billion), and this has proven to be insufficient as more and more devices are being connected to the internet.

As a result, IPv6 was introduced.

IPv4 Internet Protocol version 4; uses 32 bits to represent each address.

IPv6 Internet Protocol version 6; uses 128 bits to represent each address.

Note

The problem with the limited supply of IPv4 addresses was identified many years ago and IPv6 was introduced back in 1995; however, the widespread implementation and rollout has taken several decades and is still not complete.

Many older routers, switches and devices have hardware that is not capable or configured for IPv6 and will stop working when IPv4 is no longer used. Therefore both standards are used on all new devices for both backwards and forwards compatibility.

While IPv4 uses 32 bits for each address, IPv6 uses 128 bits and is typically represented in hexadecimal. This provides over 3.4×10^{38} possible addresses.

Public and private IP addresses

REVISED ○

Before the full rollout of IPv6, a working solution for the shortage of IPv4 addresses is to separate IP addresses into public and private IP addresses.

Public IP addresses must be unique so that networks connected to the internet can be addressed.

Private IP addresses are only used within networks. These must be unique within that network, but can be re-used in other networks.

There are three main classifications for private IP addresses:
+ The 10 range (10.0.0.0 – 10.255.255.255) with a subnet mask of 255.0.0.0
+ The 172 range (172.16.0.0 – 172.31.255.255) with a subnet mask of 255.240.0.0
+ The 192 range (192.168.0.0 – 192.168.255.255) with a subnet mask of 255.255.0.0

Public IP address An address that can be accessed from any device on the internet.

Private IP address An address that can only be accessed within that network.

Public addresses are classed as routable because a device on another network can directly address a device with a public IP address on another network.

Private addresses are classed as non-routable because a device on another network cannot directly address a device with a private IP address on another network.

Routable An address that can be accessed from any device on the internet.

Non-routable An address that can only be accessed within that network.

Dynamic Host Configuration Protocol (DHCP)

REVISED

The assignment of private IP addresses within a network is handled by a DHCP server.

Dynamic host configuration protocol (DHCP) is a process which simplifies the process of configuring a device to connect to a network and avoids the accidental duplication of an IP address within a network which can occur if configuring the addressing manually.

Dynamic host configuration protocol (DHCP) A system for issuing private IP addresses within a network.

The configuration provided by the DHCP will include an IP address and subnet mask.

✚ A new device connecting to a network will send a request to discover a DHCP server. The DHCP server will then offer a configuration to the new device which can accept or decline the configuration.

✚ Once the client has accepted the configuration, the DHCP server records this so that it cannot offer the same configuration to another device.

✚ Each DHCP configuration will have an expiry time so that if that device is disconnected from the network it can retain temporary ownership of that configuration (and IP address) for the next time it connects as long as that is within a reasonable period.

On a small network a DHCP process would typically be handled a single device that functions as a switch, router and DHCP server all in one.

Now test yourself

TESTED

65 What are the **two** active versions of the IP standard called?

66 Why is IPv6 necessary?

67 Is the IP address 192.168.10.4 public, or private?

68 Explain why private addresses are non-routable.

69 Describe the process for assigning an IP address connecting to a network for the first time.

Answers available online

Network Address Translation (NAT)

REVISED

When a device with a public address sends a request, for example to a webserver, the response is sent to the sender's IP address.

When a device with a private address sends a request then this address is non-routable, and the response cannot be returned directly to that IP address.

In this situation a router uses network address translation (NAT) to change the sender's IP address to a public IP address.

✚ For example, a router has a public IP address of 230.117.156.130 and a computer inside the network has a private IP address of 192.168.0.3.

Network address translation (NAT) Substituting a private IP address for a public IP address, or vice versa.

207

+ The computer inside the network sends a request for a web page. The router changes the sender's IP address on the packets to 230.117.156.130 so that the response will be returned to the router.
+ When the response is received the router changes the destination IP address for each packet to 192.168.0.3 and the computer inside the network receives the packets.

> **Note**
>
> The form of NAT described here works well if only one computer inside the network needs to communicate, but if two or more computers are requesting web pages at the same time then the router will not know which device to send the responses to.
>
> In this case dynamic NAT can be used, with the router using a pool of public IP addresses, issuing a different IP address for each device so that the router knows which private IP address to send each response to.

Port forwarding

REVISED

Port forwarding can be used in conjunction with network address translation by inspecting port numbers to aid the process.

When a device with a private IP address sends a request the router will use NAT to change the sender's IP address and can also use the port number in order to help identify which device to send the response to.

If one device has sent a web request on port 80 and another has sent an email request on port 20 then the router will know which device to send each response to even though both responses are returned to the same public IP address.

Port forwarding Using the port number of a packet to identify which private IP address should be used.

> **Note**
>
> Port forwarding can also be used when multiple devices inside a network want to use the same port number. A router can be configured so that all messages received on a given port number, such as 4000, are forwarded to one private IP address, and all messages received on another port number, such as 4010, are forwarded to another private IP address. This is useful when hosting a server inside a private network.

> **Now test yourself**
>
> TESTED
>
> 70 Which device is responsible for carrying out network address translation?
> 71 Why is network address translation required?
> 72 When a response packet arrives back at the network, how can the intended private IP address be identified?
>
> **Answers available online**

Client–server model

REVISED

Client–server

In the client–server model the server controls access to a centralised resource.
+ When a client wants to access a resource (such as a file or a web page) then the client sends a request to the server.
+ The server processes the request and returns an appropriate response (which could be the requested resource, a login page, a refusal, or something else).

In the case of many websites, rather than simply storing a series of HTML files, the data that makes up the content of the website is stored in a database.

When a request to view a webpage is sent, the server queries the database in order to generate the exact content on the webpage based on the current

Server A device that controls access to a centralised resource.

Client A device that makes requests of a server.

values in its database. This means that websites can be automatically updated to reflect live data (such as view counts, likes, new posts, etc.).

The basic client–server model is relatively passive, with the server only responding when a request is received from a client. In some situations, however, a more interactive communication is required.

Using the Websocket protocol a full-duplex socket connection is opened between a web browser and a server, using a TCP connection. This means that both client and server have a persistent connection and either device can communicate at any time during the process.

CRUD and REST

Connecting to a database can be carried out using a variety of methods, including:
+ A shell connection (SSH) using SQL commands
+ A programmed solution using REST

REST stands for representational state transfer and uses HTTP request methods in order to communicate with the database. This allows program code, such as JavaScript, to communicate with the database server using the HTTP protocol.

In the manipulation of databases the acronym CRUD is used to refer to the main database operations. Using REST, HTTP request methods are used in their place, as follows.

Database operations	SQL command	HTTP request	Meaning
Create	INSERT	POST	Add data to a database
Retrieve	SELECT	GET	Search, or query, a database
Update	UPDATE	PUT	Update or change a record
Delete	DELETE	DELETE	Remove a record

Making links

Databases are a critical component to understanding modern data storage and the implementation of a huge number of systems. Chapter 10 explains the principles of database design as well as the DDL and SQL syntax used to create and work with database tables.

The REST application programming interface (API) runs on the database server. In order to access the commands:
+ HTML pages that are stored on a web server include JavaScript code.
+ The HTML pages are accessed through the client's web browser, which then executes the JavaScript code on the client side.
+ The JavaScript code makes calls to the REST API on the web server which then processes the request using REST to communicate with the database server over HTTP and returns the required data from the database to the web server, and then on to the web browser.

Data communication between the server and the client web application is commonly carried out using one of two formats: JSON (JavaScript Object Notation) or XML (Extensible Markup Language).

Websocket A communications protocol using TCP to create a full-duplex connection.

Full-duplex Both devices can send transmissions at the same time.

Note

Ideally, the database server and web server should be separate in order to improve security; however, it is possible for both to be run from the same server.

REST Representational state transfer. A software style that allows web services to interact.

JavaScript A programming language often used for web applications.

CRUD A mnemonic for the four main database operations.

Note

Programmers create their own APIs, and APIs that use REST are referred to as RESTful.

Application programming interface (API) A tool that allows other programs to make calls or requests.

JavaScript object notation (JSON) A file format for human-readable text used to transmit data objects.

Extensible markup language (XML) A file format for human-readable text used to transmit data objects.

XML (Extensible Markup Language)	JSON (JavaScript Object Notation)
| ```
-<document>
 -<person id="1">
    <first-name>Dave</first-name>
    <last-name>Smith</last-name>
    <email>dave@smith.com</email>
  </person>
 -<person id="2">
    <first-name>Nicola</first-name>
    <last-name>Tandy</last-name>
    <email>nictandy@hotmail.com</email>
  </person>
 -<person id="3">
    <first-name>Hermione</first-name>
    <last-name>Belicchi</last-name>
    <email>minniebel@gmail.com</email>
  </person>
</document>
``` | ```
{
    "ID": 1,
    "Firstname": "Dave",
    "Lastname": "Smith",
    "Email": "dave@smith.com"
},
{
    "ID": 2,
    "Firstname": "Nicola",
    "Lastname": "Tandy",
    "Email": "nictandy@hotmail.com"
},
{
    "ID": 3,
    "Firstname": "Hermione",
    "Lastname": "Belicchi",
    "Email": "minniebel@gmail.com"
}
``` |

Figure 9.11 (left) An XML document for storing details of users; (right) A JSON document for storing details of users

JSON is generally preferable to XML as it is:
+ easier for a human to read
+ more compact
+ easier to create
+ easier and, therefore, quicker for computers to parse (process).

> **Parse** Process a string of symbols or letters.

Exam tip

You are not expected to write exact syntax using either JSON or XML, though you should be able to recognise which is which. Remember that XML looks a lot like HTML with its use of tags.

Now test yourself

TESTED ◯

73 What protocol is used to create a full-duplex connection between the client and the server?
74 State the REST calls for each of the following database commands.
   a SELECT
   b INSERT
   c DELETE
   d UPDATE
75 What **two** formats are typically used to send data between the server and the web application?
76 Give **two** advantages for using JSON.

Answers available online

Check your understanding and progress at **www.hoddereducation.co.uk/myrevisionnotesdownloads**

Thin- versus thick-client computing

REVISED

Thin-client computing is a model where the client is a low-powered computer with limited processing power and limited memory. The majority of the processing is carried out by the server and so a high level of system performance for the client is not needed.

One recent example of a thin client is a Google Chromebook, in which the user mostly uses a web browser to access software and files stored online. The Chromebook needs very little computing power as the programs are all run on the server and the browser simply needs to render the results to the screen.

Many offices and companies make use of desktop thin-client systems as the thin-clients are cheap to produce and require very limited software. They are very easy to manage are very easily replaced as the device itself does very little other than access the server's resources. The devices can often be very small as well.

Thin clients are generally used where processing requirements are low; for example, for office or productivity software such as word processing, spreadsheets and email.

Thick-client computing is a model where the client is at least a reasonably powerful computer with appropriate processing power and memory. A thick client carries out much more of the processing.

A desktop PC or laptop is an example of a thick client. The computer may be used to access files stored on a server; however, the editing and processing of these files is carried out on the client itself.

Thick clients are more expensive and require more powerful components, however they are also more flexible and can be used even if the connection to the server is not available at that time.

Thick clients are generally used for more powerful tasks such as image editing, audio editing, video rendering and animation.

> **Thin-client** Almost all processing is done on the server side.

Now test yourself

77 A Google chrome book is an example of what kind of client?

78 What kind of client would be most suited to 3D rendering for a digital animation?

79 Give **two** advantages for using a thin-client.

80 Give **two** disadvantages for using a thin-client.

Answers available online

TESTED

> **Thick-client** A significant amount of processing is done on the client side.

Summary

Communication

+ Serial transmission involves sending one bit at a time down a single wire
+ Parallel transmission involves sending bits simultaneously down multiple wires
+ Parallel transmission is hampered by crosstalk and data skew
+ Synchronous data transmission requires an additional timing signal to be transmitted
+ In asynchronous data transmission, start, stop and parity bits are added to provide the receiver with timing data and error detection
+ Baud rate refers to the number of state changes per second in a transmission
+ The bit rate is the maximum number of bits that can be transferred per second
+ The bit rate can be higher than the baud rate if each signal can represent more than one value
+ The bandwidth describes the range of values that can be sent in a single signal
+ The bit rate is directly proportional to the bandwidth
+ Latency refers to the time taken for the first part of a transmission to reach its destination

Networking

+ A protocol is a set of rules or standards
+ A topology describes the physical or logical structure of a network
+ In a star topology all devices are connected to a central switch
+ In a bus topology all devices are connected to a central cable or bus
+ Star topologies require more cabling, but cope better with high levels of traffic and are more secure
+ A physical star topology can act as a logical bus network by using a hub which forwards all transmissions to all devices
+ In client–server networking a server controls access to a centralised resource and a client requests access to that resource
+ In peer-to-peer networking all devices have an equal status and can act as a client or server in any interaction
+ Wi-Fi is a protocol to provide a wireless network over a small area using radio frequencies
+ A wireless network adapter allows wireless devices to connect to a network
+ A wireless network access point provides a connection point to the wired part of the network →

9 Fundamentals of communication and networking

+ Wireless networks require encryption as any device in range can potentially pick up the signals
+ Each wireless network has an SSID, which can be enabled for ease of access or disabled for security
+ A wireless network can use a MAC address whitelist to block or allow individual devices from accessing that network
+ CSMA/CA is used by wireless devices to prevent them from broadcasting at the same time as other devices on the network
+ RTS/CTS involves sending a request to send and waiting for a clear to send response before transmitting

The internet

+ The internet is a global connection of millions of networks in a mesh topology
+ A router is a device for connecting networks together that use the same protocol
+ A gateway is a device for connecting networks together that use different protocols
+ Data is split into packets and additional data is added to a header before the packet is transmitted
+ Packet switching means that each packet can be routed across a different route in order to avoid routes that are slow, busy or have failed
+ A URL, or uniform resource locator, is a method of addressing an online resource and contains a protocol, a domain name and a path
+ An IP address is a numeric address that uniquely addresses a device on a network
+ Domain names are used in web browsers in preference to IP addresses as they are easier to remember, easier to type accurately and are more meaningful
+ A hostname appears before the domain name and specifies the host, or device, which is being addressed; for example, in mail.awebsite.com and www.awebsite.com the hostnames are mail and www
+ A fully qualified domain name (FQDN) must include both a hostname and a domain name
+ DNS (domain name system) is used to look up domain names to find the corresponding IP address
+ Internet registries assign IP addresses to networks in order to avoid accidental duplication
+ A firewall can be a software or hardware service used to stop suspicious transmissions
+ Packet filtering involves stopping packets based on their IP address or port number
+ A hardware firewall can act as a proxy server if it sits between a private network and a public network by providing a layer of anonymity
+ Stateful inspection involves examining the data content of a packet in order to decide whether it is suspicious
+ Symmetric key encryption means using a cipher in which the same key is used to encrypt and decrypt a message
+ Asymmetric key encryption means that a different key must be used to either encrypt or decrypt a message
+ Private/public key encryption uses two mathematically related keys – one public and one private
+ The sender encrypts the message using the receiver's public key so that only the receiver can decrypt the message using their private key
+ A digital certificate is issued by a certification authority in order to ensure that the public key is accurate and genuine
+ A digital signature is a digest or checksum that is used to check that an encrypted message has not been altered in any way
+ The digest is encrypted using the sender's private key so that the receiver knows that it is genuine once decrypted using the sender's public key
+ Malware is a term meaning malicious software (or software that causes harm)
+ A virus is a form of malware that attaches malicious code to an existing program and can self-replicate when executed
+ A Trojan is a form of malware that pretends to be a helpful program but causes damage when executed. It is not self-replicating
+ A worm is a form of malware that replicates itself across a network without attaching itself to another program
+ Malware can be protected against using firewalls, anti-virus programs, improved user education and improved code quality

TCP/IP

+ TCP/IP is a fundamental communication protocol, and is split into four layers
+ The application layer deals with the formatting of data specific to an application; for example, HTTP
+ The transport layer adds a packet number and port number to each packet so that the packets can be reassembled and the completed data passed to the correct application layer protocol
+ The network layer adds the IP address of both the sender and the recipient as well as adding error checking bits
+ The link layer is used to transmit the packet over a physical medium; for example, wired (ethernet) cable, Wi-Fi, and so on.
+ The four layers of the TCP/IP stack can be remembered using the mnemonic All Teachers Need Llamas
+ A socket is an endpoint for communication based on an IP address and a port number
+ A MAC address is a unique physical address linked to an individual network interface card installed in a device
+ Well known ports include 80 and 443 for web traffic, 25 and 110 for email, 21 for file transfer and 22 for shell access
+ Application layer protocols include FTP, HTTP, HTTPS, POP3, SMTP and SSH
+ FTP is used for file transfer
+ SSH is used for remote management using a TCP connection to a remote port
+ HTTPS and HTTPS are used to transfer HTML from a web server to a web browser which it renders into text, images and other media
+ POP3 and SMTP are used for email
+ An IP address is split into a network identifier and a host identifier
+ A subnet mask is used to identify the network identifier part of an IP address
+ IPv4 is used throughout the AQA specification, but IPv6 is a newer format with a much wider range of possible addresses

Check your understanding and progress at **www.hoddereducation.co.uk/myrevisionnotesdownloads**

+ IP addresses in the 10, 172 and 192 range are only used inside private networks and are non-routable because they can be duplicated in other networks
+ Public IP addresses are routable because they are unique across the internet
+ DHCP automates the process of assigning private IP addresses in a network
+ Network address translation replaces a sender's private IP address with a public IP address so that the response can be received over the internet
+ Port forwarding uses the port number in a socket with a public IP address so that the router in a private network knows which device to forward the response to
+ In a client–server model, a client (for example, a browser on a laptop) sends a request message to a server (for example, a web server), which responds with a message back to the client

+ The Websocket protocol allows a full-duplex connection between a web browser and a sever over TCP
+ A web browser can connect to a database using a RESTful API
+ CRUD is an acronym for database operations Create, Retrieve, Update, Delete
+ Each database operation has an equivalent REST function
+ Data is transferred using JSON or XML
+ JSON is generally preferred as it is easier to read, easier to parse, easier to create and is more compact
+ A thin client is a device with little processing power and memory, used with a more powerful server as most processing is done on the server side
+ A thick client is a device with more processing power and memory, used in situations where most processing is done on the client side

Exam practice

1 The number 82 is sent using asynchronous transmission at a rate of 30 megabits per second
   a) Explain the difference between the baud rate and the bit rate of the data transmission. [2]
   b) State the maximum bit rate of the transmission if the bandwidth is doubled. [1]
   c) Explain why increasing the bandwidth of the transmission will not improve the latency. [2]
   d) Copy and complete the table below to indicate the data that will be transferred, using even parity. [3]

Stop bit	Parity bit							Start bit

2 A network is configured using a physical star topology
   a) Explain the operation of a star topology. [2]
   b) Explain how a physical star topology can function as a logical bus topology. [2]
   c) The network is to be extended to allow Wi-Fi connections. Identify **two** advantages for allowing wireless connections. [2]
   d) Identify **two** pieces of hardware required to create a Wi-Fi network. [2]
   e) Describe **two** methods of ensuring that a wireless network can be secured. [4]
   f) CSMA/CA with RTS/CTS are used to reduce the number of collisions on the wireless network.
      Explain the steps involved in CSMA/CA and RTS/CTS. [5]

3 A private network is connected to the internet using a router
   a) State the name of an alternative device that can be used to connect a private network to the internet, and the circumstances in which this device would be chosen. [2]
   b) A user enters the URL for a webpage.

Describe the process by which the web browser finds the IP address for the webpage as well as how it retrieves and displays the content of that webpage. [5]
   c) The webpage is transmitted using a secure protocol.
      Justify the decision to use asymmetric rather than symmetric encryption. [2]
   d) Explain the principles of operation of asymmetric encryption and the significance of using a digital certificate. [5]

4 A router connecting a private network to the internet uses the public IP address 17.43.0.61 and the private IP address 10.0.0.1.

The private network contains several workstations, a file server, a DHCP server and a printer.
   a) Why does the router have two IP addresses? [2]
   b) Explain how, when a device connects to the network, it is possible to ensure that it is given a unique IP address. [2]
   c) When an email request is sent to a public email server, the workstation sending the request initially has a non-routable address.
      Explain what this means and identify one concept that can be used to overcome this problem. [3]
   d) A user on the network wishes to download a file from the file server and a socket is used.
      State what is meant by a socket and identify **two** pieces of information that will be required to connect to the file server. [3]
   e) The network is to be subdivided into several subnets. Each subnet will use a 27-bit network identifier and will include one switch and one printer.
      Write the subnet mask that will be needed and state the maximum number of workstations that can be connected to one subnet. [2]

Conceptual models and entity relationship modelling

Data models are made up of entities and relationships (the links between them).

+ An entity is a type of object which we wish to describe.
+ Each entity is made up of attributes, or characteristics, of that type of object

For example, we might be designing a data model with an entity called 'Doctors'. For the data model we are considering, the attributes of the entity 'Doctors' might include their name, ID number and area of medical specialism. A different data model might define different attributes – it depends on the purpose of the model. Relationships between entities can be described as:

+ one-to-one
+ one-to-many
+ many-to-many.

> **Entity** A type of real-world object about which data should be stored.
>
> **Relationship** The way in which two entities relate to each other.
>
> **Attribute** A single characteristic of an entity.
>
> **E-R diagram** An entity-relationship diagram.

These relationships can be represented using an entity-relationship diagram (E-R diagram). In an E-R diagram, the entities (or tables in a database) are represented as boxes, and the relationships are represented by lines.

For example, patients are registered with a doctor's surgery. But each doctor's surgery has many different patients. This is an example of a one-many relationship:

Figure 10.1 An E-R diagram showing a one-many relationship

The single line connected the left-hand box represents the 'one' and the forked lines on the right represent the 'many'. The surgery can have many patients, but each patient only has one surgery.

Within the doctor's surgery, it is however possible for a patient to see more than one doctor. This is an example of a many-many relationship:

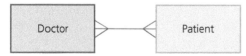

Figure 10.2 An E-R diagram showing a many-many relationship

Many-many relationships are not easily implemented in databases – instead we wish to turn the many-many relationship into two one-many relationships. To do this we add a third entity.

In this example, when a doctor sees a patient we can define another entity called Appointment. This allows us to create the following E-R structure which is much more straightforward to implement in a database:

Figure 10.3 An E-R diagram showing a three table database using two one-many relationships

Check your understanding and progress at **www.hoddereducation.co.uk/myrevisionnotesdownloads**

In the above diagram we can say that:
+ Each doctor can have many appointments, but each appointment is with one doctor
+ Each patient can have many appointments, but each appointment is with one patient

It is quite common to be asked to draw in the relationships between entities, and this includes both the direct relationships and the indirect relationships.

In this case we would draw in the many-many relationship between the doctor and the patient.

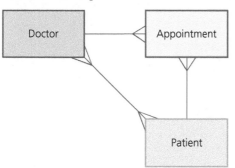

Figure 10.4 An E-R diagram showing all of the relationships between three entities

Sometimes a four-entity structure is used. In these cases there are up to six possible relationships:

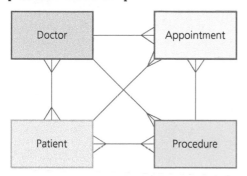

Figure 10.5 An E-R diagram showing the relationships between four different entities

E-R diagrams can also be written in a format that shows the attributes within each table in brackets, for instance:

Doctor (<u>DoctorID</u>, FirstName, LastName, Specialism)

Patient (<u>PatientID</u>, FirstName, LastName, PhoneNumber, DateOfBirth)

Appointment (<u>ApptDate</u>, <u>ApptTime</u>, <u>DoctorID</u>, <u>PatientID</u>, Notes)

The key fields are traditionally shown using an underline. (For an explanation of key fields, see the next section.)

Exam tip

It is a common mistake to draw the relationships the wrong way round. Say to yourself 'one doctor can have many appointments' (or the equivalent for your question) and remember that the 'many' symbol should attach to the 'many' entity.

Exam tip

It is normal to be asked to draw in three possible relationships with 4-table or 5-table examples. In these questions you should draw in the three relationships you are most confident about and should **not** draw any extras, as you will be marked down for any incorrect relationships.

Now test yourself   TESTED

1 What **two** things should be included in an E-R diagram?
2 In an E-R diagram, what is represented by a straight line with no 'prongs' at either end?
3 Draw an E-R diagram to show the structure of a database for a hotel, containing three tables – room, customer and booking.

Answers available online

Relational databases

When databases are created, each entity in a data model is represented in a database as a table.

Each attribute in a table is represented as a field.

Each time we add a new item to a table this is represented as a record.

A flat file database contains only one table.

A relational database contains two or more tables. This allows the data to be stored with minimal duplication of data.

For example, rather than storing the following data:

OrderID	FirstName	LastName	Email	ItemOrdered	Price
1	Dave	Smith	dave@smith.com	Motherboard	£89.99
2	Dave	Smith	dave@smith.com	CPU	£132.99
3	Dave	Smith	dave@smith.com	RAM	£79.99
4	Dave	Smith	dave@smith.com	GPU	£219.99

This could be split into two tables:

Table: Customers

CustomerID	FirstName	LastName	Email
1	Dave	Smith	dave@smith.com

Table: Orders

OrderID	CustomerID	ItemOrdered	Price
1	1	Motherboard	£89.99
2	1	CPU	£132.99
3	1	RAM	£79.99
4	1	GPU	£219.99

This reduces the need for data entry, for data storage and reduces data duplication. It also means that any changes to a customer's details only need to be made once, reducing the risk of inconsistencies in the data.

✚ Each entity is made up of attributes, or characteristics, of that type of object. Attributes are represented in tables as fields.

✚ Each table is populated with records, in which each record describes one item in that table.

✚ Each table requires a primary key, which is an attribute with values that uniquely identify each record in that table. This is important to avoid ambiguity. There cannot be any duplicate values in a primary key field.

✚ A primary key can be based on a single attribute or can be composed of several attributes combined. This is known as a composite primary key, or a composite key for short.

✚ A foreign key is an attribute in a table which matches the primary key in a related table. This creates the link between the two tables.

In the Customers table above, the CustomerID is a primary key.

In the Orders table, OrderID is a primary key and the CustomerID is a foreign key.

Now test yourself TESTED ◯

4 Why is it preferable for to use a relational database of a flat-file database?

5 Why is it necessary to have a primary key?

6 What term is used for a primary key made up of more than one attribute?

7 What term is used when a primary key is used as a field in another table in order to create a relationship between those entities?

Answers available online

Table The representation of an entity within a database, that is a structure for storing attributes.

Attribute A characteristic of an object.

Field A single item of data from a record.

Record The data about one item from a table.

Flat file database A database made up one table.

Relational database A database made up of two or more, related tables.

Primary key An attribute used to uniquely identify a record.

Composite primary key A primary key made up of two or more attributes.

Foreign key An attribute in one table that links to the primary key in a related table.

Exam tip

AQA sometimes refer to database tables as 'relations' and sometimes as 'entities'. Be careful not to confuse the terms 'relation' and 'relationship'.

Check your understanding and progress at **www.hoddereducation.co.uk/myrevisionnotesdownloads**

Database design and normalisation techniques

The rules around making sure that a database design is efficient are referred to as normalisation.

+ Normalisation ensures that there is less redundancy and less inconsistency in the data.
+ A poorly designed database might result in data being stored twice because the same attributes exist in different tables, or because different records include the same data (for example, storing the address for a customer every time they make a purchase).
+ A poorly designed database might result in erroneous data because duplicate data has been incorrectly updated or deleted (for example, if the address for a customer is stored every time they make a purchase but needs to be changed then it is possible to miss one or more records with the old address).
+ A fully normalised database **is atomic**. Each table, or group or attributes, cannot be broken down any further and so there are no repeating groups of attributes.

  For example:

  + a 'name' attribute could be broken down into 'first name' and 'last name'
  + an address attribute could be broken down into 'house number', 'street', 'town', 'county' and 'postcode'.
+ A fully normalised database **has no partial dependencies**. A partial dependency is when an attribute depends on part of a composite key but not the whole composite key (note, this point is only relevant to tables with composite keys).

  For example, a table for an appointment with a doctor uses a composite key:

  `appointment(`<u>`date, time, doctorName, patientID`</u>`, notes, doctorSpecialism)`

  The `doctorSpecialism` attribute depends on the `doctorName`, but not on the rest of the attributes in the composite primary key.

  The solution is to create a separate `doctor` entity:

  `doctor(`<u>`doctorID`</u>`, doctorName, doctorSpecialism)`

  `appointment(`<u>`date, time, doctorID, patientID`</u>`, notes)`
+ A fully normalised database **has no non-key dependencies**. The value of each attribute must only depend on the key. If the value of an attribute can be determined using any other attribute, then it is not independent. If this is the case, then the table normally needs splitting into two further linked tables.

  For example, an address entity is designed as follows:

  `address(`<u>`addressID`</u>`, houseNumber, street, town, county, postcode)`

  Two neighbours have a different house number, but the same street, town, county and postcode. The attributes for `street`, `town` and `county` can be determined from the postcode as well as the primary key `addressID`, as everyone on that street has the same postcode.

  To resolve this, it can then be split into two tables:

  `address(`<u>`addressID`</u>`, houseNumber, postcode)`

  `postcode(`<u>`postcode`</u>`, street, town, county)`

10 Fundamentals of databases

Note

There are several normalisation rules, and the AQA specification considers these up to and including the **third normal form**. It is not necessary to know which rule refers to which specific level of normalisation.

Normalisation Structuring a database in a way designed to reduce data redundancy and improve integrity.

Redundancy Not needed, for example data that is unnecessarily stored twice.

Inconsistency The result is not always the same.

Third normal form A database in which all data is atomic, there are no partial dependencies and no non-key dependencies.

Exam tip

If you are asked what it means for a database to be fully normalised remember that data must be atomic, and that all of the attributes in the table depend on the whole primary key (including all parts of a composite key, if the primary key is composite) and no other attributes.

Now test yourself

8 What are **two** advantages of normalising a database?

9 What does the term *atomic* mean?

10 What are **two** other requirements for a fully normalised database?

Answers available online

TESTED ○

217

It is common to be asked to write SQL code during the Component 2 exam.

Database definition language (DDL)

SQL can be used to
+ create tables
+ manipulate tables.

The code used to create tables is known as database definition language (DDL) and an example in SQL is as follows:

```sql
CREATE TABLE Purchase (

        PurchaseID INT,

        CustomerID INT,

        StoreID VARCHAR(6),

        Date DATETIME,

        TotalCost CURRENCY,

        LoyaltyCard BOOL,

        PRIMARY KEY (PurchaseID),

        FOREIGN KEY (CustomerID) REFERENCES Customer(CustomerID))
```

Figure 10.6 The DDL code to create a database table

> **Database definition language (DDL)** The language used to create database tables. A subset of SQL commands can be used as a database definition language.

In the example above it is key to note that:
+ each field is declared using its name, followed by its data type
+ SQL commands (in other words, anything not referring to the name of a table, name of an field or a value) are typically written in all caps, although this is convention and not a requirement of the syntax
+ the primary key is declared using the command PRIMARY KEY followed by the name of the field in parentheses
+ the foreign key is declared in a similar way to a primary key, followed by a reference to the corresponding field in the related table; the keys do not need to have the same name in different tables, though it is often easier to follow the structure of the database if they do.

There are many possible data types that can be used in SQL. Any valid type will be accepted but, for numeric types it is important to consider whether an integer or non-integer type should be used.

> **Note**
>
> It is possible to declare a field and indicate it is a primary key in one line; for example:
>
>   CustomerID INT
>   PRIMARY KEY
>
> Both methods are acceptable.

Example data	Appropriate datatypes	Notes
fixed length text	CHAR(10)	Each entry must be exactly the length specified.
variable length text	VARCHAR(10)	Each entry can be any length up to the specified length.
whole number	INT	Should only be used for numbers that can never be fractional.
fractional number	FLOAT, REAL, CURRENCY	FLOAT and REAL are both used for fractional numbers – they just have different levels of precision. CURRENCY should only be used for financial data.
date or time	DATE, TIME, DATETIME	DATETIME stores both a date and a time.
yes or no	BOOLEAN, TINYINT	A Boolean is ultimately stored as a 0 or 1 and in some database systems will be automatically converted to a TINYINT (an integer type that is one byte in size).

Check your understanding and progress at **www.hoddereducation.co.uk/myrevisionnotesdownloads**

Retrieve (SELECT)

To retrieve data from a query, we use three SQL commands:

```
SELECT <fields>

FROM <table>

WHERE <condition>
```

The first two are mandatory but WHERE is optional. These can also be written in one line:

```
SELECT ProductName, Price FROM Products WHERE Price < 100
```

An asterisk (*) can be used as a wildcard in order to select all fields:

```
SELECT * FROM Products WHERE Price < 100
```

It is possible to use logical operations such as AND, OR and NOT to further refine queries:

```
SELECT * FROM Products WHERE Price < 100 AND Type = "Canned"
```

The results from queries can be further improved by sorting the results using the ORDER BY command:

```
SELECT * FROM Products WHERE Price < 100 ORDER BY Price ASC

SELECT * FROM Products WHERE Price < 100 ORDER BY Price DESC
```

Complex queries

Complex queries are used to retrieve data from two or more tables. In order to complete this it is necessary to state the primary and foreign key fields, to avoid duplicate responses.

There are several possible formats for achieving this, however the most accessible format is used here. Valid answers using other formats (such as JOIN and UNION) will be accepted by AQA.

The example below is based on the following database structure:

Doctor (<u>DoctorID</u>, FirstName, LastName, Specialism)

Patient (<u>PatientID</u>, FirstName, LastName, PhoneNumber, DateOfBirth)

Appointment (<u>ApptDate</u>, <u>ApptTime</u>, <u>DoctorID</u>, <u>PatientID</u>, Notes)

```
SELECT Patient.FirstName, Patient.LastName, PhoneNumber,
ApptTime

FROM Doctor, Patient, Appointment

WHERE Date = "2023-03-26"

AND Appointment.DoctorID = Doctor.DoctorID

AND Appointment.PatientID = Patient.PatientID

ORDER BY Time ASC
```

The query above would return the first name, last name and phone number of each patient as well as the time of the appointment for all appointments on 26 March 2023. This might be needed if someone needed to send a text message reminder to all patients for that day.

Points of note:

+ There are two FirstName fields in the database, which is why the table name has been included as a prefix. This can be added to every field but is not necessary where only one field exists; for example, there is only one PhoneNumber field so we do not need to state the table it is in.

> **Note**
>
> If you are tackling a database project as part of your NEA programming project, the use of composite queries is good evidence towards a higher level of technical complexity. This refers to additional commands such as ORDER BY, SUM, MAX, MIN, and AVG applied to the results of a query.

+ It is important to add all tables used in the FROM field, but also important to exclude any tables in the database not relevant to this query.
+ In this case there are two one-many links between the tables, and so the foreign keys and their corresponding primary keys (DoctorID and PatientID) must be referenced in the query.

Create (INSERT)

To insert data into a database it is easiest to insert an entire record in one go. In order to do this, the data must be presented in the same order as the fields appear in the table:

```
INSERT INTO Appointment VALUES
("2023-03-27","13:50",113,26850,"Routine checkup")
```

It is possible to enter data by specifying the fields in a different order. It is also possible to exclude some fields altogether, if they are not required:

```
INSERT INTO Appointment(DoctorID, PatientID, ApptTime,
ApptDate)

VALUES (127,39254,"09:30","2023-04-03")
```

It is generally easiest to use the first format in exam questions.

Note that dates and times are always entered using speech marks.
+ Dates are formatted "YYYY-MM-DD"; for example, "2023-01-17".
+ Times are formatted "HH:MM:SS" or "HH:MM"; for example, "09:17:02".
+ The datetime format uses both, with the date first and a space before the time; for example, "2023-01-17 09:17:02".

Note that Boolean values can be entered as TRUE, FALSE, 1, or 0.

Boolean values must NEVER be written in quotation marks.

Update (UPDATE)

Sometimes it is necessary to change a value already in the database. This might be a single instance, or for all instances.

The structure of an update query should always read:

```
UPDATE <table>

SET <field> = <value>

WHERE <condition>
```

For example, the doctor with DoctorID 127 is ill and a replacement doctor has been brought in for the day, with DoctorID 180.

```
UPDATE Appointment

SET DoctorID = 180

WHERE DoctorID = 127

AND ApptDate = "2023-04-02"
```

Whilst there are two conditions here, note that only one condition may be needed.

Check your understanding and progress at **www.hoddereducation.co.uk/myrevisionnotesdownloads**

Delete (DELETE)

A delete query is used to remove data from the database.

This command can be used to remove a single record, a number of records, or all records from a table.

```
DELETE FROM Doctor

WHERE DoctorID = 128
```

To delete all records, no `WHERE` clause is needed.

Though presented in a different order here, the four main types of database manipulation can be remembered using the acronym CRUD. This stands for:

- create
- retrieve
- update
- delete.

Making links

Databases are often run on servers, with clients accessing databases remotely. In order to achieve this over a web interface, a RESTful API must be used which maps HTTP requests to the equivalent SQL command. More detail on RESTful APIs and web-based database access are discussed in Chapter 9.

Database manipulation	SQL implementation
Create	`INSERT INTO <table>` `VALUES (…,…,…)`

Retrieve	`SELECT <fields>`
	`FROM <tables>`
	`WHERE <condition>`
	`AND <condition>`
	`SORT BY <field> DESC`

Update	`UPDATE <table>`
	`SET <field> = <value>`
	`WHERE <condition>`

Delete	`DELETE FROM <table>` `WHERE <condition>`

Revision activity

Using the W3Schools website you can create your own database tables using SQL syntax.

Go to www.w3schools.com, scroll down to *Learn SQL*, and then click the *Try It Yourself* button.

1 Use the command `DROP TABLE <tablename>` to delete the existing tables.

2 Choose a past paper question and create the tables using SQL code.

3 Make up some suitable data and add this to the database using an `INSERT` query.

4 Create `SELECT` queries, including complex queries, according to the questions on the paper.

5 Create `UPDATE` and `DELETE` queries to alter the data in the database, running `SELECT` queries after each one to check the results.

Client–server databases

In a client–server database system it is possible for two clients to attempt to access, or alter, the data in a database at the same time. This is referred to as concurrent access.

If two or more clients attempt to alter data concurrently then it is possible that the integrity of the database will be compromised.

For example, a bank balance is currently £1000.
+ A payment of £10 is made into the account and so the balance is checked, £10 added to the figure and the new balance of £1010 is written to the account. The write process was slightly slow, however.
+ At the same time, another transaction took place in which the account holder spent £800. This processing was slightly quicker and the balance was reduced to £200; however, the first transaction had not yet completed and, when it did, the balance was overwritten as £1010.

There are several possible methods to preserve the integrity of the data.
+ **Record locks**: When a record is initially accessed it is locked and cannot be accessed again until the lock has been removed. In the case above the record for that customer would be locked by the first transaction until it was complete. Only then could the second transaction be processed.
+ **Serialisation**: The database system manages the transactions so that only one can be carried out at a time. As both transactions were received at the same time the second transaction would be held in a queue momentarily until the first transaction had completed.
+ **Timestamp ordering**: Each time access to the database is made, the timestamp is recorded. In the above example, the second transaction would change the timestamp at which the balance was last changed. When the first transaction attempt to complete it would see that the timestamp had changed and so would start again.
+ **Commitment ordering**: Transactions are arranged into an order that avoids potential conflicts, using an algorithm within the database system.

> **Concurrent** At the same time.

> **Now test yourself**
>
> 26 What does *concurrent* mean?
> 27 Why is concurrent access a potential problem?
> 28 How can record locks prevent problems with concurrent access?
> 29 Identify **two** other methods of preserving data integrity against concurrent access issues.
>
> **Answers available online**
>
> TESTED ◯

Summary

Conceptual data modelling and E-R modelling
+ Entity-Relationship diagrams show the relationships between entities as: one-to-one, one-to-many or many-to-many
+ Entities contain attributes which each describe a characteristic of that entity
+ Underlining can be used to identify the key fields

Relational databases
+ Relational databases are designed to represent data using multiple related entities
+ Data is stored in records, where each record describes one object of that type
+ A primary key is an attribute which must have a unique value in order to identify a record
+ A composite primary key is a primary key made up of two or more attributes which must have a unique combination
+ A foreign key is used to reference a primary key from another table in order to create a relationship between those entities

Database design and normalisation
+ Normalisation is the technique of ensuring that a database design reduces data redundancy and improves data integrity
+ In a database normalised to the third normal form, data should be atomic, data should have no partial-key dependencies and should have no non-key dependencies

SQL
+ SQL commands are used to create and manipulate database tables
+ Tables are created using the command `CREATE TABLE ( ... )`
+ Fields are declared by stating their name, followed by their data type
+ Text fields are declared using the data types `CHAR(n)` or `VARCHAR(n)`, where n refers to the fixed (for `CHAR`) or maximum (for `VARCHAR`) length of the text
+ Dates and times are declared using the data types `DATE`, `TIME`, or `DATETIME`
+ Primary keys are declared using the command `PRIMARY KEY (<fieldname>)`
+ Foreign keys are declared using the command `FOREIGN KEY (<foreignkey>) REFERENCES <table>(<primarykey>)`
+ The four main database manipulation commands can be remembered using the acronym CRUD
+ Creating data is done using an `INSERT` query: `INSERT INTO <table> VALUES (...,...,...)`

Check your understanding and progress at **www.hoddereducation.co.uk/myrevisionnotesdownloads**

- Retrieving data is done using a SELECT query: `SELECT <fields> FROM <table> WHERE <condition>`
- Updating data is done using an UPDATE query: `UPDATE <table> SET <field> = <value> WHERE <condition>`
- Deleting data is done using a DELETE query: `DELETE FROM <table> WHERE <condition>`
- Complex queries can retrieve data from more than one table by including additional conditions linking the primary and foreign keys; for example, `AND <table>.<foreignkey> = <table>.<primarykey>`
- Data can be sorted once retrieved by adding an extra clause `SORT BY <fieldname> ASC` or `SORT BY <fieldname> DESC`
- Dates and times are written using the format `"YYYY-MM-DD HH:MM:SS"`
- Boolean values are written as either `TRUE`, `FALSE`, `1`, or `0`

Client server databases

- In a client–server database system it is possible for two or more clients to attempt to access a record concurrently, threatening the integrity of the database
- This can be avoided using record locks, serialisation, timestamp ordering or commitment ordering.

Exam practice

1 A community cinema with a single screen wishes to use a database to store the details of film showings and ticket bookings.
   - Each film is identified with a unique number and the film's title, certificate and running length (in minutes) are recorded.
   - Each showing is identified with a combination of the film's ID, date of showing, and time of showing.
   - Each customer is identified with a unique code made up from the first three letters of their first name and the first five letters of their surname. The customer's first name, last name and email address are stored, as well as whether or not they are a member of the cinema's loyalty scheme.
   - Each ticket is identified with a unique number and the seat number is stored.

   a) The entity-relationship diagram below is incomplete.
      Draw on **three** additional relationships. [3]

      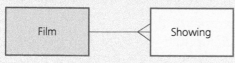

   b) The `Film`, `Showing` and `Customer` relations have already been defined.
      `Film(`FilmID`, Title, Certificate, Length)`
      `Showing(`FilmID, Date, StartTime`)`
      `Customer(`CustomerID`, FirstName, LastName, Email, LoyaltyMember)`
      State the type of primary key used in the `Showing` table. [1]

   c) Design the remaining relation, underlining the attribute(s) for the primary key. [2]
   d) The database should be fully normalised. Define what it means for a database to be fully normalised. [2]
   e) Write the SQL code needed to create the `Film` table. [3]
   f) Write the SQL code needed to add a new customer named Nicola Tandy. Their email address is nicolatandy@hotmail.com and they are not currently a member of the loyalty scheme. [2]
   g) A number of showings have had the wrong start time recorded incorrectly. Write the SQL code needed to change all films scheduled to start before 9am so that they will now start at 9:30am. [3]
   h) The cinema has cancelled a Halloween special. Write the SQL code needed to delete all showings for the 30 October 2023. [2]
   i) Write an SQL query to show a list of all the names and email addresses for loyalty scheme members. [3]
   j) Write an SQL query to show the title and start times for all 18 certificate films on the 23 May 2023. [5]
   k) The owners of the community cinema are considering splitting the building into several screens, each with a different number of seats. Describe the changes that would need to be made to the database in order to accommodate this, ensuring that tickets could only be booked for seats that exist, and are available. You do not need to provide any SQL code. [4]
   l) Customers can book tickets in the cinema, and also online, allowing concurrent access to occur. Describe **one** problem that could occur. [2]
   m) Identify **two** possible methods for avoiding issues caused by concurrent access. [2]

Big data

Defining Big Data

Modern computer systems can be required to collect and process a huge amount of data that lacks structure. This is referred to as Big Data.

Simply having a lot of data doesn't necessarily mean that this is Big Data. There are three characteristics that are used to define Big Data: volume, velocity and variety.

Volume

This refers to an amount of data so large that it cannot fit into a single server.

Such a large volume of data must be processed across multiple servers simultaneously. This has an impact because relational databases do not work well across multiple devices. Therefore, even structured data becomes hard to analyse and process if there is a lot of it.

Velocity

This refers to the rate at which data is generated or collected – for example social media platforms receive hundreds of millions of digital images per day.

A high velocity of data means that one server would be unable to cope with processing the data, particularly if the processing relies on data currently stored on another server.

Variety

This refers to the unstructured format of data and the different forms of data being received or captured, including images, video, audio, text and numeric data.

The variety of data means that it will not fit into a row-and-column format that is required for processing in a traditional database table.

These three issues combined make it difficult to store data, retrieve data and process data on demand.

Machine learning techniques are often used to process Big Data, as they allow the system to identify patterns in the data which make it easier to extract meaningful information.

Typical sources of Big Data include:
+ systems with networked sensors
+ video surveillance systems
+ social media platforms.

Processing Big Data

When there is so much data that it cannot fit on one server, the data storage and data processing must be distributed across multiple devices. This is known as distributed processing.

Big Data Data that cannot easily be stored, retrieved, and processed because it is too varied, too large or acquired too rapidly.

Volume The quantity of data to be stored, typically too much to fit on a single server.

Velocity The rate at which data is generated or collected.

Variety Data in many forms; that is, unstructured.

Exam tip

If you are asked what constitutes Big Data, remember the three Vs of volume, velocity and variety, but ensure that you explain your answers. Simply recalling the word will not be sufficient to show understanding.

Now test yourself

1 What are the three Vs of Big Data?

2 Why is it a problem if data is captured by the system in a wide range of forms?

3 Suggest **one** source of Big Data.

Answers available online

Distributed processing A system that uses multiple processors or servers to process data.

Functional programming is an effective solution for distributed processing as it is easier to write correct code that can be distributed to run across more than one server.

Functional programming supports three main features which help with distributed programming: immutable data structures, statelessness, and higher-order functions.

+ **Immutable data structures**: Rather than changing data and re-assigning a new value to a variable, data is not changed in functional programming. Instead, the data is processed by a series of functions, and the result is returned, leaving the original data unaltered.
+ **Statelessness**: The functions in a functional program don't change depending on another factor elsewhere in the program. This means that the state of another part of the system will not impact the process being applied. This is important for distributed processing as it may not be possible to check the states of other parts of the system.
+ **Higher-order functions**: Higher-order functions can take another function as an argument. This means that functions can be chained together to produce a result rather than having to store the intermediate values in additional variables.

> **Making links**
>
> Functional programming is a different paradigm, or style of programming, to procedural and to object-oriented programming. Your ability to understand and to write functional programs is assessed in Component 2 and this topic is explored in much more detail in Chapter 12.

> **Functional programming** A programming paradigm based around using functions to process data.
> **Immutable data structures** Data structures that cannot be changed.
> **Statelessness** A system in which the processing does not depend on the state of another part of the program.
> **High-order function** A function that can take another function as a parameter.

> **Now test yourself**
>
> 4 What is meant by *distributed processing*?
> 5 What type of programming is typically used in distributed processing?
> 6 What are the **three** main features of that type of programming?
>
> **Answers available online**
>
> TESTED ○

Representing Big Data

REVISED ○

Big Data can be represented by a fact-based model, in which each fact captures a single piece of information.

A fact-based model is commonly drawn using a graph schema.

A graph schema uses nodes and edges to describe facts, and the relationships between facts.
+ Oval nodes are used to represent objects.
+ Rectangle nodes are used to represent individual items of data.
+ Solid edges are used to represent relationships between objects.
+ Dashed edges are used to represent links between objects and their data.
+ Edges can be directed.

> **Graph schema** A graphical tool for representing fact-based models.
>
> **Node** An item in a graph.
>
> **Edge** A connection between nodes in a graph.

Figure 11.1 A graph schema with nodes (the shapes) and edges (the lines) showing facts about staff and students at a college

My Revision Notes AQA A-level Computer Science Third Edition

In this example:

+ the teacher and the students are objects and so they are shown in ovals,
+ each object has some data that relates to that person, which is shown in rectangles.
+ dashed edges are used to connect the data to the person (for example, Freya is in tutor group 12AP)
+ solid edges are used to connect the objects (in this case, people).
+ sometimes, no arrow is shown (for example, Freya and Dave are siblings) because this is not a one-way relationship.
+ sometimes, an arrow is shown because Andrea teaches Dave and Nicola (they don't teach Andrea)
+ for all solid edges, a label is added to describe the relationship.

Summary

+ Big Data refers to data that does not fit into standard data structures
+ Big Data can be described as data that has one or all of the following characteristics: volume, velocity, and variety
+ Volume: data can be classified as Big Data if the volume is so big that it will not fit on one server
+ Velocity: data can be classified as Big Data if it is being generated or captured at an extremely high rate
+ Variety: data can be classified as Big Data if it is unstructured, and hence cannot be represented using the table structures within relational databases
+ Machine learning techniques are often used to identify patterns and to extract meaningful information from Big Data
+ Distributed processing is often required in order to process the large quantities of data across multiple servers
+ Functional programming is often used as the programming paradigm of choice for processing Big Data because it lends itself to distributed processing
+ Functional programming supports immutable data structures, statelessness and high-order functions
+ Big Data can be represented using a fact-based model
+ A graph schema is a graphical representation of a fact-based model
+ Objects are represented using an oval node
+ Items of data are represented using a rectangular node
+ Connections between objects are represented using a solid edge, which can be directional
+ Connections between data and objects are represented using a dashed edge

Now test yourself

7 In a graph schema, what is represented by a rectangular node?
8 What is represented by an oval node?
9 What kind of edge should connect an item of data to an object?
10 Using the figure above, state **three** things you know about Dave Smith.

Answers available online

TESTED

Exam practice

1 Describe **three** characteristics that might result in a set of data being classified as Big Data. [3]

2 Explain why functional programming is a suitable method to use for processing Big Data. [2]

3 This is a graph schema for a fact-based model:

Copy and complete the graph schema, adding the following information. [4]

+ Andy Frey is 32 years old.
+ Rahal Meyrick treated a cat called Shadow. The cat is black.
+ Both vets are employed by a vet surgery called Soucek's Pets, based in Crewe.
+ The email address for the vet surgery is info@soucekspets.co.uk.

Check your understanding and progress at **www.hoddereducation.co.uk/myrevisionnotesdownloads**

Functional programming paradigm

Function type

A function is a rule that takes a value from a set of inputs (A) and assigns it to an outputs that is contained within set B:

For example, a function f that takes a positive integer as an input, and produces an output which is the double of each input, can be written as follows:

```
f: {0,1,2,3,4,…} → {0,2,4,6,8,…}
```

The domain is the set that contains all of the input values.

The co-domain is the set that contains all of the output values.

It is not necessary for all values in the co-domain to be included in the output. For instance, in this example the co-domain does not contain the numbers 1, 5 and 9. However, all of the values in the co-domain are natural numbers.

The domain and co-domain are always subsets of objects of a given data type (for example, integers, rational numbers, characters, and so on). In the function above, the domain is the set of natural numbers ($\mathbb{N}$).

The co-domain is also the set of natural numbers ($\mathbb{N}$), although not every value from that set will be included.

A function f has a function type:

```
f: A → B
```

A is the argument type and B is the result type. They refer to the data types from which the domain and co-domain are taken. For instance, for the example above where the domain and co-domains are taken from the set of natural numbers (integers), we can say:

```
f: ℕ → ℕ
```

or

```
f: integer → integer
```

However, this notation only describes the data type of the domain and co-domain and does not indicate the purpose or effect of the function.

> **Function** A rule that takes one or more values as an input and produces an output.
>
> **Set** A collection of objects.
>
> **Domain** A set from which all input values are chosen.
>
> **Co-domain** A set from which all output values are chosen.

> **Making links**
>
> When describing the domain and co-domain it is important to be familiar with the main sets of $\mathbb{N}$, $\mathbb{Z}$, $\mathbb{Q}$ and $\mathbb{R}$, as well as the principles of subsets. The sets are described in Chapter 5. The topic of subsets and their mathematical descriptions are discussed in Chapter 4.

First-class object

A first-class object is an object that can:
+ appear in expressions
+ be assigned to a variable
+ be assigned as an argument
+ be returned from a function.

In most programming languages a numeric value is a first-class object.

```
FUNCTION AddOne(StartNum)

    EndNum = StartNum + 1

    Return EndNum

ENDFUNCTION
```

> **First-class object** An object that can be assigned as an argument or returned from a function.

227

Here, the value of StartNum has been passed as an argument and used in an expression. The value resulting from that expression has been assigned to a variable and returned from the function.

In functional programming, a function is also a first-class object. This means that functions can be passed as arguments returned from other functions. This does not mean that the function is called, and the result is passed, but that the function itself is passed in its entirety.

A higher-order function is a function that takes a function as an argument, or returns a function, or both.

> **Higher-order function**
> A function that takes a function as an argument, or returns a function, or both.

Now test yourself

TESTED ◯

1 A function takes a whole number as an input and returns half of its value.
   a What is the domain of the function?
   b What is the co-domain of the function?
2 A function takes a whole number as an input and returns the square of its value.
   Copy and complete the description of the function:
   f: {1,2,3,4,…} → {   …}
3 What are the **four** features of a first-class object?
4 What are the **three** possible features of a higher-order function?

Answers available online

Function application

REVISED ◯

Function application is the process of applying a function to its arguments.

For example, a function to add two values takes two integer arguments as an input and produces a single integer result as an output.

add(6,2) → 8

The domain of the function is described as $\mathbb{Z} \times \mathbb{Z}$, which is the Cartesian product of $\mathbb{Z}$ and $\mathbb{Z}$. This means that the input contains two values, both of which are integers.

Note

The Cartesian product of two sets contains ordered pairs of the values from both sets.

For example:

{0,1,2,…} × {0,1,2,…} = {(0,0),(0,1),(0,2),(1,0),(1,1),(1,2),(2,0), (2,1),(2,2),…}

This means that the function call must be either add(0,0) or add(0,1) or add(0,2) or … etc.

Since the domain only contains integers, the call add(1,0.5) would not be accepted.

The co-domain for the function is $\mathbb{Z}$.

The type of the function is written as:

f: $\mathbb{Z} \times \mathbb{Z} \to \mathbb{Z}$

It is important to note that this function only takes one argument, but that argument is a pair of values, such as (6,2).

Partial function application

REVISED ◯

Partial function application is about providing some of a function's arguments and producing a function that takes the remainder of the arguments.

Imagine that, when the function add is given an argument of (6,2), a new function is created:

fx: add (6,2) becomes fy: add_six (2)

> **Partial function application** Providing some of a function's arguments and producing a function that takes the reminder of the arguments.

The function `add_six` will add 6 to a single integer (since it takes an integer input, and produces an integer output): `fy:` $\mathbb{Z} \rightarrow \mathbb{Z}$

For example: `fy:` $2 \rightarrow 8$

Note that the new function is an anonymous function and does not need to be written by the programmer; it is simply a method of describing how the partial function application occurs.

The whole process can be described by saying that the function `add` takes one integer input in order to create a function that takes the second integer input. The result of carrying out the new function produces an integer output.

This is written as: `fx:` $\mathbb{Z} \rightarrow (\mathbb{Z} \rightarrow \mathbb{Z})$

which means that function `fx` takes an integer argument and produces another function that takes an integer argument, which produces an integer output.

This can also be written as: `fx:` $\mathbb{Z} \rightarrow \mathbb{Z} \rightarrow \mathbb{Z}$

Composition of functions

REVISED ○

Functional composition involves combining two or more functions together.

Function `fx` takes an integer input and returns the double of that value:
`fx a = 2a`

For example: `fx:` $2 \rightarrow 4$

Function `fy` takes an integer input and returns the square of that value:
`fy b = b`^{2}

For example: `fy:` $3 \rightarrow 9$

Function `fz` takes an integer input and finds double the value of the square of the input.

For example: `fz:` $4 \rightarrow 32$ ($4^2 = 16$; $2 \times 16 = 32$)

Function h can be described as the composition of `fx` and `fy`, and can be written as: `fx ∘ fy`

This can be read aloud as 'fx of fy'.

We can also state that: `fx ∘ fy a =` $2(a^2)$

It is important to apply the functions in the correct order. In the case of `fx ∘ fy`, the function `fy` is applied to the original input and the function `fx` is applied to the result returned from function `fy`.

In terms of domains and co-domains it can be said that:

`fy:` A $\rightarrow$ B (A is the domain of function `fy` and B is its co-domain)

`fx:` B $\rightarrow$ C (B is also the domain of function `fx` and C is its co-domain)

> **Functional composition**
> The process of combining two or more functions.

> **Note**
> Functions can have a range of identifiers. In some scenarios functions will be given a single letter to identify them,

> **Now test yourself**
> TESTED ○
>
> 5 A function `fx` takes a two positive integers as arguments and returns the product of those arguments: `fx [a,b] = a*b`
>   a Write the type of the function using function application.
>   b Write the type of the function using partial function application.
> 6 `fx a = 2*a`
>   `fy b = b`^{2}
>   `fz c = c - 1`
>   a What is the result of `fx ∘ fy 2`?
>   b What is the result of `fz ∘ fx 10`?
>   c What is the result of `fy ∘ fx ∘ fz 3`?
>
> **Answers available online**

Writing functional programs

For the AQA examination, a form of pseudo-code is used to represent functional programs.

A function that takes a single argument will typically be written using the following format:

```
fx a = a + 2
```

This means that when the function `fx` is called, whatever value is passed to the function as an argument, that value + 2 will be returned. For example:

```
fx 3 → 5
```

A function that takes two arguments will typically be written using the following format:

```
fy [b,c] = b + c
```

This means that when the function `fy` is called, the value returned will be the sum of the values passed as arguments. For example:

```
fy [7,4] → 11
```

A function combination will typically be written using the following format:

```
fz [d,e] = fx (fy [d,e])
```

This means that the function `fy` will be applied to the values passed as arguments. The function `fx` will then be applied to the result. For example:

```
fz[3,1] → 6 (since fy [3,1] → 4 and fx 4 → 6)
```

There are three higher-order functions that you are expected to be familiar with. Each one takes two arguments: a function, and a list.

Note

It is useful to have done some practical programming in a functional programming language. However, this is not necessary and questions will only be asked on Component 2, the written exam.

Map

REVISED ○

Map is a higher-order function that applies a given function to each item in a list of values. Once complete, a new list containing the results is returned. (Lists are described in more detail in the next section.)

The map function will typically be written in the following format:

```
fu f = map fx f
```

From the previous section, remember that `fx a = a + 2`. This means that the function `fx` will be applied to each item in the list `f`, creating a new list of values which is returned. For example:

```
If list = [3,9,25,10]

fu list → [5,11,27,12]
```

Map A higher-order function that applies a given function to each item in a list.

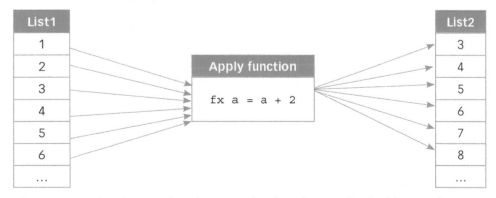

Figure 12.1 Using the map function to apply a function to a list, in this case the function will output the square of the input

Check your understanding and progress at **www.hoddereducation.co.uk/myrevisionnotesdownloads**

Filter

Filter is a higher-order function that uses a conditional operator to generate a new list.

The filter function will typically be written in the following format:

```
fv g = filter (<10) g
```

This means that the function `fv` will return a new list containing all of the values in list g that meet the criteria in parentheses (in this case, values less than 10).

```
If list = [3,9,25,10]

fv list → [3,9]
```

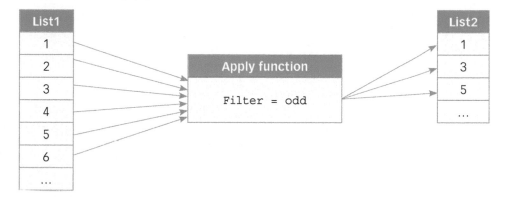

Figure 12.2 Using the filter function to create a new list according to a condition. Filters can use inequalities (for example, <10) or filters such as 'odd' or 'even'

Filter A higher-order function that produces a new list containing all items from the input list that meet a given condition.

Fold (or reduce)

REVISED

Fold is a higher-order function that reduces a list to a single value by repeatedly applying a combining function. Some languages refer to this as 'fold', some refer to it as 'reduce'.

The fold function will typically be written in the following format:

```
fw h = fold (+) 0 h
```

This means that each item in list h will be repeatedly added to the starting value of 0. The result will be a single value, which will be returned; for example, `fw list → 47`.

The process involves adding each value from the list, starting with the value of 0 as shown in the table below.

Fold A higher-order function that reduces a list to a single value by repeatedly applying a combining function.

List	Head of list	Tail of list	Result of applying combining function
			0
[3,9,25,10]	3	[9,25,10]	3
[9,25,10]	9	[25,10]	12
[25,10]	25	[10]	37
[10]	10	[]	47

If a fold function uses a product operator it is typical to see the following:

```
fw h = fold (*) 1 h
```

In this case the items in the list are combined by multiplying each of them together. The first values is multiplied by 1. If the function is defined `fw h = fold (*) 0 h`, then the first value (and each subsequent value) in the list will be multiplied by 0 then the result will always be 0.

Note

Using subtraction and division as part of a fold function is more complex, as the order in which the items are combined is more important. It is not expected that a question using a subtraction or division as a combining function would be asked.

231

Now test yourself

TESTED

7 Write a function, fx, that will multiply a number by 6.

8 Write a function, fy, that will take two numbers, and subtract the second from the first.

9 Write a function, fz, that will take two numbers, carry out function fy, and then carry out function fx on the result.

10 What will be the result of using the function map fx [1,2,3,4]?

11 What will be the result of using the function filter (even) [1,2,3,4]?

12 What will be the result of using the function fold (*) 1 [1,2,3,4]?

13 Describe the purpose of the fold function.

Answers available online

Lists in functional programming

REVISED

Lists in functional programming can be described as being made up of a head and a tail.

The list [3,9,25,10] can be described in the format 3:[9,25,10], where the head is the value 3 and the tail is a list of values [9,25,10].

✦ The head is always a single value, whereas the tail is always a list.

✦ A list can be empty, and this is represented using empty square brackets, [ ]

There are several standard list processing operations and it is expected that students will have practical experience of using each one. Although there is no specific language in which this should be carried out, the AQA pseudo-code for functional programming is similar in syntax to the language Haskell, one of the more popular functional programming languages.

Head The first item from a list.

Tail The remainder of a list, without its head.

Process	Description	Haskell code	Result
Return the head of a list.	Identifies the first element in the list.	head [1,2,3,4,5]	1
Return the tail of a list.	Identifies all of the other elements apart from the head.	tail [1,2,3,4,5]	[2,3,4,5]
Test for an empty list.	Checks whether there are any elements in the list.	let MyList = [4,8,15,16,23,42] null MyList let MyList = [] null MyList	 False True
Return the length of a list.	Identifies how many elements there are in a list.	length [1,2,3,4,5]	5
Construct an empty list.	Creates a list that has no elements in it.	let emptylist = []	emptylist []
Prepend an item to a list.	Adds an item to the beginning of a list.	let SetA = [1,2,3,4] let SetB = [0] ++ SetA	SetA [1,2,3,4] SetB [0,1,2,3,4]
Append an item to a list.	Adds an item to the end of a list.	let SetC = SetA ++ [0]	SetC [1,2,3,4,0]

Prepend Add something to the start of a list.

Append Add something to the end of a list.

It is possible to combine list processing operations, and it is common in exam questions to repeatedly combine head and tail functions. For example, consider the following operation:

```
head(tail(list)) → 9
```

This is because

```
tail(list) → [9,25,10]
```

and the head of this list is 9.

Using head and tail it is also possible to describe the application of the fold function in more detail.

Re-visit the table in the *Fold* section above to see how the head:tail structure is used to recursively call the same combining function, reaching the base case in which the tail is an empty list.

Making links

Recursion is a programming technique in which a subroutine will call itself repeatedly until it reaches a non-recursing, base case. Recursion is explored in *Recursive techniques* in Chapter 1.

Now test yourself   TESTED ◯

14 Given that list = [2,3,5,7,11,13], state the result of applying the function:
   a head(list)
   b tail(list)
   c head(tail(tail(list))).
15 How is an empty list represented?
16 State the result of [1] ++ list.
17 Explain how head and tail can be used to recursively carry out a filter function.

Answers available online

Summary

Functional programming paradigm

✦ The set that contains all of the values that can be used as the input is called the domain
✦ The set that contains all of the values that can be used as the output is called the co-domain
✦ Not all of a co-domain's members need to be outputs, so if the outputs are all even numbers the co-domain can still be described as the set of integers
✦ A first-class object can appear in an expression, be assigned to a variable, be assigned as an argument or be returned as a function call
✦ In functional programming a function is a first-class object
✦ A higher-order function is a function that can take a function as an argument, return a function, or both
✦ In function application a function is applied to its arguments; for a function that takes one argument this is written in the format f: integer → rational (or similar, depending on the domain and co-domain)
✦ If a function takes two arguments, the Cartesian product is used to describe the domain; for example: f: integer x integer → integer
✦ In partial function application a function takes some arguments and produces another function that takes the rest of the arguments; for example, add(6,4) → add _ six 4 → 10
✦ The function type of partial function application can be described as add: integer → (integer → integer) or integer → integer → integer
✦ Functional composition combines two functions so that fx o fy a → fx (fy (a))

Writing functional programs

✦ The map function is a higher-order function that applies a given function a list of values; for example: map +2 [1,3,5] → [3,5,7]
✦ The filter function is a higher-order function that filters a list according to a condition; for example: filter (>20) [7,35,41] → [35,41]
✦ The reduce or fold function that reduces a list to a single value by repeatedly applying a combining function; for example: fold (+) 0 [1,2,3,4] → 10

Lists in functional programming

✦ A list can be written in the format head:[tail], where the head is the first item in the list and the tail is the remainder of the list; for example: 1:[2,3,4].
✦ The tail can be an empty list, which is written []
✦ The higher-order functions map, filter and fold all use recursion, repeatedly carrying out their function on the head and calling itself on the tail, ending with the base case of an empty list
✦ Other commands for working with lists include:
   ✦ testing for an empty list: null listName
   ✦ returning the length of a list: length listName
   ✦ creating an empty list: let list = []
   ✦ prepend an item to the start of a list: let list = [0] ++ list
   ✦ append an item at the end of a list: let list = list ++ [5]

Exam practice

1 A list of values is defined as `list = [8,1,4,7,3]`.

The function double is defined as `double x = x * 2`.

a) State the result of applying the functions `head(tail(tail(list)))`. [1]

b) State the result of applying the function `fold (+) 0 list`. [1]

c) State the result of applying the function `map double tail(list)`. [2]

2 Four functions are defined as follows.

```
fw a = a + 10
fx [b,c] = b / c
fy d = filter (>0) d
fz e = map fx e
```

Lists of values are defined as follows:

```
m = [17,-6,28,0,-30]
n = [-2,7,16,-3]
o = [[12,3],[4,1],[24,4]]
```

a) The co-domain of function `fw` is ℤ, state the function's domain. [1]

b) The domain of function `fx` is ℤ x ℤ. State the function's co-domain. [1]

c) Copy and complete the table below by ticking each higher-order function. [2]

Function	Higher-order function?
fw	
fx	
fy	
fz	

d) Calculate the results of each of the following function calls. [3]

Function call	Result
fy m	
fz o	
map fw (fy n)	

3 The function `fold (+) 0 [5,2,6,8]` is called.

a) State the purpose of the `fold` function. [2]

b) State the result of the function call. [1]

c) Explain how you arrived at your answer to part b, and the recursive steps that you followed. [3]

13 Systematic approach to problem solving

There are many models used to describe or define approaches to software development. Whichever model is used, the stages of development are very similar.

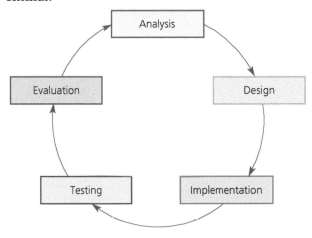

Figure 13.1 Stages of system development

Exam tip

It is not necessary to be familiar with any specific model of software development. However, make sure you are familiar with the five key stages described below.

Making links

The NEA programming project is broken down into the same five steps outlined below. It is rare for questions on this topic to appear specifically on the Component 2 examination, though the knowledge here will be very helpful to supporting you in the NEA.

Aspects of software development

Analysis

REVISED ⬤

The first stage of solving any problem is the analysis. The aim of this stage is to identify the details of that problem and to make sure that the problem is well understood.

In projects where the analysis is not given enough time or attention there is a risk that the solution will not fully solve the problem, or that the solution will not be suitable for the end-user.

The first part of the analysis is focused on understanding the problem:
+ Defining the problem

  This is usually a short summary, giving the big picture.
+ Identifying the stakeholders

  These include the client, the end-users and anyone else directly affected by the problem.
+ Understanding the current system

  This can be done by asking users how they deal with the current situation, researching the context of the problem and observing the current system in progress.

Analysis The first stage of systems development, in which the problem is identified, and solutions proposed.

Stakeholders The people with an interest in the problem or the solution.

235

The next step is to outline the potential solution.

+ Examine existing solutions

   This involves looking at existing products or solutions that already exist. For example, looking at several other stock-taking systems in order to identify what features are common, which are most used, and which are unnecessary or irrelevant to this scenario.

+ Identify required features

   Having looked at the current system, compared existing solutions and discussing the needs with a variety of stakeholders, it is important to narrow down a list of key features that the solution must include.

+ Development platforms

   It is important to consider whether the solution should take the form of a desktop program, mobile program, web-based platform or some other form. It is also important to consider what programming languages could be used in the development and details such as whether a database system or file management system is necessary.

+ Modelling

   A model for the data must be created in order to understand the problem and identify a suitable solution. Describing both the problem, and the proposed solution, using diagrams, charts and tables is an effective way to generate and refine the data model and to understand how the solution might fit together. It can also help to demonstrate ideas to a client, who may not be a computing expert.

   This is an example of using abstraction to help model aspects of the external world for use in a computer program

+ User Interface

   A user interface is an extremely important consideration for any computer system. The solution could involve a command line interface, a graphical user interface (GUI), a menu driven interface or even a voice-controlled interface. Sketches and ideas for prompts, dialog boxes and other elements of the user interface should be produced as early as possible.

> **Modelling** Graphical descriptions such as flowcharts, E-R diagrams, class diagrams and hierarchy charts.
>
> **User interface** The inputs and outputs of a program.
>
> **Agile** A method of project management in which a rough prototype is created and repeatedly improved.

Client discussion is key to analysis, both in order to help to understand the problem and to ensure that both parties agree on the proposed solution. You should show your ideas, plans, sketches and models to your client to help them understand your proposed solution and you may wish to take an agile approach, producing ever-more complete prototypes throughout the life of the project.

Making links

The agile approach makes use of rapidly built prototypes to plan and develop the project as you go. This can be a risky strategy and this is discussed in more detail in the design section.

The final stage is to create a list of detailed, formal objectives. Each objective should be SMART – specific, measurable, achievable, relevant, and timely. Any object that does not meet these criteria will be either difficult to measure, difficult to achieve, or will add little value to the overall solution.

The client may have questions to help them understand the proposal, the developer may have questions to help clarify certain parts of the problem, and the client might well have additional ideas or concerns about the proposed solution that are important to consider.

Design

REVISED ○

The design of the solution is something easily overlooked or rushed, as people are often keen to get straight into the practical development of the solution. As projects become larger and more complex, however, the time taken in the design phase becomes increasingly important to avoid problems later in the development.

The design should consist of several sections.

Top level design

A top level design gives an overview of the solution. The aim is to look at the big picture in terms of what the project aims to achieve. Details of specific algorithms can be skipped at this stage in order to provide a clear design that covers the whole solution in one place.

The nature of the top-level design will depend very much on the type of project. For example:
+ a flowchart might be ideal for a heavily algorithm-based project
+ an entity-relationship diagram might be more suitable for a heavily database centred project
+ a class diagram can help to summarise an object-oriented project
+ a hierarchy chart can help to show how a large task is split into subroutines.

A combination of two or three diagrams might be needed to give this top-level overview.

Making links

Class diagrams are an effective design tool to help describe the structure of an object-oriented program. Object oriented programming is explored in Chapter 1.

Hierarchy charts are commonly used in procedural programming to describe how subroutines are related to each other and how a larger problem can be tackled by being split into smaller sub-problems. Hierarchy charts are also discussed in Chapter 1.

Database design

If the project requires the use of a database then it is important to design the structure of the database carefully. This should include:
+ E-R diagrams
+ a data dictionary (showing the data type and keys for each table)
+ designs for all required queries; this includes INSERT, UPDATE, and DELETE queries as well as SELECT queries.

Algorithm design

Algorithms are a key component to any software project. It is therefore necessary to plan algorithms before they are programmed. It is common to create the broad, top-level design initially and then plan each individual subroutine in more detail.

It is not usually necessary to design every single algorithm as some are relatively straightforward. However, more complex and significant algorithms should always be planned in advance. This can be done with pseudo-code, flowcharts, or other forms of modelling as appropriate.

Design The second stage of systems development, in which the details of the solution are planned.

Top level design An outline design that shows how the whole program will fit together.

Flowchart A diagram using symbols to represent parts of an algorithm and arrows to show which step to follow next.

Entity-relationship diagram A diagram showing the relationship between different entities in a database.

Class diagram A diagram showing the structure of and relationship between classes in an object-oriented program.

Hierarchy chart A diagram showing which subroutines will call which other subroutines.

Making links

Databases are an essential component of many computer-based systems. Component 2 typically includes a large proportion of questions on the topic of databases, and this topic is discussed in detail in Chapter 10.

Algorithm A sequence of steps to follow in order to achieve an outcome.

Pseudo-code A form of program design that uses code which is not specific to one programming language.

237

Data structure design

It may be necessary to use abstract data structures such as stacks, queues, dictionaries, hash tables or vectors. If this is the case then it would be appropriate to describe how these could be implemented. For example, a stack can be created using a one-dimensional array and a pointer to the top of the stack.

If data is to be stored in files it is also important to consider how these files will be organised; for example:

+ will there be one file per user, or will all data be stored in the same file?
+ what format will the file take?

Modular structure

In a modular structure, each part of the program achieves one task. These modules are combined to create the overall solution by passing parameters and returning the results of each individual part of the program.

Using a modular structure means that parts of the program are loosely coupled. This means that if one part of the program needs to be replaced then the rest of the program should be unaffected. This can be achieved by avoiding the use of global variables and creating subroutines that solve a general problem (for example, a subroutine in a card game should shuffle an array of cards rather than the whole deck. This way the whole deck can be passed if needed, but a smaller selection of cards can also be shuffled if needed).

Modular programs are easier to debug, easier to update, require less code (as modules can be re-used) and modules can be re-used in future projects.

User interface

Though the user interface should have been considered in the analysis phase, the design phase is likely to be much more detailed and so a comprehensive design of the user interface should be included.

This involves designs for all screens, pages, prompts, responses, and error messages that may be required as part of the solution.

The design phase is often an iterative process, meaning that it is unlikely that the whole project would be designed in one go before being implemented. In practice it makes much more sense to design part of the project and then implement that section. This means that practical problems can be overcome quickly and future iterations of the designs can take this into account.

Agile approach

You may wish to take an agile approach to solving the problem. This involves starting with a rough prototype that is repeatedly improved. In each phase a relatively small part of the solution is quickly planned, implemented and tested.

Phases are very short and approaches can be quickly tried and discarded if not suitable. This can be an effective solution, but comes with risks as it is possible to spend several phases working towards an end-goal, only to realise that there is a critical flaw that requires a complete re-write to solve.

> **Making links**
>
> Complex data structures such as stacks, queues, dictionaries and vectors are discussed in detail in Chapter 4. Making good use of these data structures can be an effective way of demonstrating your abilities.

> **Abstract data structure** A data structure which can be implemented using a combination of other, simpler data structures.
>
> **Modular** Made up of independent units or parts.

> **Iterative** Repeating a process in order to approach an end point.
>
> **Agile** A method of project management in which a rough prototype is created and repeatedly improved.

Now test yourself　　　　　　　　　　　　　　TESTED ◯

4　What would typically be left out of a top-level design?
5　Which aspects of a database should be included in the design?
6　Why is it preferable to use a modular design?

Answers available online

Check your understanding and progress at **www.hoddereducation.co.uk/myrevisionnotesdownloads**

Implementation

Implementation refers to the creation of the algorithms and data structures required to solve the problem.

It is important to write, debug and test code in small chunks as the program is developed, rather than waiting until the end of the program. The modular design discussed in the previous section makes this much easier, as each subroutine can be tested individually as well as testing the program as a whole.

It is typical to use an iterative process to code, test and refine the implementation, with a focus on the core elements of the program first, adding in additional elements later on. There is a risk in focusing on implementing each section to perfection that time will run out and the client will be left with an excellent start, but an incomplete overall solution.

Making links

The implementation phase draws on concepts covered in Chapter 4.

> **Now test yourself** TESTED
>
> 7 What **two** things should be created during the implementation stage?
> 8 When is it appropriate to test the implementation?
>
> **Answers available online**

Testing

REVISED

Testing should be carried out throughout the development of the solution. The aim of testing is not only to focus on whether the system works with expected data, but to test that it copes appropriately with extreme and invalid data.

For example, a database designed to track shoe sizes up to and including size 13 should be tested with:
+ normal data (such as 6, 8, 11),
+ boundary data (such as 13)
+ erroneous data (such as 14, 15, 106, -2, 'orange').

This will ensure that the boundaries are set appropriately and that incorrect or invalid inputs are dealt with cleanly.

Defensive programming should be used to prevent the program from crashing. For example, exception handling should be used to deal with invalid inputs such as a string being entered where a number is expected.

Making links

Exception handling is an effective technique for dealing with invalid inputs. The syntax and structure of exception handling is discussed in Chapter 1.

Acceptance testing should also take place towards the end of the project. At this point, the client and/or end-users should be provided with the opportunity to test the solution for themselves in order to check:
+ they are happy that the solution solves the original problem
+ it functions as it should
+ it does not contain any errors or problems.

Acceptance testing should be at an appropriate time in the software development schedule so that if the feedback suggests that improvements are necessary, there is time to correct them.

> **Now test yourself** TESTED
>
> 9 What **three** types of test data should be used?
> 10 What is the meaning of *defensive programming*?
> 11 What is the final stage of testing?
>
> **Answers available online**

Evaluation

The final stage of any project is to evaluate the success of the project. To do this the original objectives should be reviewed, using the testing process as evidence, and each item marked as complete or incomplete.

+ The most fundamental aspect of an evaluation is to consider whether the original problem has been solved. It is possible to make a fully functioning, complex program that doesn't fully meet the requirements initially set out.

+ User feedback should be considered. This includes feedback from the client, from the end-users and from other stakeholders.

It is perfectly acceptable for feedback to suggest further improvements and developments for the future, and this does not necessarily mean that the project is not a success. There are always opportunities to further refine and extend any project.

> **Evaluation** The fifth and final stage of systems development, in which the success of the project is considered.

Now test yourself

12 Who should provide feedback used in an evaluation?

13 What is the fundamental question that an evaluation should aim to answer?

Answers available online

Summary

+ Large software development projects can be split into five sections

+ Analysis is focused on identifying and describing the problem, establishing system requirements from potential users, creating data models and agreeing a specification

+ Design is focused on planning the data structures, algorithms, modular structure and user interface required to solve the problem

+ Implementation is focused on the creation of the program code and data structures

+ Testing is focused on ensuring that the program works for valid data and copes well with boundary data and erroneous data

+ Testing also includes acceptance testing with intended users of the system

+ Evaluation is focused on reflecting on the finished solution and making sure that it solves the original problem

+ An iterative approach may be used at each stage as part of a prototyping/agile approach

Exam practice

1 Anne-Marie has been asked to develop a computer program for a company that manufactures vending machines.

a) Copy and complete the table by entering the appropriate letter, A–E, to match the activities with the stages of systems development. [3]

   A **Analysis**   D **Testing**

   B **Design**   E **Evaluation**

   C **Implementation**

Tasks	Stage
Creating a flowchart to describe an algorithm for part of the program	
Reviewing the overall success of the finished program	
Trying out other vending machines in order to see what features they include	
Entering invalid data to see how the program copes	
Writing the program code	

b) Identify **two** stakeholders for this project. [2]

c) List **three** things that should be included in the design for the project. [3]

d) Anne-Marie is using a modular design for the program.
Explain what is meant by a modular design and why this is useful. [3]

e) The vending machine uses a numeric keypad allows the user to enter a 3-digit number between 100 and 199 to choose their item.
Identify **three** types of input that should be tested and give an example value for each. [6]

Check your understanding and progress at **www.hoddereducation.co.uk/myrevisionnotesdownloads**

Glossary

Term	Definition	Page
Absolute error	The difference between the intended value and the actual value.	118
Abstract data structure	A data structure which can be implemented using a combination of other, simpler data structures.	238
Abstract data type	A complex data structure in which the complexity of how the data is stored or accessed is typically hidden from the programmer.	38
Abstract method	A method that has no program code and is intended to be overridden.	29
Abstraction	Making a problem simpler by removing or hiding features.	81
Acceptance testing	Testing by the client and/ or end-user to ensure that the system meets the specification.	239
Access specifier (or access modifier)	A keyword that sets the accessibility of an attribute or method.	25
Access speed	The time taken to read or write data.	178
ADC	Analogue to digital converter.	174
Address bus	A bus for transmitting memory addresses.	160
Address bus width	The maximum number of bits that can be used to address a memory location.	173
Addressing mode	Either immediate or dircct.	164
Adjacency list	A method of representing a graph by listing, for each node, just the nodes that are connected to it directly.	44
Adjacency matrix	A method of representing a graph using a grid with values in each cell to show which nodes are connected to each other.	44
Aggregation	The idea that one class can be related to another using a 'has a' relationship.	26
Agile	A method of project management in which a rough prototype is created and repeatedly improved.	236, 238
Algorithm	A sequence of instructions that are followed in order to solve a problem.	53, 71, 237
Amplitude	A measure of how large a vibration or oscillation is.	129
Analogue	A continuous signal, usually represented as a curved wave.	126
Analogue to digital converter (ADC)	Converts an analogue signal into a digital signal.	126
Analysis	The first stage of systems development, in which the problem is identified, and solutions proposed.	235
Anti-virus	Software that scans programs for malicious code.	200
Append	Add something to the end of a list.	232
Application layer	Formats data according to the application to be used.	201
Application programming interface (API)	A tool that allows other programs to make calls or requests.	209
Application software	Software intended to allow the end-user to achieve a task.	139
Arguments	The actual values that are passed to the subroutine at runtime.	19
Arithmetic	Mathematical operations such as addition, subtraction and multiplication.	162
Arithmetic logic unit (ALU)	Carries out arithmetic (mathematical) and logical operations.	162
Array	A data structure for holding values in a table	34
ASCII	A 7-bit code used for representing characters as binary numbers.	122, 188
Assembler	Translates assembly language code into object code.	143

Assembly language	Each instruction is represented as a text-based command.	141
Assignment	Changing the value stored in a variable.	11, 72
Associated class (or associated object)	A class or object that is used to make up another object.	26
Association aggregation	A type of aggregation where the container object can be destroyed without destroying its associated objects.	26
Asymmetric	Different keys are used for encryption and decryption.	135
Asymmetric encryption	Different keys are used to encrypt and to decrypt a message.	198
Asynchronous data transmission	Where data is sent without a timing signal.	188
Attribute	A single characteristic of an entity.	214, 216
Attributes	The properties that an object of that type has, implemented using variables.	23
Automation	Designing, implementing and executing a solution to solve a problem automatically.	83
Backus–Naur form (BNF)	A notation used to describe the syntax of a language.	89
Bandwidth	The range of possible signals that can be sent in one signal.	189
Barcode	A black and white image consisting of vertical bars of different widths to represent data.	173
Barcode reader	A device for reading barcodes.	173
Base case	The case in which a recursive function terminates and does not call itself.	22
Base class (or parent class)	A class whose attributes and methods are inherited by another class.	25
Baud rate	The number of state changes per second.	189
Bi-directional	Data travels in both directions.	159
Big Data	Data that cannot easily be stored, retrieved, and processed because it is too varied, too large or acquired too rapidly.	224
Binary	Numbers with base 2.	104
Binary file	A file that uses binary values to represent each item of data.	37
Binary point	Used to separate the whole number and fractional parts of a binary number.	114
Binary prefix	A shorthand used for multiples of 1024 (2_{10}) bytes; for example kibibyte, mebibyte, gibibyte.	109
Binary search	A searching algorithm in which the middle item is checked and half of the list is discarded.	62
Binary tree	A tree in which each node can have no more than two child nodes, each placed to the left or right of the preceding node so that the tree is always in order.	64
Binary tree search	A searching algorithm in which a binary tree is traversed.	64
Bit rate	The number of bits that can be transmitted per second.	189
Bitmap	An image format that uses a grid of pixels.	127
Bitwise	An operation that works on one bit at a time.	167
Block	A subdivision of the storage on an SSD.	177
Blu-Ray	A high-capacity optical disc typically used for high-definition video and large computer programs.	177
Boolean expression	A mathematical notation for logic gates and circuits.	145
Boolean identity	A relation that is always true.	152
Bottleneck	A congested path within a network.	195
Boundary data	Data on the edge of what should be accepted.	239
Branch	Jump to a labelled part of the program.	166
Breadth first search (BFS)	Searching a graph by checking every node one step from the starting point, then every node two steps away, etc.	53
Brute force	Trying every possible combination.	134

Check your understanding and progress at **www.hoddereducation.co.uk/myrevisionnotesdownloads**

Bubble sort	A sorting algorithm in which pairs of items are sorted, causing the largest item to bubble up to the top of the list.	65
Bug	A mistake in a computer program that causes unexpected results.	200
Bus	A communication system for transferring data.	159
Bus topology	A network arranged with a main cable, or bus, connecting all devices.	190
Bytecode	An intermediate code between high-level and object code which can run in a virtual machine.	145
Cache	A small unit of volatile memory placed on the same circuit board as a processor for fast access.	172
Caesar cipher	A substitution cipher in which each letter is shifted according to the key.	133
Call	The process of running a subroutine by stating its identifier, followed by any required arguments in parentheses.	18
Call stack	A data structure that stores the stack frames for each active subroutine while the program is running.	20
Capacity	The amount of data that can be stored.	178
Cardinality	The number of values in a finite set.	86
Cartesian product	The set of ordered pairs of values from both sets.	86
CD	Compact disc, typically used for audio and small computer programs.	177
Certification authority	A body capable of providing digital certificates.	199
Character set	The set of all characters that can be understood by a computer system, and their associated character codes.	121
Check digit	A single digit derived by following an algorithm, used to check for errors.	124
Checksum	A value, calculated by an algorithm, based on the contents of the original data.	124, 199
Cipher	An algorithm for encrypting data.	133
Ciphertext	The encrypted form of the message.	133
Circular queue	A queue which wraps around in a circle. If implemented using an array, the last index is followed by the first index.	39
Class	The definition of the attributes and methods of a group of similar objects.	23
Class diagram	A diagram showing the structure of and relationship between classes in an object-oriented program.	237
Client	A device that makes requests of a server.	191, 208
Client–server network	A network in which clients make requests to servers.	191
Clipart	A cartoon style image.	129
Clock	A component in the processor for generating timing signals.	162, 172, 188
CMYK	In a colour printer the colours used are cyan, magenta, yellow and key (black).	175
Co-domain	A set from which all output values are chosen.	227
Collision	Where two items of data are transmitted at the same time, causing both to be lost.	47, 194
Colour depth	The number of bits used to store the colour of each pixel.	127
Command line interface (CLI)	A text-only interface which is less user-friendly but often more powerful for knowledgeable users.	140
Common factor	A term which appears in 2 or more parts of an expression.	154
Compare	The operation used to check the condition between two values.	166
Compiler	Translates high-level code into object code as a batch.	143
Composite primary key	A primary key made up of two or more attributes.	216
Composition	Combining parts of a solution together to create a solution made of component parts.	83
Composition aggregation	A type of aggregation where, if the container object is destroyed, its associated objects are also destroyed.	26

Compression	Reducing the size of a file.	131
Computable	A problem that can be solved with a computer.	96
Concatenate	Join two (or more) strings together; for example, ABC + DEF = ABCDEF.	16
Concurrent	At the same time.	222
Condition	A comparison to see if two values are equal, or whether one is greater/less than the other.	166
Constructor	A special method (with the same name as the class) that is called when the object is instantiated.	24
Container class (or container object)	A class or object that contains, or is made up of, other objects.	26
Continuous	Can take any value, such as the length of an object.	104
Control bus	A bus for transmitting control and status signals.	159
Control unit (CU)	Decodes instructions and sends/ receives control signals.	162
Controller	A component of an SSD which manages the reading and writing.	177
Convex combination	The process of multiplying two (or more) vectors by scalar values that are both positive and add up to exactly 1.	50
Cost	This can mean the cost per device, or cost per GB.	178
Countable set	A set with the same number of values as a subset of the natural numbers N.	86
Countably infinite sets	A set whose values will go on forever, but can still be counted (for example, N).	86
CPU	Electronic device used to process instructions.	158
Crosstalk	Interference caused when two or more worse are in close proximity	188
CRUD	A mnemonic for the four main database operations.	209
CSMA/CA	Carrier sense multiple access/collision avoidance. A method of collision avoidance by checking for existing transmissions.	194
Cultural	Relating to the ideas, customs and behaviour of a society.	183
Data	Values or information.	126
Data bus	A bus for transmitting data.	160
Data bus width	The maximum number of bits that can be transferred at one time.	173
Data skew	When data that was sent at the same time arrives at a slightly different time to each other	188
Data structure	The concept of storing multiple values together with a single identifier	34
Data type	A definition of what type of data can be stored in that variable.	15
Database definition language (DDL)	The language used to create database tables. A subset of SQL commands can be used as a database definition language.	218
De Morgan's laws	Break the line, change the sign (and vice versa).	154
Debug	The process of identifying and removing errors from program code.	13, 239
Decimal	Numbers with base 10.	104
Decimal prefix	A shorthand used for multiples of 1000 (10_3) bytes; for example, kilobyte, megabyte, gigabyte.	108
Declaration	The creation of a variable in memory.	10
Declarative	A language in which the programmer codes what they want to happen, but not how.	142
Decomposition	A method of solving a larger problem by breaking it up into smaller and smaller problems until each problem can't be broken down any further.	22
Decomposition	Breaking a problem into smaller subproblems.	83
Decryption	A method of converting an encrypted message back to its original form.	133
Dedicated registers	Registers which are dedicated to holding data for a specific, functional purpose.	162
Defensive programming	Programming intended to deal with unforeseen circumstances.	239
Definite iteration, or count-controlled iteration	Iterating a fixed number of times (also known as a count-controlled loop, implemented as a FOR loop).	12

Check your understanding and progress at **www.hoddereducation.co.uk/myrevisionnotesdownloads**

Denary	An alternative less ambiguous term for base 10 numbers.	104
Dense graph	A graph with many edges.	44
Depth first search (DFS)	Searching a graph by heading in one direction until you reach a dead end, then stepping back one node at a time.	53
Design	The second stage of systems development, in which the details of the solution are planned.	237
Dictionary	A data structure based on key–value pairs.	48, 132
Digest	A checksum value used in a digital signature.	199
Digital	A discrete signal, often represented using a stepped wave.	126
Digital camera	A device for taking photographs stored as digital data.	174
Digital certificate	A digital document indicating that a public key is valid.	199
Digital signal processing	Manipulating digitised data relating to analogue signals.	161
Digital signature	A method of checking that an encrypted message has not been altered.	199
Digital to analogue converter (DAC)	Converts a digital signal to an analogue signal.	126
Direct addressing	The operand is the address of the value which is to be processed.	164
Directed graph	A graph some edges can only be traversed in one direction, shown with an arrowhead.	43
Disconnected graph	A graph in which two or more nodes are not connected to the rest of the graph.	43
Discrete	Can only take certain, countable values, such as shoe sizes or ordinal numbers.	104
Distributed processing	A system that uses multiple processors or servers to process data.	224
Domain	A set from which all input values are chosen.	227
Domain name	The identifier for an individual or organisation's online presence.	196
Domain name system (DNS)	A system for looking up domain names to find their corresponding IP address.	197
Dot product	A calculation used to help find the angle between two vectors.	50
Dotted-decimal	A format for writing an IP address with decimal values separated by dots.	197
Drum	A round device used to attract the toner.	175
Dual-core	A processor containing two CPUs, both working simultaneously.	172
DVD	Digital versatile disc, typically used for medium quality video and medium sized computer programs.	177
Dynamic	The size of, and the memory assigned to that data structure can change.	38
Dynamic host configuration protocol (DHCP)	A system for issuing private IP addresses within a network.	207
E-R diagram	An entity-relationship diagram.	214
Edge	A line used to represent the relationship between two nodes. Also known as an arc.	43, 225
Edge triggered D-type flip-flop	A logic circuit used to store the state of an input.	151
Edge-case	A problem that only occurs in an extreme setting.	200
Efficiency	Being able to complete a task with the least use of time or memory.	91
Encapsulation	The concept of grouping similar attributes, data, and methods together in one object.	24
Encryption	A method of hiding the meaning of a message.	133, 193, 198
Entity	A type of real-world object about which data should be stored.	214
Entity-relationship diagram	A diagram showing the relationship between different entities in a database.	237
Erroneous data	Data that is in error or invalid.	239

Evaluation	The fifth and final stage of systems development, in which the success of the project is considered.	239
Even parity	A method of using parity in which each block of data should have an even number of 1s.	123
Exception handling	A program technique that uses a try … catch structure to deal with errors that would otherwise cause the program to crash; for example, if the user enters a string where a number is expected.	239
Expanding brackets	The process of removing brackets by multiplying.	154
Exponent	The part of a floating point binary number which states how far to move the decimal point.	115
Exponential	An expression where the variable is used as an exponent, or power; for example, y = 2x.	92
Exponentiation	The raising of one number to the power of another.	14
Extensible markup language (XML)	A file format for human-readable text used to transmit data objects.	209
Factorial	The product of all positive integers less than or equal to a given integer.	93
Factorising	The process of removing a common factor.	154
Fetch-execute cycle	The process by which instructions are fetched from memory, decoded and executed.	162
Field	A category of data within a record or group of records.	37, 216
File	A persistent collection of data, saved for access and accessible once the program or subroutine has finished running.	37
Filter	A higher-order function that produces a new list containing all items from the input list that meet a given condition.	231
Finite set	A set with a fixed number of values.	86
Finite state machine (FSM)	A computational model which has a fixed number of potential states.	83
Firewall	A software or hardware service that blocks or allows individual packets from entering or leaving.	198
First In, First Out (FIFO)	Those items placed into the queue first will be the first ones to be accessed.	39
First-class object	An object that can be assigned as an argument or returned from a function.	227
Fixed point binary	A method for representing fractional numbers where the number of binary digits before and after the decimal point is fixed.	114
Flat file database	A database made up one table.	216
Floating gate transistor	Used as a memory cell in flash memory.	177
Floating point binary	A method for representing fractional numbers where the position of the decimal point is moved according to the value of the exponent.	115
Flowchart	A diagram using symbols to represent parts of an algorithm and arrows to show which step to follow next.	237
Fold	A higher-order function that reduces a list to a single value by repeatedly applying a combining function.	231
Foreign key	An attribute in one table that links to the primary key in a related table.	216
Frequency analysis	The process of examining how often something occurs. A useful tool for trying to break some encryption methods.	48
Full adder	A logic circuit to add three binary digits.	150
Full-duplex	Both devices can send transmissions at the same time.	209
Fully qualified domain name (FQDN)	A domain name that addresses an exact resource, including a hostname.	196
Function	A subroutine that returns a value.	19
Function	A rule that takes one or more values as an input and produces an output.	227

Check your understanding and progress at **www.hoddereducation.co.uk/myrevisionnotesdownloads**

Functional composition	The process of combining two or more functions.	229
Functional programming	A programming paradigm based around using functions to process data.	225
Gateway	A network hardware device for connecting networks that use different protocols.	196
General case	A case in which a recursive function is called and must call itself.	22
General-purpose registers	Registers that can be used to store any data.	162
Getter	A function used to return the value of an attribute to another object.	25
Global variables	Variables that can be accessed from any subroutine.	20
Graph	A data structure designed to represent the relationships between items.	43
Graph schema	A graphical tool for representing fact-based models.	225
Graph traversal	Inspecting the items stored in a graph data structure.	53
Graphical user interface (GUI)	An image-based interface that uses windows, icons, menus and pointers.	140
Half adder	A logic circuit to add two binary digits.	150
Halting problem	A specific example of a non-computable problem that proves that some problems are non-computable.	96
Halting state	A state with no outgoing transitions, and so the Turing machine will stop.	96
Hand-trace	Also known as dry run. Without using a computer, completing a table to record the values of each variable as the program is executed line-by-line.	53, 72, 170
Hard disk drive (HDD)	A storage device which saves data using magnetic film.	176
Hardware	The physical components of a computer system.	139
Hash table	A data structure for holding data that is indexed according to its key.	47
Hashing algorithm	An algorithm for calculating a key for each value.	47
Head	The first item from a list.	232
Header	Extra data added to a packet such as the destination address or packet number.	195
Heuristic	An approach to solving intractable problems in a reasonable amount of time by accepting an imperfect solution.	95
Hexadecimal	Numbers with base 16.	105
Hierarchy chart	A diagram showing which subroutines will call which other subroutines.	237
Hierarchy charts	A diagram that shows which subroutines call which other subroutines. More complex versions will also show what data is passed and returned.	22
High-level language	A programming language which uses keywords and constructs written in an English-like form.	142
High-order function	A function that can take another function as a parameter.	225
Higher-order function	A function that takes a function as an argument, or returns a function, or both.	228
Host identifier	The second part of an IP address, indicating the device on that network.	205
Hostname	The device within the network that is being addressed.	196
Hypothetical	Consideration of a 'what if…' scenario.	182
I/O controller	The physical interface between an I/O device and the internal components.	159
I/O devices	Input and output devices such as keyboard, mice, printers and monitors.	159
Identifier	A technical term for the name of a variable.	15
Immediate addressing	The operand is the value, which is to be processed.	164
Immutable data structures	Data structures that cannot be changed.	225
Imperative	A language in which commands are used to say how the computer should complete the task.	142

My Revision Notes AQA A-level Computer Science Third Edition

Implementation	The third stage of systems development, in which the program code and data structures are created.	239
In-order tree traversal	Inspecting or displaying the value of each node after checking the node on the left but before checking the node on the right.	57
Inconsistency	The result is not always the same.	217
Indefinite iteration, or condition-controlled iteration	Iterating until a condition is met (also known as a condition-controlled loop, implemented in AQA pseudo-code as a WHILE loop or DO-WHILE loop).	12
Index	A value indicating the position of a value within an array or list.	34
Infinite sets	A set whose values will go on forever.	86
Infix notation	A method of writing mathematical or logical expressions with operators placed between operands; for example, 2 + 2.	60
Information hiding	Controlling access to data stored within an object.	24
Inheritance	The idea that one class can use the attributes and methods defined in another class.	25
Instantiation	The process of creating an object based on its class definition.	24
Instruction set	The list of machine code values for each available operation.	164
Integer division	A division operation in which any fractional part is discarded, equivalent to rounding down to the nearest whole number.	63
Integer numbers	Whole numbers, including both positive and negative values.	103
Interface	A collection of subroutines that can be implemented by unrelated classes.	28
Internal components	The components essential to a computer system.	158
Internet of Things (IoT)	Physical devices able to share data or to be controlled using a connection to the internet.	187
Internet registry	A body responsible for allocating IP addresses.	197
Interpreter	Translates and then runs high-level code one section at a time.	144
Interrupt	A signal sent to the processor in order to alert it to an event.	171
Interrupt service routine (ISR)	A program which will examine an interrupt and handle the event.	171
Intractable	A problem which can be solved, but not in a reasonable amount of time (worse than polynomial).	95
IP address	A numerical address for a device on a network.	197
IPv4	Internet Protocol version 4; uses 32 bits to represent each address.	206
IPv6	Internet Protocol version 6; uses 128 bits to represent each address.	206
Irrational numbers	Any number that cannot be represented as a fraction, including π and square roots of non-square numbers.	103
Iteration	The repetition of a process or block of code.	12, 72, 166
Iterative	Repeating a process in order to approach an end point.	238
JavaScript	A programming language often used for web applications.	209
JavaScript object notation (JSON)	A file format for human-readable text used to transmit data objects.	209
Key	A value used to encrypt or decrypt data.	133, 198
Label	A named point in the program.	167
Lands	Small bumps in the track.	177
Laser	A device for creating an intense beam of light.	175
Last In, First Out (LIFO)	Those items placed into the stack most recently will be the first ones to be accessed.	41
Latency	The time taken for the first signal to reach its destination.	177, 189
Least significant bit (LSB)	The right-most bit in a binary number. The bit with the smallest place value.	105

Check your understanding and progress at **www.hoddereducation.co.uk/myrevisionnotesdownloads**

Library	A collection of modules that provide related functionality.	19
Linear	Rising in a straight line; for example, the graph of y = 2x.	92
Linear queue	A queue in which data is stored in a line.	39
Linear search	A searching algorithm in which each item is checked one-by-one.	62
Link	A physical connect between two devices.	190
Link layer	Deals with the physical medium used for transferring the data.	201
List	A data structure similar to an array, commonly used in Python in place of an array.	34
Load	Fetch a value from memory into a register in the processor.	165
Local variables	Variables that are declared within a subroutine and can only be accessed by the subroutine during the execution of that subroutine.	19
Logarithmic	The opposite of exponential. If y = 2x, then x = log2y.	92
Logic circuit	A solution to a problem that uses one or more logic gates.	147
Logic gate	Device which takes one or more binary outputs and produces a single binary output.	145
Logic problem	A puzzle which is intended to be solved using logical reasoning.	71
Logical	Operations using computation logic such as AND, OR and NOT.	162
Logical AND	The operation of applying an AND function between the individual bits in two binary numbers.	205
Logical bus network topology	A star network that uses a hub as the central device, which causes it to operate like a bus network.	191
Logical shift	An operation involving moving each bit in a given direction.	169
Logical shift left	Moving all of the bits left, doubling the value each time.	169
Logical shift right	Moving all of the bits to the right, halving the value each time.	169
Lossless compression	Reducing the size of a file without the loss of any data.	48, 132
Lossy compression	Reducing the size of a file by permanently removing some data.	132
Low-level language	A programming language which describes exactly how to interact with the computer's hardware.	141
MAC address	A physical address, uniquely assigned to each piece of network hardware.	193
Machine code	Binary code instructions which can be read and understood by a processor.	141, 162
Main memory	Memory that can be directly accessed by the CPU.	1258
Majority voting	Transmitting each bit an odd number of times in order to identify and correct any transmission errors.	124
Malware	Malicious software.	200
Mantissa	The part of a floating point binary number which provides the value of that number.	115
Map	A higher-order function that applies a given function to each item in a list.	230
Matrix	A rectangular, two-dimensional collection of values.	35
Mealy machine	A finite state machine in which each input has a corresponding output as well as a transition between states.	85
Media Access Control (MAC) address	A hardware, or physical, address that does not change.	203
Memory	The location where instructions and data are stored in a computer.	15
Merge sort	A sorting algorithm in which items are split into single items and then merged into sorted pairs, fours, eights and so on.	66
Mesh topology	A network topology in which each device can be directly linked to several other devices.	195
Metadata	Data about data. Additional data stored in a file.	128
Methods	Processes or actions that an object of that type can do, implemented using subroutines.	23
Modelling	Graphical descriptions such as flowcharts, E-R diagrams, class diagrams and hierarchy charts.	236

Modular	Independent of other subroutines.	20, 238
Module	A file that contains one or more subroutines that can be imported and used in another program.	19
Modulo	Finding the remainder when one number is divided by another.	124
Modulus	The remainder of the division of one number by another.	14
Moral	Relating to the principles of right and wrong.	183
Most significant bit (MSB)	The left-most bit in a binary number. The bit with the largest place value.	105
Motherboard	The circuit board to which all other components are connected.	158
Musical Instrument Digital Interface (MIDI)	A type of file that uses the instructions for how to create each note rather than capturing the analogue sound wave.	131
Named constant	A variable whose value cannot be changed while the program is running.	16
NAND flash memory	Memory which can be electrically erased and reprogrammed.	177
Natural numbers	Positive integers, including 0. Numbers used to count things.	103
Nested	Placing a programming structure inside another programming structure.	12, 35
Network address translation (NAT)	Substituting a private IP address for a public IP address, or vice versa.	207
Network identifier	The first part of an IP address, indicating the network.	205
Network interface card (NIC)	The component in any device that physically connects to the network.	203
Network layer	Adds sender and receiver IP addresses.	201
Node	Used to represent an item of data, drawn as a circle. Also known as a vertex.	43
Node	An item in a graph.	225
Non-computable	A problem that cannot be solved by a computer.	96
Non-routable	An address that can only be accessed within that network.	207
Non-volatile	Data is retained even when electrical power is removed.	158, 176
Normalisation	Structuring a database in a way designed to reduce data redundancy and improve integrity.	217
Normalised	The standard way of writing floating point binary, in which the first two bits are opposite to each other.	119
Number base	The number of digits available in that number system.	104
Nyquist's theorem	The rule that the sample rate should be at least double the maximum frequency that can be heard.	130
Object	A specific instance of a class.	24
Object code	Low-level code, translated from the source code.	143
Object-oriented programming	An approach to solving a problem using a model based on real-world objects that are designed to interact in a realistic way.	22
Odd parity	A method of using parity in which each block of data should have an odd number of 1s.	123
One-time pad	The key used in the Vernam cipher.	134
Opcode	An operation code, describing what operation is to be carried out.	164
Operand	A value or object that is to be operated on.	60, 164
Operation	A function to be applied; for example, +, −, AND, OR.	60
Operators	Symbols used to indicate a function.	14
Optical disk	A storage medium which uses light to read the data.	177
Ordinal numbers	Numbers used to count the order that something appears; for example, 1st, 2nd, 3rd, and so on.	104
Overflow	Where the result of a calculation is too large to be stored in the available digits.	120, 169
Overhead	Additional data added to the original values.	123

Check your understanding and progress at **www.hoddereducation.co.uk/myrevisionnotesdownloads**

Overriding	A method in a subclass re-defining a method inherited from a base class.	27
Packet	A small parcel of data, including a header.	195
Packet filtering	Stopping packets based on their IP address or protocol.	198
Packet switching	The process of sending individual packets on different routes.	195
Page	A subdivision of a block.	177
Paradigm	A particular style or approach to designing a solution to a problem.	22
Parallel data transmission	Data is sent on several wires, simultaneously	188
Parameters	The variables that a subroutine needs in order for the subroutine to run.	19
Parity bit	A single binary digit added to some data in order to help with error checking.	123, 188
Parse	Process a string of symbols or letters.	210
Partial function application	Providing some of a function's arguments and producing a function that takes the reminder of the arguments.	228
Pass	The transfer of a value, or the value of a variable, to a subroutine.	18
Pass	Travelling through a list from start to finish exactly once.	65
Path	The location of the file or folder on a server that is being addressed.	196
Peer	Of equal standing, able to act as a client or a server.	192
Peer-to-peer network	A network in which all devices are peers.	192
Peripheral	External hardware devices, on the periphery of the computer system.	139
Permutation	One of the different ways that a set can be arranged.	93
Personal data	Data that relates to an identifiable person.	183
Pits	Small indentations in the track.	177
Pixel	The smallest addressable element of an image.	127, 174
Plaintext	The original, unencrypted message.	133
Platter	A metal disk used to store the data in a HDD.	176
Pointer	A value that stores an address. In the context of queues this is usually the index of the front or rear item.	39
Polygon	A shape made of straight lines, for example, rectangle, hexagon, and so on.	128
Polymorphism	Literally 'many forms' – the ability for two methods with the same name to carry out their actions using different code.	27
Polynomial	An expression involving powers; for example, $y = 2x_2$.	92
Port forwarding	Using the port number of a packet to identify which private IP address should be used.	208
Port number	Extra data added to a packet that identifies what application layer protocol should be used to process the data.	201
Post-order tree traversal	Inspecting or displaying the value of each node after checking for all child nodes.	57
Postfix/Reverse Polish notation	A method of writing mathematical or logical expressions in which the operators appear after their operands; for example, 2 2 +.	60
Pre-order tree traversal	Inspecting or displaying the value of each node before moving on to other nodes.	57
Prepend	Add something to the start of a list.	232
Primary key	An attribute used to uniquely identify a record.	216
Printer	A device for creating a hard copy of a document, usually on paper.	175
Priority queue	A queue which stores a priority for each value so that the items with the highest priority can be accessed first.	39
Private	An access specifier that protects that attribute or method from being accessed by any other object.	25
Private IP address	An address that can only be accessed within that network.	206
Private key	A key that is kept secret. Has a matching public key.	198

251

Procedural-oriented programming	An approach to solving a problem using subroutines to tackle smaller subproblems.	22
Procedure	A subroutine that does not return a value.	19
Production rule	The set of acceptable inputs for a given symbol.	89
Protected	An access specifier that protects that attribute or method from being accessed by other objects unless they are instances of that class or a subclass.	25
Protocol	A set of rules or standards.	189, 196
Proxy server	A device that sits between a private and a public network.	198
Pseudo-code	A format for program code that is not specific to one programming language. Pseudo-code is useful for describing an algorithm that could be coded in one of several different languages.	10
Pseudo-code	A form of program design that uses code which is not specific to one programming language.	237
Public	An access specifier that allows that attribute or method to be accessed by any other object.	25
Public IP address	An address that can be accessed from any device on the internet.	206
Public key	A key that is made public. Has a matching private key.	198
Quad-core	A processor containing four CPUs, both working simultaneously.	172
Queue	A data structure in which items are stored in the order in which they should be accessed.	39
RAM	Short term storage for currently running programs and currently used data.	158
Rational numbers	Any number that can be represented as a fraction, including an integer.	103
Read/write head	The device used to read and write magnetic data to each to sector.	176
Real numbers	The collection of all rational and irrational numbers.	103
Record	A collection of related data.	37, 216
Recursion	The process of a function repeatedly calling itself.	22
Recursive	An algorithm that uses a sub-routine which calls itself.	66, 80
Redundancy	Not needed, for example data that is unnecessarily stored twice.	217
Registers	Small areas of memory inside the processor.	162
Regular expression	A sequence of characters used to describe a pattern. Used in searching and validation.	88
Rehashing	The process of recalculating the keys for all existing data using a new hashing algorithm.	47
Relational database	A database made up of two or more, related tables.	216
Relationship	The way in which two entities relate to each other.	214
Relative error	The percentage difference between the intended value and the actual value.	118
Resolution	The number of pixels per unit of length, also known as pixel density, often measured in PPI or DPI.	127
REST	Representational state transfer. A software style that allows web services to interact.	209
Return	To pass a value or the contents of a variable back to the place in the program where the function was called.	19
RFID	Radio frequency identification.	174
RFID scanner	A device for reading the data from an RFID tag.	174
RFID tag	A small device capable of emitting data using radio frequencies.	174
Rising edge	The point at which the clock signal changes from 0 to 1.	151
Robustness	How likely the device is to break or be damaged.	178
ROM	Long term storage for start-up instructions.	158
Rooted tree	A tree with a rooted node, from which all edges leading away from that root.	45
Rounding	Reducing the number of digits used to represent a value while maintaining its approximate value.	14
Routable	An address that can be accessed from any device on the internet.	207

Check your understanding and progress at **www.hoddereducation.co.uk/myrevisionnotesdownloads**

Router	A network hardware device for connecting different networks together.	195
RTS/CTS	Request to send/clear to send. A method of collision avoidance by requesting clearance to transmit.	194
Run	A series of identical values in a file or dataset.	132
Run length encoding (RLE)	A lossless compression technique of recording the length and value of each run in the data.	132
Sample rate	The rate at which samples are taken, typically measured in kHz.	130
Sampling resolution	The number of bits per sample.	130
Scalable	Used to describe a product, service or business that can cope with increased demand.	183
Scalar	A single number used to represent or adjust the scale of a vector.	48
Scalar-vector multiplication	Multiplying each element of a vector by a number in order to increase the scale of a vector.	49
Scaling	Changing the scale of a vector by multiplying the vector by a scalar.	49
Scope	The visibility of variables (either local or global).	19
Secondary storage	Persistent, non-volatile storage.	176
Sector	A small section of a track.	176
Selection	A program structure that makes a decision about which block of code to execute, typically implemented using an IF statement.	11, 72, 166
Self-documenting code	Program code that uses naming conventions and programming conventions that help other programmers to understand the code without needing to read additional documentation.	13
Sequence	Executing instructions in the order they are written.	72
Serial data transmission	Data is sent down one wire, one bit after another	188
Server	A device which controls centralised access to a resource.	191, 208
Set	A collection of objects.	227
Set comprehension	A collection of rules to define which values are in a set.	86
Set theory	A branch of mathematical logic in which sets are collections of objects.	86
Setter	A procedure used to allow another object to set or update the value of an attribute.	25
Shortest path	The route between two nodes on a graph that incurs the least cost. In an unweighted graph the cost for each path can be assumed to be 1.	67
Signal	The electric or electromagnetic impulses that are used to transmit data.	126
Single-core	A processor containing a single CPU.	172
Size	The pixel dimensions measured as the width x height of an image in pixels.	127
Socket	The endpoint, or final destination, of a packet. Described using both the IP address and port number.	203
Software	The programs that run on a computer system.	139
Solid state disk drive (SSD)	A storage device with no moving parts that uses flash memory and a controller.	177
Source code	Code written by a programmer.	143
Space-wise complexity	A measure of how much memory will be required to complete an algorithm.	91
Sparse graph	A graph with few edges.	44
SSID	Service set identifier – an identifier, or name, for a wireless network.	193
Stack	A data structure in which items are added to the top and removed from the top, much like a stack of plates.	41, 171
Stack frame	The collection of data associated with a subroutine call.	20
Stakeholders	The people with an interest in the problem or the solution.	235
Star topology	A network arranged with a switch (or hub) at the centre.	190
Start bit	A bit sent at the start of a message in order to provide timing data.	188

Starting state	The state a Turing machine is in when it starts its program.	96
State transition diagram	A diagram showing the states, inputs and transitions in a FSM.	84
State transition table	A table showing the states, inputs and transitions in a FSM.	84
Stateful inspection	Inspecting the data contained in a packet.	198
Statelessness	A system in which the processing does not depend on the state of another part of the program.	225
Static	The size of, and the memory assigned to that data structure is fixed and cannot be changed.	38
Static method	A method within a class that can be called without the need to create an object of that class.	29
Stop bit	A bit sent to mark the end of a message.	188
Store	Copy a value from a register in the processor and save it in memory.	165
Subclass (or child class)	A class that inherits the attributes and methods from another class.	25
Subnet	A subdivision of a network.	205
Subnet mask	A 32-bit number used to isolate the network identifier in an IP address.	205
Subroutine	A named block of code designed to carry out one specific task.	18
Subset	A selection of the values found in a set.	87
Substitution cipher	A cipher in which each plaintext letter is replaced with a ciphertext letter.	133
Substring	A series of characters taken from a string.	17
SWITCH	An alternative selection structure to an IF statement that is slightly quicker to execute if used with exact values rather than a range.	11
Switch	A device that receives and forwards data on a network.	190
Syllogism	An argument that uses logical reasoning.	71
Symmetric	The same key is used in encryption and decryption.	135
Symmetric encryption	The same key is used to encrypt and to decrypt a message.	198
Synchronous data transmission	Where data is sent along with a timing signal.	188
Syntax	The strict rules and structures used within a specific programming language.	10, 89
Syntax diagram	A diagram used to describe BNF graphically.	90
System software	Software intended to allow the computer system to run.	139
Table	The representation of an entity within a database, that is a structure for storing attributes.	216
Tail	The remainder of a list, without its head.	232
TCP/IP stack	The use of the TCP/IP layers to add header data which is then processed in reverse order.	201
Terminal	A single value that cannot be broken down into smaller parts.	89
Testing	The fourth stage of systems development, in which the program is tested to ensure it functions as it should.	239
Text file	A file that uses text encoding (such as ASCII or Unicode) to store data.	37
Thick-client	A significant amount of processing is done on the client side.	211
Thin-client	Almost all processing is done on the server side.	211
Third normal form	A database in which all data is atomic, there are no partial dependencies and no non-key dependencies.	217
Time-wise complexity	A measure of how much time, or how many steps, will be required to complete an algorithm.	91
Toner	A powdered form of ink with a static charge.	175
Top level design	An outline design that shows how the whole program will fit together.	237

Check your understanding and progress at **www.hoddereducation.co.uk/myrevisionnotesdownloads**

Top level domain (TLD)	The right-most term in a domain name, such as .com or .uk	196
Top-down approach	A method of planning solutions that starts with the big picture and breaks it down into smaller subproblems.	22
Topology	The physical or logical arrangement of connections in a network.	190
Trace table	A table for recording the values of variables as a program runs.	72, 170
Track	A concentric ring on a platter.	176, 177
Tractable	A problem which can be completed in a reasonable amount of time (polynomial time or less).	95
Translation	Moving a vector by adding another vector to it.	49
Translator	Systems software for converting one form of code into object code.	143
Transmission Control Protocol / Internet Protocol (TCP/IP)	One of the main protocols used in network communications.	201
Transport layer	Adds a port number, packet number and error detection data.	201
Tree	A graph which has no cycles (it is not possible to loop back around to a previously traversed part of the tree).	45
Tree traversal	Inspecting the items stored in a tree data structure.	57
Trojan	A malicious program that pretends to be a useful program, does not self-replicate.	200
Truncation	Removing any value after a certain number of decimal places.	14
Truth table	A table showing the possible inputs and their corresponding outputs.	145
Turing machine	A model of computation with a single program which manipulates symbols on a strip of tape.	96
Two's complement	A representation of binary numbers that includes both positive and negative values.	111
Underflow	Where the result of a calculation is too small to be stored in the available digits.	121, 169
Uni-directional	Data only travels in one direction.	160
Unicode	A variable size character set in which each character code can be 8, 16 or 32 bits in length.	122
Uniform resource locator (URL)	A standard structure for addressing an online resource using alphanumeric strings.	196
Universal Turing machine (UTM)	A Turing machine that takes the description of another Turing machine and its tape as inputs. It can simulate any conceivable Turing machine.	98
Unsigned binary	A system that is only capable of representing positive numbers (0 or larger).	109
User interface	The tools that are provided for a user to interact with a computer system.	140, 236
Variety	Data in many forms; that is, unstructured.	224
Vector	A data structure used to represent a position (for example, a two-dimensional vector represents a position on a 2D plane).	48
Vector addition	Adding two vectors together in order to perform a translation.	49
Vector graphic	An image made of lines and shapes.	128
Vector primitive	Simple objects which can be combined to create a vector graphic.	128
Velocity	The rate at which data is generated or collected.	224
Vernam cipher	A cipher which uses a randomly generated key and is mathematically unbreakable.	134
Virtual machine	Software that emulates or simulates a computer system.	145
Virtual memory	A portion of secondary storage used to store the least frequently-used instructions and data.	158
Virtual method	A method that may be overridden (this is the default in many languages).	29
Virus	Malicious code that attaches to another program and self-replicates when executed.	200
Volatile	Data is lost when electrical power is removed.	158, 176
Volatile memory	Memory which can only store a value when supplied with power.	151
Volume	The quantity of data to be stored, typically too much to fit on a single server.	224

Websocket	A communications protocol using TCP to create a fullduplex connection.	209
Weighted graph	A graph in which each edge has a value or cost associated with it.	43
Whitelist	A list of things considered to be acceptable or trustworthy.	193
Wi-Fi	A set of technology standards that allows devices to communicate using radio frequencies.	193
Wireless access point	A hardware device for allowing other devices to connect to an existing wireless network.	193
Wireless network	A network that allows devices to transmit data using radio frequencies.	193
Wireless network adapter	A hardware device for enabling devices to communicate using Wi-Fi.	193
Word	The maximum number of bits that can be processed in one instruction.	173
Worm	A malicious program that copies itself over a network.	200
XOR	A logical operation which checks whether both inputs are equal, or different.	134

Check your understanding and progress at www.hoddereducation.co.uk/myrevisionnotesdownloads